GET READY
FOR
IMMORTALITY

GET READY FOR IMMORTALITY

A Doctor's Guide

Lawrence E. Lamb, M.D.

HARPER & ROW, PUBLISHERS

New York, Evanston, San Francisco, London

"This book is also available under the title, STAY YOUTHFUL AND FIT."

FIRST EDITION

Designed by Ann Scrimgeour

Library of Congress Cataloging in Publication Data

Lamb, Lawrence E
  Stay youthful and fit.

  1. Aged—Care and hygiene. 2. Aging. 3. Age
factors in disease. I. Title. [DNLM: 1. Hygiene—
Popular works. 2. Longevity—Popular works
QT180 L218s 1974]
RC952.L33   1974   613'.04'38   73-4101
ISBN 0-06-012494-6

Contents

PART IV   THE FUTURE

Acknowledgments

One of the main interests of physicians is the preservation of life and health. Most of us must content ourselves with dealing with sickness, and many have little time or opportunity to explore the problems of the optimal in health and longevity or what might have been. A physician may spend his entire lifetime with no chance to gain experience in optimal health. It is not the healthy individual who comes to the hospital, the clinic, or the doctor's office, but the person who is sick or thinks he is sick. For this reason I am especially grateful for my 11 years with the U.S.A.F. School of Aerospace Medicine. As chief of the medical sciences I studied health among fliers and eventually established and carried out the medical examinations for the selection of the nation's astronauts. With this vast source of data and opportunity to study the effects of such factors as diet, exercise, relative obesity, cigarettes, coffee, and a variety of living habits, I found a new appreciation of what can be done to stay young and healthy.

Fortune was kind to me, and my unique experience in health was followed by my years as professor of medicine at Baylor College of Medicine in Houston, Texas. Here I received firsthand, on-the-spot, day-by-day information on the artificial heart, the heart transplant saga, and the inside story of the efforts of the modern "youth doctors," Denton Cooley and Michael DeBakey, to undo the ravages of time and disease. Fate also had put into my background a greater awareness of the history of transplanting. My boyhood in Kansas had been filled with the lore of Kansas's famous organ transplanter Dr. John Brinkley, the charlatan who transplanted goat testicles into men seeking to regain their lost vigor.

To prepare an actual description of the changes attributed to age I have drawn freely from standard medical reference texts in physiology and applicable medical specialties as well as scientific journals and various government publications dealing with the medical, psychological, and social aspects of aging. Worthy of special mention are the technical presentation in the **Hand-**

book of **Aging and the Individual,** edited by James E. Birren (The University of Chicago Press, Chicago and London, 1959), and **Working with Older People: A Guide to Practice,** Vol. IV, **Clinical Aspects of Aging** (U.S. Department of Health, Education, and Welfare, U.S. Public Health Service, 1971).

Many versions of the well-known DNA-RNA story and the ingenious work of the scientists who made this knowledge possible were essential to my own understanding of how close the medical profession is to solving the riddle of immortality and defining the difference between true time-dependent aging (inherited) and aging experienced because of events and illnesses. There is a great difference between preventing or curing illnesses common with increasing years and the fascinating opportunity open to man with the solution of the aspects of inherent aging.

I wish to express my appreciation to Dr. Bertram Brown, Director of the National Institute of Mental Health, for his help in identifying important government reports that had a bearing on the subject of this book.

The Social Security Administration was especially helpful in providing information on the U.S. centenarians and data on the longevity of our oldest citizens.

I am especially grateful to Joyce Boston of the San Antonio, Texas, Manpower, Inc., office for final typing of the manuscript and her cheerful cooperation during the difficult task of fitting all the pieces together. The illustrations are the result of the patient work of Miguel Martinez and Malvan Jordan.

I am also indebted to Robert Metz and the other members of the editorial staff of Newspaper Enterprise Association (NEA) for their interest and encouragement. The thousands of letters from readers of my medical column for NEA have provided me a solid basis for understanding the problems people experience with age.

Many more people have helped in one way or another to write this book. I hope that the final product in gathering a general description of the aspects of aging and the future opportunities will stimulate further efforts to realize man's full potential within the scheme of the universe.

L. E. L.

PART 1

The Basis of Life and Aging

One Hundred Plus

It was a special day in Bazavu, Azerbaijan. Shirali Mislimov, Russia's oldest living person, was celebrating his 166th birthday. Over 200 relatives came to drink to his health, but Mislimov drank only lemonade. He credited his long life to hard work and lemonade. He had risen early that morning and carried out his daily chores in the orchard and garden as was his custom.

The modern world's oldest living man lived happily for two more birth dates. Then in 1973 he died at age 168 after an undisclosed serious illness. Some scientists have doubted the Russians' claim about Mislimov's age, but there are many long-lived individuals among the Abkhasians and other Caucasian peasants. It is not unusual to find Abkhasians over 100 years of age in good health. Men often continue an active sex life beyond the age of 100. In 1963 a study of one man aged 119 demonstrated that he had live sperm and was fully potent. Many even at advanced age still have good eyesight and teeth. Their posture remains erect, and they look a vigorous 70 rather than past 100 years old. They remain lean throughout their lifetime; their attitude is that to be fat is to be ill.

The Soviet Union has established the Ethnographic Institute in Sukhumi. Dr. G. N. Sichinava of the Institute of Gerontology in Sukhumi has studied the working habits of the Abkhasians past 100 years of age. In one group of men a little more than half slowed down in work between 80 and 90; the rest decreased their work activities between 90 and 100. The women's work pattern began to slow down after 80. Many men and women over 100 regularly averaged four hours of work a day on collective farms.

The Abkhasian diet is close to that which has been recommended for the prevention of heart and circulatory diseases in the United States, Scandinavian countries, and other industrialized nations. Most importantly, the caloric intake is almost one-fourth less among the Abkhasian peasants than among their industrial counterparts from the cities, who have a higher rate of heart and vascular disease. Abkhasians eat meat as infrequently as once or twice a week. Much of their diet consists of a cornmeal mash, goat cheese, buttermilk, and generous amounts of fresh fruits and vegetables. The long-lived Abkhasians do not smoke or drink coffee or tea. The only alcoholic beverage commonly used is a locally produced red wine of low alcoholic content, taken in small amounts with meals. Sugar is essentially unknown, and honey is used for sweetening.

Numerous investigators from Russia and other nations have noticed the limited evidence of atherosclerosis—fatty blockage of the arteries—in the Abkhasian peasants. Dr. Samuel Rosen, an ear, nose, and throat specialist, found that the Abkhasian peasants had much better hearing than workers in Moscow who lived the standard industrial life of plenty. In his opinion the remarkable hearing acuity of the older Abkhasian peasants was associated with their freedom from atherosclerosis.

Another facet of the Abkhasians' life of importance in aging is their continued interest in life and a sense of responsibility. Even centenarians feel needed. Their family structure is such that age is still respected. By remaining useful even in later years they continue to give something to those around them. There is no such thing as "retiring." This concept is unknown to the Abkhasian peasants, and they expect to work according to their ability from childhood until death. They have very few illnesses and remain physically active throughout life. The apparent key to the long-lived Abkhasian's youth and vigor is his way of life, which is simple and close to nature.

Living beyond 100 years of age is unusual but not rare in our society. At the beginning of 1972 there were 6200 individuals 100 years or older listed by the Social Security Administration. In addition, the Social Security Administration estimates there are another 1800 persons not listed —or a total of 8000 people in the United States who are 100 years old or older. Of the 6200 recorded by the Social Security Administration their ages are as follows:

100 years	41.9%
101	24.2
102	13.5
103	18.3
104	2.9
105	3.4
106	1.9
107	1.4
108	0.6
109	0.4
110 and over	1.5

One of the oldest living Americans was Sylvester Magee, who was born May 29, 1841, and died in 1970 at age 129. His age was certified by the state of Mississippi after investigation of the supporting evidence. His mother was literate and had recorded his birth date in the family Bible. He was known to be old by young people's standards in 1910. He fought with the Union army at the Battle of Vicksburg during the Civil War, and the key points of his story were verified. His mother died in 1939 at the age of 119 and his father in 1922 at age 104. Among the interesting aspects of Sylvester Magee's life was the report that he fathered a child at age 109.

Another long-lived American is Charlie Smith, who claims to have been born in 1842 in Liberia. His original name was Mitchell Watkins. He tells of being lured on board a slave boat to see the boat and being captured as a boy. He remembers that the captain of the slave ship was named Legree. There were two Legree brothers who were captains of slave boats at that time, and no doubt the memory of the name Legree among the slaves provided this name for Harriet Beecher Stowe's classic *Uncle Tom's Cabin*. When the ship docked at Galveston, Texas, the boy was taken to the slave market in New Orleans, became the property of Captain John Smith, and was sent to a ranch near Galveston. All of the events as Charlie Smith remembers them fit with established facts. He has chosen July 4 as his birth date.

Carl Smith claims to have been born on December 25, 1858, and has been followed by the Social Security Administration since 1959. His story too seems to be accurate.

The oldest living woman with well-documented evidence of her age is Mary Nolte of Saint Louis, Missouri. She was born October 2, 1861, and educated in Lutheran schools with records establishing her age during her school years.

Not far behind is Kathrine Holman of Durham, North Carolina, born March 17, 1865, in North Carolina, three weeks after the Civil War ended. She retired from a tobacco company in 1940. Because her social security number had been issued before that date and it was common for people to claim to be younger than their actual age to avoid retirement without benefits at that time, she is probably at least as old as she claims to be.

Through the ages there have been long-lived individuals. The presumed criteria for longer life have remained relatively constant. Even 2000 years ago some people were believed to live as long as 150 years. Lucius Annaeus Seneca (4 B.C.–65 A.D.), the Roman historian and philosopher, observed that "the more a man follows nature, and is obedient to her laws, the longer he will live, and . . . the further he deviates from these, the shorter will be his existence."

> It is not the rich and the great, not those who depend on medicine, who become old; but such as use much exercise, are exposed to the fresh air, and whose food is plain and moderate, as farmers, gardeners, fishermen, laborers, soldiers; and such men, as perhaps never employed their thoughts on the means which have been used to promote longevity. It is among these people, chiefly, that the most astonishing instances of it are observed. Sometimes, in these situations, man still attains to the amazing age of 150 years, and upward.*

Despite the obvious capacity to live well past 100 years most individuals from industrial societies do not. At birth the life expectancy for a white woman in the United States is 74.9 years; for a white man it is only 67.5 years. For nonwhites the life expectancy is 67.5 years for women and 60.1 years for men. The average life expectancy of a man who has already reached 50 in the United States is 70, but on the island of Cyprus 50-year-old men have a life expectancy of 83; in Iceland, 79; and in Sweden, 78. Since these are averages, many have longer or shorter lives. In the United States in a population of 100,000 white males aged 40 to 44 years, 1877 die each year of atherosclerotic heart disease, a complication of atherosclerotic blockage of the arteries. Atherosclerosis is responsible for many changes often ascribed to old age.

As recently as 1900 the average life expectancy in the United States was only 47 years, because of infant mortality and early deaths associated with infectious diseases. People who reached the fifth decade of life often had a longer life expectancy than we do today. There is no better example than the history of the presidents of the United States. Excluding George Washington (who you might say was assassinated by medical ignorance because his physicians bled him—a practice common in his day) and all of the presidents who have been assassinated, there has been a marked change in the longevity of presidents (see table on p. 7). From Adams to Van Buren, the first seven presidents following Washington had a life span between 73 and 90 years with an average of 81 years, very nearly that touted for the Cypriots and a full 11 years longer than the life expectancy of a 50-year-old man today.

By contrast, the presidents from Harrison to Roosevelt (excluding those assassinated) had an average life span of only 66.7 years, below that of the American male today. Of these 20 presidents only three (Fillmore,

* From an editorial by Dr. Crawford W. Adams in *Chest*, Vol. 27, p. 308, 1970.

Adams, J.	90	Adams, J. Q.	80
Jefferson	83	Jackson	78
Madison	85	Van Buren	79
Monroe	73		

Average = 81 years

Harrison, W. H.	68	Arthur	56
Tyler	71	Cleveland	71
Polk	53	Harrison, B.	67
Taylor	65	Roosevelt, T.	60
Fillmore	74	Taft, W. H.	72
Pierce	64	Wilson	67
Buchanan	77	Harding	57
Johnson, A.	66	Coolidge	60
Grant	63	Hoover	90
Hayes	70	Roosevelt, F.	63

Average = 66.7 years

Buchanan, and Hoover) lived longer than Monroe's 73 years, the earliest death of our first seven presidents after Washington.

To illustrate how disease has continued to affect the longevity of the presidents, study of the subsequent presidents, from Wilson to Johnson (excluding Kennedy, who was assassinated), reveals that six of the eight had heart or vascular disease. If Harding's known heart disease and high blood pressure caused his sudden death, four (Wilson, Harding, Roosevelt, and Eisenhower), or half of the eight presidents, either had a stroke, died, or had a heart attack while in office as a result of heart and vascular disease—atherosclerosis. In addition, Coolidge died of a heart attack, and Johnson had heart attacks before and after his presidency.

Individual groups have been identified as living longer than others. For example, the Seventh-Day Adventists, who neither drink nor smoke and eat sparingly of meat, have a life span six years longer than that of the average American. According to a 10-year study by Dr. Richard T. Walden of Loma Linda University Medical School in California, they have their first heart attack a full decade after most Americans. In general, groups whose living habits are simple and include the features advocated by Seneca and practiced by the peasants of Abkhasia live longer in good health.

One way to increase the length of life is to obviate the major illnesses causing death and disability—mainly heart attacks, strokes, and cancer. Some authorities on aging think this would extend the life span only a few years, as would indeed be the case if one looked at the average. However, for young men 40 to 44 years of age who die from heart attacks, eliminating this problem would significantly increase the life span. For the vast majority of individuals, the first hurdle in lengthening life is doing away with heart and vascular disease and cancer. It is generally believed that if satisfactory solutions to these major medical problems of modern society are found many individuals can live in good health to the centenarian mark. One should emphasize that the interest here is in increasing the active middle years of life—that is, delaying the onset of old age. Many individuals who die before their time really begin to have the things we associate with old age sooner: heart attacks in their 40's and 50's, strokes, loss of physical ability, impotence, and other manifestations of sexual decline accompanied by loss of physical prowess.

These are short-term objectives. More dramatic is the belief of a group of scientists that the life span of man could be increased manyfold. The suggestion is that aging can be not only delayed but possibly even reversed. These scientists envision life spans approaching that of the biblical Methuselah, who lived 969 years. They believe that a quantum leap is possible in solving the problem of aging, and that immortality is not just a dream but a genuine possibility. The thought is that genetic engineering and control of the chemical factors at the cellular level which determine the ability of the body to constantly regenerate and replace itself can bring about immortality.

Living with all of one's faculties, health, and vigor, with the full joy of living, is one thing, but to be disabled, isolated, unloved, and ill is another. The difficulties here are well exemplified by the case of Elisha Campbell, an 81-year-old retired ironworker of Miami, Florida. His wife, also 81 years of age, was in ill health and needed to be placed under full-time nursing home care. Neither Campbell nor his children could afford this expense. While discussing the problem with his son and daughter, he told them he thought he had the answer. He got up, turned to his children, and said, "Mom and I have lived too long. I think I have a solution." Before his children or their mates could guess his intent, he had disappeared into the bedroom and they heard two shots. He had shot his wife and himself to death.

The unhappiness of aging is not limited to Western society. A similar situation has developed in Japan in recent times. Oldsters unsatisfied with their lot in life, trying to cope with their loneliness, miserable living conditions, and poor economic situations, have taken to committing suicide. In a culture where age was once revered, the elderly are now shunned. The traditional Japanese family system broke down after World War II, and the children became either unable or unwilling to care for their elders. The biggest problem in Japan is money. Many firms have a mandatory retirement age of 55 which leaves most middle-aged workers with at least one or two decades of life without means of support. Although annuities and pensions cover a limited number of workers, they are inadequate. About three-fourths of the Japanese over 65 have little income of any kind.

There are social problems to be solved as well as medical and health problems, if one is to enjoy a long life. Even so, it is not possible to deny the rewards of being able to live longer in good health with full vigor and as a meaningful part of one's society and environment. Aside from dreams for the future, there are solid facts to support what the individual can do to help achieve this goal now: specifically, understand the changes that occur with the process of aging, and learn how to delay the adverse changes, and maintain youthfulness and energy. It is entirely possible for most people to add years of healthy vigorous living to their life span. Usually a change in some living patterns is required, as well as the development of a disciplined personality. But the person who loves life and wants to *live* while he lives can do something about it.

two

From Atoms to You

Man is at the threshold of immortality. Most of the secrets of life are now known, though still unanswered are questions about what switches vital processes on and off, the identification of new chemical and physical inter-actions, and how to fit them together into a time sequence. There is every reason to believe that the ability to synthesize life will soon be common-place, permitting even complex creatures like man to be manufactured within the physiochemical laboratory. Perhaps even sooner, it will be possible to reverse the time-sequence pattern and replace aged and mal-functioning cells with youthful, healthy ones, providing the key to immortality.

Single-cell organisms already have a form of immortality. They simply divide and continue living as their children. In higher forms of life with sexual differentiation, mating is necessary, which inevitably results in continuous mixing of the gene pool that controls heredity.

Living cells have the ability to renew or even replace themselves. As organized systems within the cell deteriorate, they too are continuously replaced. In early life cells are constantly dying and being replaced. New cells must be formed for continuation of the growth process. Then suddenly growth stops. Maturation is achieved, and finally cells lose their capacity to renew or replace themselves and the inevitable decline begins. When the mechanism that stops the dynamic renewal process is understood and mastered, immortality will be possible.

INORGANIC COMPOUNDS

The concepts of heredity and cellular renewal are related to genes or DNA and its chemical helper RNA. To understand the life process, aging, youth, and reproduction as related to DNA, it is helpful to understand some simple chemistry. Everything in the universe is composed of little more than 100 chemical elements. These are around us in the form of metals like copper and iron and in the gas we breathe, containing mostly oxygen and nitrogen. The smallest unit of an element is called an atom. Thus there are atoms of oxygen, nitrogen, iron, and copper. The atoms are the building blocks which can combine to form molecules, the smallest units of a substance containing the atoms of two or more elements. Water is a common example, built from two atoms of hydrogen gas and one atom of oxygen to form one molecule of water. Common table salt is another example, made by combining one atom of sodium with one atom of chlorine to yield sodium chloride salt.

Sodium chloride salt dissolves in water to form salt water. In the process the elements of sodium and chlorine separate into individual atoms bearing unequal electrical charges. The sodium is electrically positive and the chlorine electrically negative. In this unstable state they are called ions. The positive sodium ions and negative chlorine ions give the water an electrical character. Literally thousands of electrical charges may be floating in a glass of plain salt water. A liquid with such charges is called an electrolyte and is a good conductor of electricity. Seawater contains salt (sodium chloride) and is an electrolyte. Salt water is a major part of our bodies and of all other living creatures on earth. Salt in the blood and other body fluids outside the cell has about the same concentration found in seawater. Some scientists think this is the consequence of the evolution of life from the sea.

Inside the cells there are different salts composed of potassium, chlorine, and phosphate (oxygen and phosphorous). The element potassium belongs to the same small group of elements that sodium does. Potassium chloride has a somewhat sharper taste than sodium chloride and is often a major component of salt substitute used by people who cannot use sodium for any reason. A salt solution of potassium chloride also separates into electrically charged atoms forming an electrolyte solution. Nearly 70 percent of the body weight is composed of salt-water solution of sodium or potassium salts.

Simple chemical compounds of salt or other combinations of atoms are called inorganic compounds. The study of their interactions is called inorganic chemistry. Many of these compounds, such as sodium chloride, potassium chloride, and plain water, are essential to life. Inorganic compounds are also found freely in inert materials unrelated to life processes.

ORGANIC COMPOUNDS

Another group of chemical compounds all contain the atom carbon and are found in living structures. These are called organic compounds, and the study of them is called organic chemistry. The food we eat, animal or vegetable, is nutritious because it contains organic compounds. Carbohydrates, proteins, fats, alcohol, and vitamins are all organic compounds, meaning that they contain carbon atoms.

The atoms of each element are different and are exceedingly complex electrical structures. The number of electrical charges influences how an atom can be used as a building block. For our purposes we need only think of an atom as a tiny ball with one or more hands that can be joined with the hands of other atoms to form compounds. Let us return to the simple sodium chloride salt concept. The sodium atom has only one hand, and the chlorine atom has only one hand; thus only one sodium atom and one chlorine atom can hold hands to form a molecule of sodium chloride salt (Fig. 1). The same is true of potassium in forming a molecule of potassium chloride salt.

Fig. 1

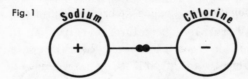

Ordinary water is a little more complex. Hydrogen, like sodium, has only one hand, but oxygen is more versatile and has two hands. A simple oxygen atom holds hands with two hydrogen atoms to form a molecule of water (Fig. 2).

Fig. 2

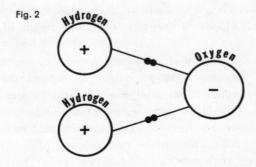

Nitrogen, essential to the formation of protein, has three hands and combines with three one-handed hydrogen atoms to form simple ammonia (Fig. 3).

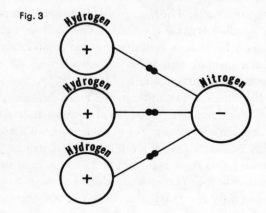

Fig. 3

Carbon, the central building block for organic compounds, has four hands, the maximum number of any atom. It holds hands with two oxygen atoms to form carbon dioxide, the gas we breathe out of our lungs (Fig. 4).

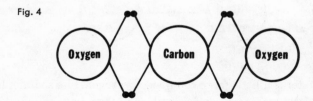

Fig. 4

Or carbon can combine with four one-handed hydrogen atoms to form the common methane gas (Fig. 5).

The most complex chemical compounds in the life system are based on the formation of chains of carbon atoms. The hands of the carbon atoms that are not used for the chain can be used to hold other atoms, frequently hydrogen or oxygen (Fig. 6).

With the apparently unlimited variations of connections and three-dimensional chain configurations that can be formed from the various chemical elements, an infinite variety of organic compounds, including enzymes and hormones, are formed. These are the basic building blocks that make the living cells. The protein used to build cells is manufactured within the cells from smaller units called amino acids. There are only 20 amino acids that are used to build all of the complex proteins that form

Fig. 5

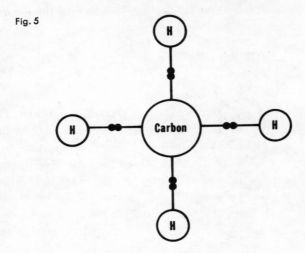

all of the cells of the body and the important chemical enzymes and hormones. Using the amino acids to build the proteins from food sources is part of the life process.

Proteins, fats, and carbohydrates are all long-chain carbon compounds. Only the proteins contain nitrogen. All of these foods are used in building cells and all can be destroyed by cells to provide energy.

Fig. 6

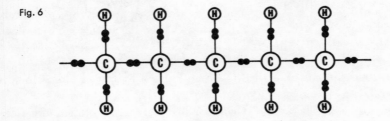

The organic compounds that dissolve in water in the same manner that common salt does are called hydrophilic (water loving) compounds. These are the amino acids used to build body protein and the sugars. They form ions in water, creating an electrolyte solution. These and simple salt enable the inner body to transmit electricity easily. Other organic compounds do not dissolve in water and are called hydrophobic (water hating). They are the long-carbon-chain fatty acids. Since they do not dissolve to form ions, fatty areas of the body do not conduct electricity readily. They do, however, make excellent building materials to maintain insoluble structures within living organisms. Nature uses these compounds to build cell walls or partitions within living matter.

THE CELL

The outer limits of a cell are recognized by its cell membrane. This may be thought of as a sheet of thin plastic which can take various shapes to encase the material within the cell unit. Electrolyte solution consisting mostly of water and salt is both inside and outside of the cell membrane. Clearly the cell membrane must not be soluble in water or it will not act as a suitable partition, yet it must still interact with the chemicals in solution for life processes. Nature solves this problem handily using the ubiquitous carbon chain. The inner layer of the cell membrane is formed by interlocking carbon chains of fatty acids, which are not soluble in water, and the long carbon chain connects to the atoms of phosphorus compounds near both of its external and internal surfaces. Such chemical structures are called phospholipids. The phosphate end is more soluble and forms ions. It interacts with the chemical solutions within and without the cell. Thus by properly arranging complex phospholipids, nature constructs a cell membrane which is insoluble in its inner layers yet soluble at its surfaces, almost melting into the more liquid environments.

For a functional analogy it is easy to visualize the chicken egg as an example of a cell. Compare the shell to the unique outer cell membrane, the yolk to the cell nucleus, and the white of the egg to the cell cytoplasm. The cell nucleus, like the yolk, is surrounded by a membrane similar to the external cell membrane. However, it is much more porous, allowing easier movement between the contents of the nucleus and the cytoplasm than occurs between the inner cell and its external environment.

Within the nucleus are rod-shaped bodies called chromosomes. These are literally the instructions for forming new cells or controlling heredity. Herein rests the secret of life and regeneration. The chromosomes divide when new cells are formed. There are 23 pairs or 46 chromosomes within each cell nucleus. Attached along the rod-shaped chromosomes are the units of heredity that control blood type, hair, eye color, and all body characteristics. Each unit is called a gene. There are more than 100,000 genes in man. The chemical structure of the gene has been identified, and it is the life-giving substance DNA—a combination of three chemical compounds, a complex *sugar molecule* (2-deoxy-D-ribose), *phosphoric acid* (hydrogen, phosphorus, and oxygen), and an organic compound called a *base* containing nitrogen. (The D is for the sugar, the N for nitrogenous base, and A for phosphoric acid.) DNA is formed in long continuous strands or chemical chains alternately using four chemically different nitrogenous bases: adenine (A), guanine (G), thymine (T), and cytosine (C). It is convenient to think of the DNA chain as two long ribbons. Both ribbons are constructed of interlocking units of sugar and phosphate from phosphoric acid. The two parallel ribbons are loosely attached to each other by bridges of the four nitrogenous bases A, G, T, C. Each nitrogenous base is fixed to its ribbon strand at one end and has, as it were, one free hand to grasp its partner base fixed to the other ribbon. If A is fixed to one ribbon, it will be holding hands with T fixed to the other sugar-phosphate ribbon. The hand holding between the two bases holds the two strands of DNA together. The entire double ribbon is then twisted like a spiral staircase (Fig. 7).

Fig. 7

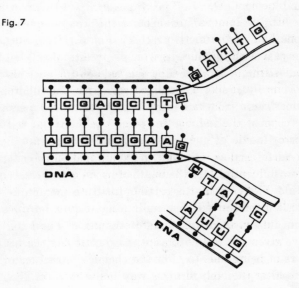

There is a simple code relationship between the two DNA strands. An easy way to understand it is to compare it to a simple color code. Assume that the four chemical bases are four colors: black (A), white (T), green (G), and red (C). Nature's scheme is that only white can be matched with black and only green with red. Now, if the colors attached to one strand of DNA are in the sequence of black, green, red, white, using the rule that only black matches white and only green matches with red, the opposite or matching ribbon color code would be white, red, green, black. Thus the hand from the bases A, G, C, T holds the hand from its mate T, C, G, A.

Either strand of DNA can interact with spare parts in the cell to form its opposite strand. DNA has been isolated and its ability to generate more DNA established. This finding has given rise to the concept that some DNA is really the initial model or master gene and much of the remaining DNA is factory copies or slave DNA.

Within the multiple variations of DNA strips are the chemical blueprints for building, renewing, and even stopping cellular actions. With reproduction half of the genetic chromosome material from the female and half from the male unite to provide a full complement of chromosomes, and the varied results provide the gene mixture from the parents. The newly fertilized egg contains in its nucleus the entire chemical blueprint for the whole body. All subsequent cells contain the genes that are a copy of the master blueprint. Dr. J. B. Gurdon of Oxford demonstrated this phenomenon with his famous frog experiment. He removed the nucleus (containing one-half of the mother's chromosomes) from an unfertilized egg and replaced it with the nucleus from an intestinal cell containing all the chromosomes from a tadpole. The egg then had a nucleus with a full set of chromosomes just like a fertilized egg, with one difference—all of the chromosomes came from one tadpole. The result was a tadpole which was a genetic copy of the tadpole providing the intestinal cell nucleus.

The old horror movie of one person's spirit invading another person's body is not so farfetched as it seems. An experiment with bacteria demonstrates just how influential DNA is in affecting an organism's characteristics. Dr. Oswald T. Avery of Rockefeller Institute extracted DNA from dead pneumonia bacteria and by implanting it into harmless bacteria converted them into virulent pneumonia organisms. These and other experiments have given rise to the concepts of genetic engineering. They are the forerunners of being able to alter the chemical structure of the genes and thereby to alter the body. In this way many medical problems, particularly birth defects, may be corrected.

Viruses are considered bad because we think of them as causing diseases. A virus is merely a small amount of DNA or its related chemical chain RNA coated with a layer of protein. It is an intermediate form between the living and nonliving chemical world. A virus particle can take over bacteria and replace their genetic characteristics with its own. From here it is a short step to manufacturing viruses, and—the important point—good viruses as opposed to bad ones may well be manufactured that can replace the gene characteristics of a cell, altering it favorably. Since viruses live and multiply within cells, they could chemically reconstruct the body just as we now know they afflict the body in an adverse way. There is much evidence to suggest that these chemical bits of nucleic acid or actual viruses may be involved in the disorganized cellular overgrowth of cancer.

The story of life doesn't end with DNA, which is confined to the cell nucleus. The cells must form many complex proteins from the 20 different amino acids used for building blocks. Proteins must be synthesized for the life-giving hormones and enzymes. The processing unit is in the cytoplasm surrounding the nucleus. The main part of the processing plant is another chemical chain much like DNA. Instead of thymine (T) it contains another nitrogenous base, uracil (U). Thus, U replaces T in the code system. The complex sugar in the chemical ribbon is slightly different, called D-ribose, giving rise to the chemical name ribonucleic acid (RNA). RNA is only a single ribbon strand rather than the double strand necessary for DNA.

Most of the RNA in the cell is clumped aggregations within the cytoplasm. Here amino acids in the cytoplasm are assembled in definite sequences to form new protein molecules. This is no random process. The RNA ribbon with its chemical code acts like a complex assembly line far more intricate than anything yet envisioned by the automotive industry. Piece by piece the carbon chain selects varied amino acids, and they are fitted together building a specific structure called for in the original blueprint of the DNA within the cell nucleus. Such an ordered sequence is necessary to produce the proteins essential to complex life structures. Otherwise, like a house built without planning but constructed of its component parts, it would be nonfunctional.

The RNA in the cytoplasm gets its orders from the DNA in the nucleus by an astonishingly simple mechanism. DNA manufactures a special messenger RNA strip (mRNA; short strips are called transcript RNA) in the nucleus which then migrates to the cytoplasm bearing a genetic code message to activate the cytoplasm RNA. The DNA makes a photographic negative of itself in the following way. A segment of the double ribbon uncoils or parts right down the middle. In this segment the nitrogenous base components stop holding hands and turn their backs on each other. Each open outstretched hand is available to sort out materials around it and form a single ribbon that complements it, a facsimile of the opposite strip of DNA. The same rules apply in the code sequence on the single strand of RNA, only U replaces T in the sequence. Thus, if the single strand of unraveled DNA has a code of A, G, C, T, the messenger RNA strip would read U, C, G, A. Once these strips of mRNA are formed, the double strips of DNA are reunited.

In bacteria the mRNA may last only a few minutes, but during that time it can form many molecules of protein. In higher forms of life mRNA may last several days, forming thousands of protein molecules. Whenever more protein building is necessary, the DNA forms more mRNA. So life continues until for some reason the DNA quits forming RNA, and production of new protein to replace old protein slows, then stops.

There is still another specialized facet of the life process. Since all cells contain the same blueprint in their nucleus, why do some become kidney cells, others heart, and still others liver cells rather than all being the same? The blueprints are literally under wraps. A protein substance is wrapped around the DNA chain except those portions that are to be active in building a particular cell. It is much like an orchestra. Even though the full musical score is there, each instrument plays only its part. In the liver cells only the liver segment is played; in the heart, only the heart segment. The proteins that wrap around the inactive portion of the DNA chain are called repressors. Certain enzymes which can inactivate or uncoil the repressor proteins and activate the repressed segments of DNA are called inducers. The repressors and inducers, with their own controlling enzyme systems that activate and deactivate them, may well be important in the aging process. It is already known that special proteins—histones—are involved in the mechanism. Dr. Vincent Allfrey of Rockefeller University demonstrated a 400 percent increase in RNA by removing histones, which meant that many previously inactive segments of DNA became activated. To the extent that aging is related to inactivated segments of DNA such studies suggest a means for perpetuating DNA action and life itself.

In addition to the RNA chemical processing plant to build proteins the cells contain another processing plant to dismantle organic compounds or food. Called the mitochondrion, this is another membrane composed of complex chemical compounds. To provide more area the membrane is crumpled into a pile much like an irregularly folded sheet. Enzymes and other important chemical compounds needed in the tear-down process are attached to its surface. The food particle starts along the disassembly line. Here is where the body uses oxygen. The oxygen interacts with the food compounds, a process called oxidation (a fire is a common physical example of oxidation). As the chemical bonds between the atoms in the food compounds are broken, energy is liberated, just as fire liberates heat. The energy is used for body processes or to form new high-energy compounds that can break down later without oxygen to provide energy (adenosine triphosphate—ATP). The oxidation process liberates carbon dioxide and water as well.

Thus, the cell contains its own individual blueprint for its structure within the genes (DNA) on the chromosomes in the cell nucleus. These are self-perpetuating. The cell also provides the coded blueprint in the form of RNA to manufacture new proteins, and it contains a disassembly plant to metabolize or consume food material.

three

The Causes of Aging

Inherent in the concept of aging is the belief that everything has a "natural life span." Automobiles, chairs, buildings—all inanimate objects wear out with time and use or misuse, and so do living things. This thinking is also expressed in the second law of thermodynamics: that systems tend to become disordered with time. The concept is called entropy. Some scientists believe it applies to man; eventually our well-ordered biological system becomes disordered or aged. The time required for entropy to occur "naturally" is not known.

The problem in applying the concept of entropy to living things is that the basic nature of protoplasm is to replace itself. The parts of a cell are not old parts but newly manufactured parts. The liver of a 100-year-old man does not contain 100-year-old cells but is made up of cells of fairly recent vintage. The constant replacement of cells and the constant renewal of organized components in the cells cause them to be distinctly different from nonliving systems.

For an analogy, think of purchasing a new automobile, then replacing all of its parts piece by piece during each two-year span. After 10 years, the resulting automobile would be, not a 10-year-old system, but a system of component parts no older than two years. The body literally does just this, and its component parts are the food we eat, the energy we absorb, and the air we breathe.

DOUBLING

One means of studying protoplasm's ability to divide and grow (doubling) indefinitely is to study isolated tissue cultures. By growing tissue in the laboratory one can measure the number of times the cells are able to double. Dr. Leonard Hayflick of Stanford University observed that human cells were not immortal but lasted only through 50 doublings. Even so, the characteristic of so-called aging occur in man well before 50 doublings of his cells have taken place. Even Hayflick does not believe that deterioration and death are the result of reaching the ultimate doubling capacity in man. Moreover, not all living cells are limited to 50 doublings. Cultures of mouse cells have been said to divide indefinitely, as do those from many other living creatures. These *immortal cells*, however, may be abnormal or mutants of the real thing. Whatever they are, the point remains they are living protoplasm with the characteristics of immortality—abnormal or not. The immortality characteristics as noted in some tumors suggest that there may be a very fine line between the disorganized growth of cancer cells and cell mechanisms basic to immortality.

At present we do not know all of the essential steps in turning on or off the actions of DNA and RNA essential to perpetual regeneration. Consequently we do not know or understand the complete process of cell or tissue aging. Tissue cultures such as used in Hayflick's experiments on doubling tell us that unless we learn the missing steps and apply them to human tissue, cellular and hence human aging is inevitable, resulting in loss of cell function and finally cell death. Herein lies much of the confusion in studying and defining aging. *The end result, loss of cell function and death, is the same outcome brought about by disease processes.* A cell is just as dead if it dies from lack of oxygen as if it passes its 50 doubling limit. Impairment of the circulation to the brain can cause loss of brain cells just as surely as if their death depended upon a time factor. The same applies to cell damage in death from most human ills, whether they are caused by toxic chemicals, physical factors such as radiation, virulent organisms, or injuries from heat, cold, or mechanical factors. This fact makes it difficult to differentiate between "time-dependent changes" and the accumulated results of damage or disease which are "acquired changes."

ACQUIRED VERSUS TIME-DEPENDENT AGING

Many of the health problems, disability, and the deterioration now associated with age are "acquired changes" rather than simply the result of the passage of time. A social attitude has evolved that because of a person's age he is expected to have these changes; therefore, they can be disregarded. *The simple truth is that most older people in our society are not just old. They are sick and have as much right to society's concern as infants or adolescents.* At age 70 a person may have reached only the halfway mark of the possible life span if the 50 maximal cell doublings were achieved. Many disabilities of the 70-year-old person are from acquired defects that we have not learned to prevent or cure rather than from time-dependent aging. The first step in managing these problems is recognizing that they are illnesses—not just the ravages of time.

For example, fatty deposits may plug the arteries and interfere with circulation, causing, in turn, heart attacks, strokes, and other diseases. The resulting dead heart cells, brain cells, and cells of other organs are dead because of a disease process, not because of time. Death from cancer in older people occurs because something has gone wrong in the body, not because of time. It is true that increasing age seems to decrease the body's ability to withstand these disease processes and other environmental challenges, but even that observation isn't absolute. Doctors may examine the heart of a 26-year-old man and note that it "is as old as a 70-year-old man's," and what they mean is that the changes in the arteries are as advanced as those often seen in older men; but in neither case are the changes caused by time. The occurrence of heart attacks and cancer and even early osteoarthritis in young people reminds us that we are dealing with "acquired changes."

Because the end results of aging and of common diseases are the same, no doubt there is an overlapping between the effects of "acquired changes" and "time-dependent changes."

The causes for aging may be placed in two main groups—those causes of acquired changes which we will call "acquired aging," such as heart attacks and strokes, and the causes related to time, hereafter called "genetic aging." In the first group are heart and circulatory diseases, cancer, arthritis, other diseases, and general disability common in the older people in our present society. In the second are the basic chemical actions involved in DNA-RNA cellular functions that are essential to protoplasm's ability to continue its constant replacement or cellular immortality.

GENETIC FACTOR

The most widely accepted theory of aging is that it is determined by one's genes. Dr. Bernard L. Strehler of the National Institute of Child Health and Human Development states flatly, "There is absolute certainty that maximum life span possible for the member of a given species is determined by the nature of the DNA that species contains." According to this view, a person is born with a life program or script which will be played out in the course of time. It is true that the age teeth erupt, the onset of puberty, the time of the menopause, and many other events occur at nearly the same time frame. Being born with a life program doesn't mean it won't be altered along the way. The events of one's life are fed into the program and ultimately determine how much of the program will be played and literally in what key.

Having a genetic program does not mean that longevity as we know it is determined by our parents' longevity. The acquired changes in the program resulting in acquired aging are such an overriding factor that people grow old or die of these rather than because they have reached the end of their original program. Whether your parents were long-lived or short-lived will not usually be a factor in your own life span. Studies by Dr. Erdman Palmore of Duke University's Center for the Study of Aging and Human Development failed to show any correlation between a person's life span and his parents' age at death. Similar results were obtained in the Russian studies by Dr. D. F. Chebotarev. These investigations and others refute the old axiom that the way to live a long life is to select long-lived parents. At some future date when the deleterious effects of acquired aging can be eliminated, a stronger case for familial longevity may be possible.

The current genetic concept is that certain substances cease to be formed at least in sufficient quantities to permit the normal DNA-RNA action of protein synthesis, thus shutting off the recycling mechanism necessary for immortality. This may also be tied in with the "repressors" and "inducers" which control the amount of DNA codes that can be used for reproduction. The extension of life by controlling the time-dependent factors will come from the final understanding and management of these basic cell mechanisms or possibly what has been termed the master gene which may control these functions.

CELLULAR FACTORS

A number of theories of aging involve changes in cell structure. These could be related to genetic factors or acquired factors. One concept is the exhaustion theory: that harmful substances accumulate in the cells impairing their normal function. Another, the error theory, has it that eventually the errors in DNA-RNA function cause errors in protein formation interfering with vital enzyme formation and cell division. Still another theory believes that the chemical chains of complex molecules in the cells join together at certain points or become "cross-linked." Such accumulated chemical changes are believed to interfere with the chemical compounds' normal action. The "cross-linked' theory was first proposed by Dr. Johan Bjorksten in 1941 and has since fallen into disfavor. Many scientists believe any cross-linking is really a result of aging rather than a cause.

Somewhat related to exhaustion is the idea that the DNA can produce only so many copies before the copies become faded, like the twelfth carbon copy in a typewriter, and illegible for reading.

Although many cellular changes are known to occur with both acquired and genetic aging, one in particular may be important: the development of a brown pigment substance called lipofuscin that accumulates in the heart, brain, testes, and other organs. It is often called the age pigment. Its exact role is in dispute, with some scientists stating it is just an accompaniment of the important changes and others believing its accumulation affects the cell's function.

The free radical concept advocated by Dr. Denham Harman of Nebraska proposes that certain substances with carbon chains having free hands not attached to other atoms such as hydrogen (unsaturated chains) are free to interact with basic cellular substances and form chemical combinations that interfere with cell function, leading to aging. Whether this would be a genetic time factor or acquired aging is a moot point. Harman's concept is related to the cross-linked idea but has won greater acceptance mostly because he has obtained some success in lengthening life span of animals by using chemicals he believes to prevent free radical actions. It is possible, though, that those chemicals achieve their effect by other means. Thus his observations may not prove his theory.

AUTOIMMUNE THEORY

Not completely unrelated to some of the concepts previously mentioned is the autoimmune theory of aging. The body naturally reacts against foreign elements, including bacteria. This defense mechanism provides immunity against disease. Under certain circumstances the immune mechanism that reacts against or destroys foreign substances turns upon a natural substance in the body, destroying it or making it ineffective. In a sense we become allergic to natural substances in our body. A group of diseases caused in this manner are called autoimmune diseases. The concept has been extended by some scientists to include aging, on the assumption that the immune mechanisms attack essential cell materials, leading to abnormal function, suppression, and eventually death.

ENVIRONMENTAL FACTORS

A host of environmental factors have been implicated in aging. In fact, one example, decreasing body temperature, lengthens the life span. Cell doubling can be arrested by freezing cells in liquid nitrogen. Much later, when they are reconstituted, they resume doubling exactly where they stopped to complete their allotted number of doubling cycles. The temperature control studies suggest that a limited amount of active energy is available and can be used slowly or rapidly. Radiation, nutrition, oxygen, and other factors are important to life span. The necessity for these in optimal amounts does not mean that they are involved in the time-dependent sequences that result in aging. It only means that certain optimal conditions must exist for the original life program to be played to its conclusion.

DISEASE FACTORS

Some scientists believe aging is a result of the cumulative toll of insults to the body, particularly diseases. Dr. Hardin Jones of the Donner Laboratories at the University of California proposes that there is a relationship between childhood diseases and degenerative diseases. He has even estimated that the low level of childhood diseases in recent years in the United States will add 15 years of useful life to the life span. He credits the long life expectancy of 50-year-old men in Cyprus (to age 83) to the remarkably low incidence of infectious diseases there.

WEAR AND TEAR

One of the almost universal changes in the older people in our society is osteoarthritis, sometimes called degenerative arthritis. It particularly afflicts the knees, hips, and weight-bearing joints. It is common to say that these joints become "worn out." This is a good example of the concept of wear and tear in aging. Other tissues in the body are also assumed to "age" because of wear and tear. Certainly osteoarthritis is one of man's oldest diseases, and evidence of it has been found throughout the animal kingdom including ancient dinosaurs. The theory of wear and tear, however, is in conflict with the general concept that protoplasm is able to replace itself. Total replacement of cells—for example, in the knee—would exchange old cells for new cells. The changes seem to be more complex than that.

There is evidence that protoplasm can replace itself and in fact replace joints, cartilage, and bony tissue. One of the best examples is the common lizard. When the lizard loses its tail, it simply grows another one—a naked, arrogant display of protoplasm's capacity to regenerate itself. Apparently what happens in humans and other mammals is that many lost cells and tissues are not regenerated. The program that is responsible for replacing these cells ceases to function.

The baseball pitcher who develops osteoarthritis or traumatic arthritis of the elbow because of wear and tear may have replaced his cells so often that he has reached their maximum doubling capacity and is unable to renew damaged or destroyed cells. If this is the case, learning to control the mechanism for turning on the instructions for regeneration and replacement should immediately solve the problem of osteoarthritis and other degenerative problems of this nature in the body, making the wear and tear concept obsolete.

There is already evidence that one can regenerate limbs in mammals, just as the lizard grows back its tail. Dr. Robert O. Becker, an orthopedic surgeon at State University of New York, Upstate Medical Center, has amputated the forelimbs of rats at the shoulder and then, using small amounts of electrical current applied to the stumps, caused the limbs to grow back as far as the elbows. Dr. Becker thinks that the electrical current stimulated the growth process and that his experiments prove that regeneration is possible. This may be only one of several external mechanisms which may in some way reactivate the special type of RNA that stimulates cell growth as seen in the growing phase of mammals before they reach maturation. The wear and tear concept of aging is a legitimate theory but one which is not totally divorced from the concept of a genetic program. Clearly one could solve the problem of wear and tear by learning how to turn off and on appropriate portions of the genetic program as desired. The same principle applies to loss of elastic tissue in the arteries. If this substance can be replaced with new elastic tissue, the arteries can literally be rejuvenated by simply recycling the cells' own master program utilized in the earlier years.

DISUSE FACTOR

Certainly many of the problems noted in older people which we attribute to aging are the direct result of disuse. There is clear evidence of loss of muscle cells and decrease in size of muscles if they are not used, just as there is evidence that the amount of muscle mass can be increased with appropriate exercise, as long as the blood supply for the developing muscle is adequate. Disuse of bodily systems not only affects skeletal muscles but can affect the heart muscle, decreasing the heart's capacity. It can affect the lung's capacity and almost every bodily system. Nature seems to follow a simple principle: "If you don't use it, you lose it."

A good example of this principle is what happens in the formation of red blood cells. Everyone destroys a certain number of red blood cells every day by normal physical activity. The simple mechanical process of circulating blood causes mechanical wear and tear on blood cells and brings about this destruction. The older cells apparently are the weaker ones and are the ones usually destroyed. If an individual maintains a relatively constant level of activity, the bone marrow will form enough red blood cells each day to replace those that are destroyed. In this way the necessary balance of red blood cells is preserved within narrow limits. If a person becomes inactive, the cells are not destroyed so rapidly and the bone marrow stops producing as many. It literally becomes inactive and may take as long as three weeks to be fully reactivated when one resumes more vigorous physical activity.

An analogy can be made to the metabolism of sugar. Individuals who do not use sugar or sweets of any type do not need to develop metabolic mechanisms to handle a sugar load. Insulin, normally produced by the pancreas, makes the utilization of the substances possible, and if no large loads of sugar substances are presented to challenge the mechanism, the pancreas just does not have to produce as much insulin. So it begins to rest or decrease its range of capacity. If the individual is then challenged with a large load of sugar, as in a sugar tolerance test, he won't be able to metabolize it and his blood sugar level will rise and stay high as it does in a diabetic. This is only transitory, and if the individual consumes large amounts of sweet substances over three or four days the pancreas will regain its ability to produce increased amounts of insulin and utilize the sugar.

There are countless examples, whether reference is to chemical systems or more obvious mechanical systems like bone and muscle, to show that the range of capacity of the human body's functions is dependent upon using it. Physical strength comes from using the body; chemical ability, from exercising the chemical system of the body. Loss of the normal range of these functions is not genetic aging; it is the body's response to disuse. Perhaps lack of activity in some way turns off some of the basic cellular mechanisms, but this is theory. In any case disuse is an important component in the weakening, loss of function, and loss of the full range of capacity of function seen so often with increasing years. Most of these changes are within the voluntary control of the individual.

ATHEROSCLEROSIS

Atherosclerosis is the accumulation of fatty deposits in the arteries. This can occur anywhere in the body. If it affects the arteries to the heart muscle, it causes heart disease; to the brain, it causes strokes; to the legs, it interferes with walking; to the genitals, it can interfere with a man's capacity to have erections or affect his testicular function; to the kidneys, it can alter their normal function. Because atherosclerosis leads to blockage of the arteries, it interferes with circulation. Cells will then be deficient in oxygen and nutrients and accumulate end products of metabolism like carbon dioxide. These adverse effects on the cells limit their capacity to regenerate and hinder their growth and response to use, thereby contributing to the disuse problem. In their extreme form they can result in cell death.

Through causing heart attacks, strokes, and kidney disease and its multiple problems, atherosclerosis accounts for approximately half of the deaths in the United States. It occasions untold numbers of cases of senility because of brain damage and a host of other medical problems. The amount of fatty deposits in the arteries clearly increases with age, and it was therefore once assumed that atherosclerosis was an aging phenomenon. This is obviously a false assumption since atherosclerosis also occurs in young people, particularly in the arteries to the heart in men as young as 22 years of age and in sufficient amounts to cause heart attacks in these individuals. Nevertheless, because it increases with age, the changes it brings about are often considered as aging. They are, of course, acquired changes.

There are several different ways in which the fatty deposits can accumulate in the walls of the arteries and lead to this problem. First, the fatty particles in the blood stream itself are the same type as those found in the arteries, and apparently the more fatty particles there are in the blood, the more will deposit in the walls of the arteries, causing atherosclerosis. It is for this reason that the blood fats are commonly measured. They can be measured by a number of methods, depending on the characteristics of the fatty particles, which are composed of triglycerides, cholesterol, and one of the blood proteins. This is why they are called lipoproteins, *lipo* meaning "fat."

One sophisticated way of gauging the importance of the blood fats is to measure the number and size of these fat particles by various means. Some investigators feel that the smaller particles are less important than the larger particles in causing atherosclerosis. The fatty portion of the lipoprotein is made up of fatty acids, which combine with glycerol to form triglycerides. Glycerol is a three-carbon chain molecule and therefore combines with three different fatty acids to form the triglyceride. Another laboratory procedure is measurement of the amount of triglycerides as an index of the likelihood of atherosclerosis.

The fatty acids themselves may be of several different types, and the chains of fatty acids may be of different lengths, all of which affect the size of the lipoproteins. Attached to the triglyceride is cholesterol. Most of this substance is produced by the liver, but part of it can come from the diet. The more cholesterol there is in the blood, the greater the number of fatty particles and apparently the greater the probability of atherosclerotic blockage to the arteries. Thus cholesterol measurements are a common laboratory procedure in studying atherosclerosis.

A second important group of factors related to atherosclerosis is comprised of the physical factors. The higher the blood pressure, the more fatty particles in the blood stream are forced out into the wall of the arteries. As a result, increased blood pressure is associated with increased amounts of atherosclerosis and complications such as heart disease and strokes.

The blood pressure in the arteries to the lungs is normally much lower than in the arteries to the rest of the body. Consequently in normal people the arteries to the lungs are spared significant atherosclerotic blockage. This is an excellent example of the role of blood pressure as a factor in causing atherosclerosis. Obviously measures which lower the blood pressure are of major importance in promoting health and longevity.

Even the physical angulation of the arteries is important since fatty deposits appear to accumulate at the site of branching of the arteries.

A third cause of atherosclerosis is related to what happens in the cells of the walls of arteries themselves. If the wall of the artery is injured in some way, it is more likely to accumulate blood fats and develop atherosclerosis. An injury can be mechanical, or due to a disease process, or perhaps even nutritional. There is some evidence, at least in animals, that diets markedly deficient in vitamin C can lead to an accumulation of fatty deposits in arteries, and actual experiments have shown that this material is eliminated when the vitamin C deficiency is corrected.

Most of the attention has really been directed toward the problem of fatty particles in the blood. Yet many secondary factors may be involved, including the diet. Individuals who eat too much of any type of calories seem to develop increased amounts of fatty particles and atherosclerosis. Female hormones apparently produce types of blood fat particles that are lower in cholesterol and less likely to cause atherosclerosis. Exercise is thought by some authorities to be important, as are many other living and habit patterns. Heredity is also a factor to be considered; perhaps one could alter the metabolic machinery of the body if one could control the genes, thereby favorably influencing the body's ability to prevent atherosclerosis. At present, since such management is not possible, atherosclerosis has to be approached much like diabetes, which is also related to an individual's gene pattern, and treated by preventing it or by reversing it through improved living patterns and sometimes medicine.

CANCER

Cancer is the second most common cause of death in the United States, accounting for 15 percent of all deaths. It is apparently directly related to basic cell DNA-RNA mechanisms. A cancer is a sudden wild uncontrolled growth of any of the body tissues. Lung cells can go berserk and form lung cancer, which can invade the spine and other parts of the body. Breast cancer is breast cells that have suddenly started growing in a disorganized and confused manner, and the same applies to cancers originating in the liver, colon, rectum, kidney, brain, or even the skin. One can have as many types of cancers as one has types of tissue in the body.

There is probably more than one mechanism that causes the loss of orderly cell growth and replacement. Viruses, which are small bits of DNA or RNA coated with protein, have long been suspected as a cause of cancer. Dr. Howard Temin of the University of Wisconsin showed that a tumor virus under proper circumstances could upset the usual DNA-mRNA sequence and cause mRNA to start producing DNA. The new

DNA in turn triggered cell division for abnormal cells that were cancer. A virus may also alter the DNA-RNA cell characteristics and take over, just as the dead pneumonia bacteria experiment showed how normal non-infectious bacteria could be converted to virulent pneumonia organisms.

Another prominent concept of cellular dynamics in producing cancer is that a special type of RNA exists until maturation is achieved and then ceases to function. If it persists or is activated later, it stimulates growth to resume in an abnormal fashion or induces cancer.

Still another idea is that cell growth is limited by the presence of the cell membrane. If the cell membrane is damaged or destroyed, perhaps by a virus, the cell's internal DNA-RNA mechanism gets no "turn off" signal and simply keeps on producing cells by rapid division which leads to more and more tumor cells and finally an established cancer.

Regardless of how the cancer growth is started, it requires a blood supply to continue growing and eventually to spread. The development of a blood supply is dependent on forming an enzyme that stimulates blood vessel formation.

There appear to be two primary approaches to curing cancer. One is to shut off the berserk DNA-RNA action by transmitting a chemical genetic message to the cell. To carry the message into the cell an RNA virus may be used since it is known that such viruses can invade cells. The viruses would invade the berserk DNA-RNA cells and shut off their mechanisms. The other approach would be to prevent the formation of the enzyme that enables the tumor to establish a blood supply, perhaps also through a virus-coded message.

Tumor cells are examples of immortal cells, and in learning how to turn off runaway life processes one might discover the mechanisms of turning on and off DNA processes. Thus the major unsolved aspects of immortality and cancer may be parts of the same problem.

PART II

How the Body Changes

four

The Nervous System

The nervous system is a complex bioelectrical network that runs the body. Without it there would be no awareness of existence. Its specialized cells are called neurons and the human brain is thought to contain 10 billion of them. These must all be organized with connections that permit the passage of electrochemical impulses in an orderly fashion for normal function. The 10 billion neurons are all developed by the time of birth. While the fetus develops, the neurons are formed by the simple expedient of repeated cell division and growth. At birth this method of neuron multiplication ceases, and for the most part the cells in the brain and spinal cord are not able to regenerate. Thus it is true that a person is as old as his neurons. The DNA-RNA mechanism literally turns off the mechanism to form new neurons. The brain cells then must repair any cell damage that occurs if they are to remain functional. It is little wonder that the brain is particularly susceptible to acquired aging and genetic aging.

The brain contains many cells that are never activated. All of us have both male and female brain cells that affect our personality and behavior. In the presence of adequate male hormone during fetal development the male cells are activated while the female cells remain dormant. Without male hormone the female cells develop and the male cells remain dormant. In this situation the female brain develops its rhythmic activities for the normal female menstrual cycle.

Some adaptations to damage in the nervous system are possible. Recent studies suggest that healthy cells can send out sprouts to form new connections or detours around or through damaged areas. In this manner the network can create new ways to perform old tasks. A hind limb of a rat may be functional after its controlling neurons have been destroyed because the cells that control the front limb take over this function as well.

Older people tend to lose 20 to 40 percent of their brain cells, and the size of the brain shrinks. Many of the remaining cells show changes that apparently interfere with their normal function. The "aging" neurons contain twisted strands of chemical fibers, but are they evidence of genetic age or formed by factors that can damage the sensitive nerve cells, including virus diseases, chemicals, metabolic disorders, or other causes of acquired aging?

The marvels of the progressive development of the brain continue after birth. The anxious parents look to see whether the baby recognizes them. Without the development of the nervous system no recognition is possible. The early years are packed with learning. As the mind and personality develop, the nervous system organizes response patterns essential for physical skills. The first piano lesson begins the gradual building of patterns within the nervous system that may evolve into the complex patterns necessary for a concert pianist. So it is that even the most exacting manual skill is just as dependent upon the nervous system as is the most abstract thought process. Electrical measurements deep inside the brain have demonstrated that as an animal learns a new skill there is a change in electrical behavior. This is an extremely important concept since it means that a basic chemical change occurs in the cell with learning. Accordingly the complex chemical structures within the cell must be the end result of inherited chemical structures modified by acquired experiences.

The components of the mind and nervous system grow progressively but sometimes at different rates. Skills of one nature are learned early in life whereas other forms of knowledge may be acquired only after years and years of training and preparation. In contrast to these years of learning and constant expanding of capability is a period of decline in which there is a loss of memory and the ability to learn begins to diminish. Awareness of one's environment—even self-awareness—lessens. As deterioration progresses, the spark of youth disappears and only old age and senility remain. The older, decrepit individual, no longer conscious of those around him, may live in a strange and distorted world.

The brain may shrink. The body may be partially paralyzed because of damage to certain areas of the brain. Speech may become impossible. Few among us would not choose to have a nervous system that continues to demonstrate the characteristics of youth with the constant expansion of knowledge and continued capacity to learn, resulting in increased total capability of the nervous system and consequently the body.

In addition to the deterioration of the nervous system there are other changes usually attributed to aging, even though they are actually caused by diseases. Foremost among these are strokes, technically called cerebral-vascular accidents, the result of destruction of brain cells. They are usually caused by atherosclerosis of the blood vessels to the brain. Strokes are the third most common cause of death in the United States, being exceeded only by heart attacks and cancer. There are approximately 200,000 deaths from strokes alone in the United States each year, and about half a million new strokes annually. Laboratory studies have demonstrated that the circulation to the brain in people with atherosclerosis may be reduced by 20 percent. This may be a significant observation in relation to the mental changes noted in many older people.

Changes attributed to aging of the nervous system are not necessarily inevitable. A great deal is known which can be applied to prevent them. Chances of avoiding a stroke can be improved by adjusting living habits. Eventually, perhaps, means of treating the nerve cells will be developed which will go a long way toward preventing other aspects of aging.

WHAT IT IS

The nervous system has been likened to a computer, yet even the most sophisticated computer is simple compared to it. A general concept of the nervous system, however, can be used to clarify the aging process and how it affects man.

There are really four major parts of the nervous system: (1) the brain, (2) the spinal cord, (3) the cranial nerves, and (4) the spinal nerves. The brain dominates the entire nervous system. It is here that signals of all types are received and integrated. It is here that actions that control the body are effected. Although there are lower-order functions in the nervous system that can be carried out independently of the brain, under normal circumstances the brain usually maintains overriding control of the functions of all other parts of the nervous system.

It is not necessary to have a detailed, anatomical concept of the brain to understand how it functions. The nervous system can be regarded as a complex electrical mechanism with many electrical circuits, some confined to the brain and others connected outward to other parts of the body. The brain itself anatomically continues into the spinal cord, extending down the back of the spine. The brain and spinal cord together are called the central nervous system.

The main tracks or electrical circuits for transmitting signals to major parts of the body pass through the cord upward to the brain. The cord is even divided into segments, one segment of the cord corresponding to each vertebral level.

Two types of nerves reach out from the brain and spinal cord. Twelve pairs of nerves extend directly out from the brain and are called cranial nerves. The first of these is connected to the nose and transmits signals to the brain for smell. The second is the optic nerve that connects the brain to the eyes. Other cranial nerves are responsible for transmitting the signals to move the eyes upward, downward, or sidewise or to rotate them. Still other nerves are related to hearing, balance, movement of the jaw, lips, face, and tongue, and swallowing. Basically the cranial nerves are responsible for signals of all types to and from the head region.

Beginning with the junction of the spinal cord with the brain, paired nerves pass out of the bony spinal column to all parts of the body. There is one pair of nerves for each vertebral level. Cervical nerves match the level of the cervical vertebrae; thoracic nerves, the vertebral level for the thoracic spine; lumbar nerves, the lumbar spine; and sacral nerves, the sacral spine.

Nerve roots that come off the spinal cord pass singly or join with each other to form a network of nerves, much like a complex wiring circuit, reaching to the muscles of the body, the skin, the internal organs, and other parts of the whole body.

HOW IT WORKS

Despite their complexities, the functions of the nervous system can be grouped into five general categories. The first function, and one of the most exciting, is that of the mind, which defies anatomical description. Many of its facets, particularly within the cells, are not understood. This function of the nervous system includes the characteristics of learning, memory, planning ability, emotional reactions (love, fear, hate, happiness, rage), thinking capacity (both creative and systematic), personality traits, general character, intelligence, instincts, conscious awareness of such things as pain, heat, cold, sex urges, and hunger, awareness of body position, pleasure, passion, self-image (including body image), evaluation of self-worth, social sense, knowledge, and a host of others. It is in this area that many changes in the function of the brain are encountered with aging and disease.

A second function of the nervous system is to make it possible for the body to be aware of its internal and external environment. Sometimes this awareness is accomplished through special senses. For example, through the eyes the brain is in contact with its visual environment. Through the ears the brain is in contact with the sound environment. Through many different pathways, both inside the body and on the external surface of the body, the brain perceives pain and discomfort. It is entirely correct to say that without the brain's awareness of the body itself, we would not know when we were ill or injured. The burning pain in the pit of the stomach exists only because the brain recognizes a disorder that produces it. The brain's function of making it possible to be conscious of our internal and external environment enables us to have an awareness of body position, including the location of hands, feet, or other parts of the body.

A third function of the nervous system is to play a role in bodily actions. If you move your hand, the nervous system must be involved. The simple act of moving the tongue and lips in speech involves the nervous system. The movement of the legs in walking is in relationship to sensations received from the feet and other sensations that identify body position. These sensations are integrated with other complex bits of information in the brain, and a signal is transmitted downward out of the nervous system through the spinal nerves to cause the leg muscles to contract and enable one to walk. Walking is a good example of "voluntary action."

The large bulk of muscles in the body are called voluntary muscles because they are moved at will. The parts of the nervous system involved with voluntary motions comprise the voluntary nervous system. Another large group of actions are effected by the involuntary nervous system. These actions occur automatically without the necessity of conscious effort. A good example is the change in the size of the pupil of the eye, depending upon whether one looks into bright light or is walking at night. The change in light stimulus automatically causes the normal pupil to change its size—quite independently of any thought process. When a response occurs rapidly to some stimulus, such as light in this instance, it is called a reflex action. Involuntary actions are controlled by the autonomic nervous system (which means automatic). It is this part of the nervous system that is responsible for the changes in heart rate, regulation of blood pressure by altering the size of the arteries and veins, the nerve impulses that stimulate the muscular contractions of the digestive tract, how much acid is formed by the stomach, sweating, functions essential to the sex act and many other important body functions.

Some of the autonomic functions are carried out by nerves from the spinal cord; others, by nerves that come all the way from the brain. The autonomic nervous system is, in turn, divided into two functional parts. These often act as a governor on the automatic action of the body. One part of the autonomic nervous system is called the sympathetic nervous system. It is made up of a group of nerve fibers that come out of the spinal cord and combine to form a chain of nerve fibers. Sympathetic nerve fibers may stimulate the heart to beat faster.

The other part of the autonomic nervous system is generally called the parasympathetic system, and although there are exceptions, for the most part the nerve fibers of the parasympathetic system come from the tenth cranial nerve or vagus nerve. Its fibers more or less oppose the actions of the sympathetic nervous system. Thus fibers from the vagus nerve, or parasympathetic system, will slow the heartbeat. By balancing the effects of the sympathetic and the parasympathetic nervous system, the brain is able to bring about the speeding up or the slowing down of the heart.

The fourth important function of the nervous system is to act as a monitoring center for the body. Within the brain there are small areas which constantly keep track of how the body is doing. One of these is the temperature center, which may be thought of as the body thermostat. When impulses reaching it from all over the body signal that the body is overheating, the thermostat will cause a number of changes directed toward lowering the body temperature. These are usually effected through the autonomic nervous system. Among these adjustments may be an increased blood flow through the skin so that the hot blood can reach the surface of the body and lose some of its heat. Sweating may be initiated so that evaporative cooling can occur. A respiratory center controls the normal speed and depth of breathing. Of course, one can voluntarily override this rate under normal conditions, but usually it is not necessary for one to think about respiration. Similarly, there are centers which can raise or lower the blood pressure, or speed up or slow the heart rate, and centers which respond to sleep and hunger. In a sense the nervous system can be considered a mission control center for the body.

The fifth function for the nervous system has to do with its neuroendocrine relationship. The sympathetic nervous system is directly connected to the chemical actions of the body. The transmission of nerve impulses at the ends of the sympathetic nerve fibers to various organs is accomplished through a chemical, mainly adrenaline or an adrenalinelike substance. Most of the adrenaline in the body is produced by the adrenal glands, which rest above the pole of each kidney. The center of the adrenal glands is truly a hybrid between the endocrine system and the nervous system.

In addition, the nervous system is directly connected to the pituitary gland, located underneath the brain directly behind the eyes. The pituitary gland is connected anatomically by a stalk to the floor of the brain, an area technically called the hypothalamus which is directly related to transmitting impulses of human emotions, temperature, and many other activities of the brain. The pituitary gland can be affected by a chemical which is formed by the brain to activate the pituitary. This is exceptionally important because the pituitary gland is the master endocrine gland of the whole body. The hormones it generates cause the thyroid, the adrenal cortex, the testicles and the ovaries to function, and regulate other endocrine glands. The pituitary produces the hormones that make the ovum mature, leading to ovulation. The joint functions of the endocrine system and the nervous system are referred to as the neuroendocrine functions.

Any or all of the five major functions of the nervous system can be affected with aging. The changes in the mind that are associated with senility are well known. The ability of the brain to perceive its internal and external environment can be lessened by failure of sense organs, like blindness or loss of hearing, or through damage to any of its spinal nerve fibers by pressures on the nerves due to arthritic changes. The ability of the body's voluntary or involuntary actions can be affected by strokes or damage in any way to the nervous system. The paralysis of half of the body, secondary to a stroke, is often included among the changes attributed to aging, even though it is really understood to be caused by disease. Reflex movements may become slower than those noted in younger years.

Damage to any of the monitoring centers which can occur as a complication of vascular disease can affect how the body acts. Body temperature tends to be lower in older than in younger people. Differences in sleep patterns are commonly observed. The endocrine system can be affected. Anxiety and depression may ultimately take their toll in the body by acting upon the autonomic nervous system. For example, anxiety may stimulate an outpouring of adrenaline leading to an increased heart rate, tremulousness, and other reactions. Changes in the level of metabolism are often observed in a depression.

DISORDERS OF THE MIND

The nerve tracks, which may be thought of as electrical connections responsible for functions such as walking, are easily defined. The functions of the mind are not so clearly set forth. Lack of a precise definition makes them seem more complex than they are. Basically, disorders of the mind can be divided into three categories. First are structural changes, including tumors, infections, injuries of any sort, and the cell changes commonly attributed to aging, such as those caused by poor circulation.

Second are the functional psychoses. These may occur at any age. The two major functional psychoses are schizophrenia and the manic-depressive group. Individuals with schizophrenia suffer from hallucinations and delusions. The intellectual functions may or may not be severely damaged. The manic-depressive psychoses are characterized by wide swings in mood, from marked overactivity in the manic phase to deep depression in the depressive phase. Delusions, flights of fancy, and being out of touch with reality are hallmarks of this disorder too. In both schizophrenia and manic-depressive disorders the manifestations of abnormal behavior are quite apparent and far exceed merely exaggerated personality traits.

Third are the disorders of personality and neurotic symptoms. Unlike the functional psychoses, these may be exaggerations of personality traits, and they include problems of anxiety, depression, and hysteria. Although they may make the individual decidedly uncomfortable and can interfere with his normal levels of performance, they do not present the degree of disability associated with functional psychoses. Personality disorders and neurotic symptoms are often within the range of the psychodynamics of personality expression occurring in normal life.

Vascular disease and many ailments which structurally alter the brain cause symptoms commonly observed in older people. The dividing line between these manifestations of acquired aging and genetic aging (if it occurs) of the brain is not clear. Studies of older people with no apparent or with minimal evidence of disease have shown that they retain their vocabulary skills. The portions of intelligence tests which are restricted to vocabulary skills and skills learned in a distant past show no significant change with aging. The decrease in functions is very often confined to test procedures that depend on "psychomotor skills." These are tests requiring arrangements of block designs or other picture arrangements, or actual mechanical inputs. In older people the ability to carry out such tasks is decreased. It is not clear, however, that this is a true aging phenomenon or, in fact, even a change within the brain.

Many psychomotor skills that are used to test older people are really dependent upon the sensors. Thus, when vision is poor, it is difficult to carry out tasks that depend upon vision regardless of how well the brain functions. Unfortunately, tests in this area have frequently been used to assess the function of the brain in older people. This is an error in logic comparable to assuming that a person inside an automobile at night has poor eyesight because he cannot see beyond the car without headlights. If the headlights are not working, it is a failure of a peripheral component of the automobile which has nothing to do with the function of the driver. So it is also with skills that are dependent upon hearing, if the hearing has been deranged. These are some of the factors which have made it difficult to assess accurately the changes in the function of the nervous system with age.

A number of learning tests suggest that as one gets older his learning capacity diminishes. This change may be closely related to the common observation of loss of memory that occurs with age. The memory is an important and poorly understood aspect of the mind. It is known that there are two phases of memory. The first is the initial, or rapid, memory, which is transitory. A person may remember something for a few minutes, but an hour or so later the memory is gone. Memories which are retained for hours, days, or even years become the long-term memory. Under certain conditions the long-term memory can be enhanced. If the learning process is interfered with immediately after the initial learning phase, the long-term memory does not develop. This outcome is irrespective of age and has been observed in numerous animal studies.

The exact nature of the long-term memory is not understood, but a great deal of evidence points to its relationship to the formation of RNA in the cells. One plausible theory is that it takes some time for the memory process to initiate the formation of sufficient RNA in the cells and for duplication of the RNA pattern throughout the brain cells to develop the long-term memory. There is no specific anatomical location for long-term memory in the brain; storage appears to be diffuse. This finding supports the concept of the generalized synthesis of RNA diffusely throughout the brain as part of a total knowledge package of the mind. Older people seem to have lost the RNA-synthesizing capacity, and as a result their memory begins to fail. The same concept in part explains why they retain their memory for old events while being unable to remember recent events. The suggestion is strong that a metabolic change takes place in the cell's RNA formation. This does not mean that it is a normal, inevitable consequence of age. When the DNA-RNA functions are better understood and methods are available to influence their formation, a great deal can be done to influence their memory capacity in both young and old.

The loss of long-term memory affects learning ability. Since remembering new words, new numbers, and new facts has become exceedingly difficult, comprehension is affected. Loss of attention span and decreased comprehension are characteristic of the older person. Many psychological tests show decreased function with increasing years simply because of loss of memory.

The evidences of organic change in the brain associated with aging progress until the individual has lost the normal functions of the mind and is no longer in touch with reality. He is said to be withdrawn into a narrow environment and usually lives on the stored memories of the past. The changes in the function of his mind may not be grossly apparent until after he has sustained one or two strokes. Then, suddenly, the manifestations of brain damage become plain, with loss of memory, decreased comprehension, and inability to think clearly or plan.

In addition to the organic brain changes occurring with age, there is a definite increase in problems related to personality disorders. Depression is a frequent accompaniment of age and no wonder. The reactions of the human being are related to his contact with his environment. As the person grows older, he is constantly faced with loss of elements of his life which are of great value to him—loss of his mate, his friends, his close relatives. Age is a progressive series of losses. In addition to the loss of human companionship, he sees the change in his body, which in turn affects his body image. He sees the physical evidence of the loss of his youth. Men in particular lose their opportunity to participate in the social structure, as gainful employment ends and retirement is upon them. A major portion of their social contact has disappeared. Here is an objective manifestation of society's rejection of their worth or need, and it occurs at a time when they are least able to cope with alterations in their fundamental living patterns.

The changes associated with the psychosocial environment of the older individual cause problems which are parallel to the adolescent's. Like the adolescent, the older person frequently experiences an identity crisis of age. He has to reidentify himself in a social setting and face the fact that his bodily condition is undergoing change. How he thinks of himself and identifies himself as an older individual has a lot to do with his overall personality and behavior patterns. A great deal can and should be done in this area to prevent some of the undesirable neurotic symptoms and depressions that often develop with age. One of the most important elements in helping individuals with age is a supportive emotional environment which continues to stress the need and value of the individual. The older person who knows that he is needed and that he is contributing to society is less likely to have significant problems from an identity crisis.

five

The Eye

Cataracts, glaucoma, and floaters are just a few of the problems of the eye associated with aging. The eye is really an extension of the brain. It uses light energy to implement chemical reactions that initiate nerve impulses to the brain which enable us to see. What we see is processed and stored in the visual memory by electrochemical processes. The eyes are a vital environmental link between the visual environment and the mind. Through the eyes the visual environment affects the DNA-RNA system of the neurons and, consequently, affects what we are.

The eye evolves from the formation of a suction-cup-like projection from the developing brain. The open end of the suction cup attaches to a segment of the material that normally forms the skin. The skin segment becomes the lens of the eye. This fact may have something to do with the subsequent growth of cataracts.

HOW IT WORKS

Look at your eye for a moment. The white of the eye is a tough outer covering which envelops all of the eyeball and is called the sclera. The colored disk is the iris, and its black center is the pupil. Actually the white sclera becomes transparent at the edge of the iris. This transparent portion is called the cornea. It is the window to the eye; if it were not transparent, one would be unable to see and the iris and pupil would not be visualized.

The cornea bulges forward like a cap at the front of the eye. The outer attachment of the ringlike iris to the cornea forms the front (anterior) chamber of the eye, which is normally filled with clear fluid. The inner rim of the iris rests on the lens behind it. The iris can open or close like the shutter of a camera, regulating the amount of light which can pass through the lens.

Behind the iris, between its outer circular margin and its inner contact with the lens, is the back (posterior) chamber of the eye. It too is filled with fluid. Normally clear fluid passes between these two spaces in front of and behind the iris through the pupillary opening. A buildup of pressure in these chambers in front of the lens is the beginning of glaucoma (Fig. 8).

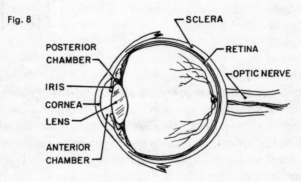

Fig. 8

POSTERIOR CHAMBER

IRIS

CORNEA

LENS

ANTERIOR CHAMBER

SCLERA

RETINA

OPTIC NERVE

The lens is directly behind the iris. Only a portion of it can be seen through the pupillary opening. It is a rounded disk, attached at its outer rim by muscle fibers (ciliary muscle) to the wall of the eye. The lens is the back wall of the two-chambered system at the front of the eye that contains clear fluid. Near the muscular attachment of the lens and in front of it is the ciliary body, a specialized gland that forms the clear fluid for the chambers in front of the lens and is often an important factor in glaucoma. The fluid provides the nourishment to the lens and cornea, since there are no blood vessels in these structures to cloud normal vision.

The lens acts like the lens of a camera. By changing its shape, through the action of the ciliary muscle around its rim, it can change the focus of the eye. Changes in the lens occurring with age affect the vision. Opacities in the lens are the common cataracts.

Just behind the lens is the largest chamber of the eye. It is filled with a clear gelatinous material. With age, some of this material liquefies, forming small pockets of fluid in the gel-like substance. The remaining gel contracts. The contractions then transmit light unevenly, and with eye movements cast shadows on the retinal screen. These shadows cause "floaters."

The cup-shaped chamber containing the gelatinous material is lined with a highly specialized membrane called the retina. The images of objects seen are transmitted through the cornea and projected by the lens through the gelatinous vitreous onto the retinal screen. Defects of the retinal screen can cause loss of vision. The retinal screen is affected by a number of disorders including diabetes, high blood pressure, and vascular diseases. It is no ordinary screen, being composed of specialized cells that are involved in complex chemical changes to permit vision and color discrimination. There are two types of vision cells in the screen, called rods and cones because of their shapes. The cones provide the eye with the ability to make fine discriminations; the rods, the ability to see general shapes in a broader field. The difference in function is achieved by an ingenious method of connecting a single cone cell to one nerve fiber which ultimately leads to image formation in the brain, whereas many different rod cells, covering a range but not a specific point, are connected to a single nerve fiber to the brain.

Good lighting is necessary to see sharp points with the cone cells because only one cell at each point transmits the light energy along one nerve fiber to effect sight. A dimmer light is adequate for general sight because it can stimulate many rod cells, which combine their light energy to stimulate one nerve fiber. The result is that we can see better with the rod cells in dim light but it is a general field vision and not a sharp point. In the dark we become more dependent upon the rods for vision, and images are less distinct.

The cone cells are concentrated in the center of the retinal screen on a straight line with the pupil in a small rounded depression called the macula and fovea area. It is slightly lighter in color than the orange color of the entire retinal screen.

Located in an eccentric position closer to the nose area of the cuplike retinal screen is a white round disk where the optic nerve attaches to the eye. Naturally, each eye has one, and the optic nerves extend backward from the eyes to meet underneath the brain directly behind the eyes. From there, the nerve pathways go to the visual centers in the brain. The point in each eye on the retinal screen where the optic nerve is attached is called the optic disk. Since it has no rods or cones, it creates a blind spot in the field of vision. If you cover one eye and keep looking straight ahead and then place objects at different areas around the eye, you can map out the field of vision for a single eye. There will be a blind spot in the center of the field which is the area that would be covered by the line of sight from the optic disk. If an object happens to be in this spot, it cannot be seen by that eye. One reason for having two eyes is that their fields of vision overlap, thus eliminating blind spots.

Other changes in the field of vision can be induced by changes in the retinal screen. If any of the cells are not functioning properly because of a change in blood supply to them or because of disease, the image on the retinal screen will be affected, as if you had scraped off a spot on the luminescent screen for your movie projector. Spotlike areas of this nature where the vision is diminished or lost are called scotomata.

Piercing the optic disk are an artery and a vein which provide blood supply to the retinal screen. The artery divides like the branches on the limb of a tree and do not connect. Consequently, if one branch is damaged or goes into spasm, that specific area of the retinal screen does not receive enough blood and its vision will be diminished or lost. The retinal screen is the only place in the human body where the doctor can see the nature of the arteries and veins during a physical examination. With his lighted scope, he can look through the lens directly at them. Changes in the arteries and veins are noted in a variety of diseases. High blood pressure causes the arteries to compress the veins that pass underneath their branches. In atherosclerosis, fatty deposits will be seen in the walls of the arteries. Beneath the retinal screen is a large vascular area called the choroid which participates in the circulation to the retina and adjacent eye structures. Outside this layer is the fibrous white capsule of sclera.

GLAUCOMA

Glaucoma is the second most frequent cause of blindness in the United States, accounting for about half of all cases. Basically, it is an increase in the fluid pressure in the eyes. The increased pressure begins in front of the lens. Remember that the lens is anchored all around its rim to the eyeball, and in front of the lens are two chambers, one behind and the other in front of the iris, just underneath the transparent cornea covering the eye. In the young normal eye, the fluid pressure is amazingly constant. The amount of fluid formed to fill the chambers exactly equals the amount which drains out through complex little canals.

After age 40, 1 to 2 percent of people begin to have a gradual increase of pressure, because of a defect in drainage or overproductivity of clear fluid. The blockage of the drainage system can be caused by the progressive increase in the size of the lens or changes which occur in the eye after an infection.

Initially, glaucoma causes no symptoms, and the only indication of it is the increased pressure detected by a careful eye examination. A small pressure gauge is placed on the surface of the eyeball and pushed down gently to measure the actual pressure at the front of the eye. If this pressure is significantly elevated, further tests determine whether it is an early indication of glaucoma.

At first the circulation to the eye undergoes some adjustments to compensate for the increased pressure within the eyeball. But gradually these deteriorate, and suddenly marked changes in vision occur. The first symptom may be some increase in brightness around the rim of objects, or the ability to see things only in direct line of sight and not in the outer visual field.

Glaucoma is a disorder that requires the patient to have utmost faith in his physician. The treatment for the early buildup in pressure may cause some loss of vision in the beginning. However, the treatment is absolutely necessary to prevent future blindness. Without treatment the pressure builds up behind the lens, causing the optic disk (where all the nerve impulses are transmitted to the brain for sight) to degenerate and damaging the visual centers in the retina.

Increased pressure is sometimes noted in young healthy people. Moderate elevation in pressure was observed in several of the candidates for the astronaut program among healthy top-notch pilots. Because early glaucoma, in the stages when it is best treated, can be discovered only by an eye examination, it is exceedingly wise for a person to have a complete eye examination once every three years between the ages of 25 and 50, and at least once a year after that.

THE LENS

The lens of the eye in young people is very pliable. It has an external capsule which is quite elastic and is filled with fibrous, easily compressed tissue. The cells in the lens behave very much like those in skin, which is no surprise since in its development it begins as a pinched-off piece of skin. Just as the skin forms new cells, which it sheds, the lens of the eye is constantly forming new cells and fibers at its outer edge. The problem is that there is no place to shed the old cells, and as the number of fibers increases, the central fibers are compressed more and more. The coagulation of cellular protein brought about by the compression causes opacities and eventually becomes recognized as cataracts. The lens gradually increases in size. At age 65 it is usually about one-third larger than it was at age 25, and it has lost a lot of its elasticity. The normal mechanism of compressing and changing the shape of the lens so that an object may be properly focused on the retina has become faulty. This function is called accommodation.

Because of the characteristics of the lens or the eye itself, some individuals are farsighted (hyperopic). The mechanism in this case is that the lens causes the image to be focused at a point behind the retinal screen; thus the image is out of focus. Young people are able to accommodate to this problem by changing the shape of the pliable lens—literally to focus the image on the retinal screen just as the lens on a movie projector is changed to focus an image on the screen. Actually, about 80 percent of children are normally born with a slight degree of farsightedness. A person is said to be nearsighted (myopic) when the image focused by the lens falls short of the retinal screen. About 5 percent of newborn children have this problem, and only about 15 percent of the newborns have normal vision.

After birth the globe of the eye gradually increases in size until age 8. From 8 to 25, visual problems tend to correct themselves, although the majority of people retain a slight farsightedness. Individuals who are nearsighted at birth are likely to have increased trouble throughout adolescence, but the problem usually stabilizes at about 25.

The young person can compensate for a number of his visual difficulties, but as time passes, the soft, pliable characteristic of the lens is lost and it becomes stiffer and more rigid. At about age 45, people usually begin to have a hard time focusing on near objects. This condition is called presbyopia, which means a loss of the normal accommodation ability of the lens. When measured properly, it gives a good estimation of the person's age.

With aging, an interesting phenomenon is observed, called second sight. Suddenly the older person who has been having visual difficulties for a long time is able to throw away his reading glasses and read without trouble. Normally, light rays are bent by the eye lens for focusing. Because of the changes in the lens with age, the rays of the light become bent in such a way that near vision is markedly improved. However, the same individual usually cannot see very well at distances greater than 10 feet. Since the interest of many older people is primarily focused on near objects, this is not a great handicap, and it is often a source of amazement to see grandparents throw away their glasses and read with the naked eye after years of having to use glasses to read. Although this phenomenon is interesting, it is usually a sign that cataract surgery will soon be required.

The formation of cataracts is the leading cause of blindness in the

United States. Most cataracts are caused by age and for this reason are called physiological cataracts. The loss of the elasticity of the lens is the result of changes in the protein within its cell structures. Opacities are formed, and eventually, if sight is to be preserved, the cataracts must be removed.

There are a number of disease conditions which contribute to the incidence of cataracts. Cataracts are more common in diabetes. They may follow severe electrical shocks such as being struck by lightning. They are also associated with certain hereditary diseases and birth defects.

Another theory of the origin of cataracts is that the coagulation of the protein in the lens is due to long-standing exposure to ultraviolet light and in some instances to the thermal effects of infrared rays. Many of the harmful rays that come from sunlight are absorbed by the first clear covering of the eye, the cornea, and by the lens. In this way, they protect the sensitive retinal screen from damage. An observation supporting this idea is that the lower part of the lens, which receives the most intense light, is the place where the opacities generally begin. In tropical regions where sunlight is abundant—for example, in India and Egypt—cataracts are much more common than in the temperate latitudes. Excluding the polar areas, which have other effects from snow and ice, the incidence of cataracts increases from the temperate zones to the equator, and they are more frequent in outdoor workers than in city dwellers. This theory deserves more study. Clearly, if the ultraviolet light is a factor, the proper use of soft contact lenses could help to prevent cataracts.

Apparently chemical changes in the body associated with the high levels of blood sugar in diabetes cause the proteins in the lens to be more easily coagulated by light. This condition may account for the fact that diabetics have cataracts much earlier than nondiabetics.

Other chemical factors may be associated with the changes in the lens. The amount of a chemical in the lens called glutathione diminishes with age, and it may offer some protection against the lens's reaction to light. Additional factors in relation to cataract formation are of interest. There may be fluorescent bacteria on the surface of the eye which help protect the lens, and certainly with age fluorescence of the eye decreases. It is suggested that ultraviolet light kills these fluorescent bacteria. Cataracts are also formed earlier in glassblowers on account of exposure to infrared rays. Individuals exposed to excess radiation often develop cataracts. Animals exposed to neutron radiation will develop cataracts in a few weeks or months after exposure. In rats, opacities in the lens can be created by feeding them a diet rich in lactose (milk sugar) or galactose.

THE RETINA

The vascular choroid area provides the nourishment to the central part of the retinal screen or the fovea and macula area responsible for central vision.

A number of changes in vision with age are caused by defects in the retinal screen, characteristically the central area or the fovea and macula. Because the macula is usually involved, this condition is called macular degeneration. The loss of visual cells in this area means a loss of sharp visual acuity, so that the person is more dependent upon the rod cells, which do not provide a sharp focus. He complains of difficulty in reading and does not see faces clearly. The central area of the visual field is affected, whereas the outer or peripheral parts of the field, which provide less clear images, remain intact. Objects like telephone poles, doors, windows, and trees appear crooked or wobbly. There may be dark spots, and the person loses his ability to carry out tasks requiring prime vision such as driving or reading.

The retina is often affected by diabetes, which leads to loss of function. This is not strictly a disease of age, but since it occurs with increasing frequency from youth to age, it is mentioned here. Incidentally, it is the third leading cause of blindness in the United States.

Many disorders of the macula and retinal screen are caused by poor circulation, which limits the nourishment and oxygenation of these highly sensitive cells. It is worth noting, therefore, that cigarette smoking can also decrease the oxygenation of the retina by causing an accumulation of carbon monoxide. In a young healthy person smoking three cigarettes can produce enough carbon monoxide in the blood to decrease his ability to see at night by 25 percent.

A number of other changes occur in the eye as age progresses. For example, a whitish-gray ring may form around the outer margin of the iris. This ring is called arcus senilis and is some evidence of aging. The pupil often becomes quite small and is limited in its reflex capacity and its response to light. Other normal reflexes associated with the functions of the eye begin to slow. These and a few changes which can be demonstrated on examination are seldom noted by the individual as altering his visual acuity, possibly because of far more important changes that are taking place.

six

The Ear

The ear is another specialized organ that enables man to maintain contact with his external environment. It has two parts, one related to the balance mechanism and the other to the hearing mechanism. The latter converts physical sound energy into electrochemical impulses that are transmitted to the brain. The electrochemical process is stored in the brain, enabling an individual to recognize a birdcall because the pattern for the sound is already recorded within the brain's memory bank. A familiar tune is recognized because the character of the music is likewise recorded in the brain's auditory memory. Thus, physical sound influences the basic electrochemical state of the brain. Without the ability to detect sound and convert it to electrochemical processes, man would be deprived of one of the environmental inputs that affect his brain and in turn his body.

Hearing loss is characteristic of older people. It is increasingly necessary for their friends and family to speak louder to them. Often much of the conversation about them is lost. They become tired of asking others to speak louder, and their associates become tired of making the extra effort. Thus a pattern is set up wherein the individual with a hearing problem tends to withdraw from situations requiring hearing as an essential part of human communication. Unless care is taken, he can become a neurotic recluse. Loss of hearing is an important factor in the isolation of age.

SOUND

The best way to think about sound is to consider it as a series of vibrations or waves. Sound energy can be defined in terms of the waves of the ocean. The number of waves arriving on the beach in a given time is the frequency. If the waves follow each other immediately the frequency is high. If they occur at long intervals, the frequency is low. Sound waves are classified the same way. If they occur rapidly, there is a high-frequency sound. If a small number of sound waves occur in a unit of time, there is a low-frequency sound. The other important characteristic of sound is its loudness or intensity. This can be equated to the height of the waves of the ocean as they arrive at the beach. Large waves have considerable force. A small wave may have very little force. Thus, the height of the wave is related to its intensity. The same is true of sound. The height of the recurring sound waves is the measure of intensity of the sound—loudness, or forcefulness.

The two aspects of sound of particular interest to the ear, then, are frequency and intensity. Both aspects must be known in order to define adequately the characteristics of the sound. The frequency is referred to as cycles per second (c.p.s.). These obviously can vary from one c.p.s. to thousands of c.p.s. Intensity is measured in a somewhat more cumbersome fashion. The level of sound pressure that is just barely audible to the normal ear is the level of intensity described as zero decibels. This applies to sounds within the frequency range of normal hearing, or those with the frequency of approximately 1000 to 2000 c.p.s. This reference level of hearing of zero decibels is used to compare all other sounds or noises in terms of intensity. A sound that has an intensity of 10 decibels is 10 times as loud as one that is only zero decibels. A sound with an intensity of 20 decibels is 100 times as loud as the threshold of hearing. And a sound having an intensity of 60 decibels is a million times as loud as a sound that is barely audible. This level of sound intensity corresponds to the normal-voice conversation.

As an index of the intensity of various sounds: If you were standing 4 feet away from a person who was whispering, the sounds you would hear would have an equivalent intensity of approximately 20 decibels. At the same distance, the conversational voice could be 60 decibels. If you were 35 feet away from a riveter, the noise would have an intensity of 100 decibels or 10 billion times the intensity of barely audible sound at zero decibels. This brief description provides some idea of the range of hearing capacity of the human ear.

The sound of the normal conversational voice has a frequency between 200 and 7000 c.p.s. Actually, most of the sounds fall within a range of 200 to 2000 c.p.s. All of the essential components of conversation can be heard within this frequency range. However, some sounds extend upward to approximately 7000 c.p.s. Thus, it would be appropriate to say that the sound of the conversational voice has a frequency of 200 to 7000 c.p.s. with an intensity of 60 decibels.

To measure hearing range, the ear is examined for its ability to detect sounds of different frequency at different levels of intensity. The most common test is the simple clinical audiogram. A series of sounds is generated at various frequency levels, usually from 125 to 8000 c.p.s. These sounds are varied in intensity from zero decibels to 110 decibels. Let us take an example. A sound with a frequency of 125 c.p.s. and an intensity of zero decibels is generated. If the subject hears it, his ability to hear sounds of that low intensity for that particular frequency range is established. Then another sound with a frequency of 250 c.p.s. is generated. If the subject first hears this sound when it has an intensity of 10 decibels, that describes his hearing threshold for sounds of that frequency. Progressively, sounds with increasing frequency are presented to the subject at different levels of intensity, and at each point the threshold of hearing is marked. A perfectly normal human ear will be able to hear all the sounds with a frequency range of 125 c.p.s. to 8000 c.p.s. at a level of intensity very near the zero-decibel level with minor variations for different subjects.

The hearing in young healthy people with normal ears actually covers an approximate range between 20 c.p.s. and 20,000 c.p.s. The ear has increasing difficulty hearing sounds of low frequency. Sounds below 100 c.p.s. usually must be louder to be detected by the human ear. A low-intensity sound below 30 c.p.s. is not likely to be heard. An application of this principle is made in listening to the human heart. Some of the vibrations it makes fall below 30 c.p.s. and are so low in intensity that they cannot be heard by the human ear. However, since they are vibrations, they can be felt by the tips of the fingers. This is one reason why the doctor frequently places his hand over the heart when he is examining a patient: to feel vibrations which may be present that his ear is unable to detect. Sounds with a low frequency of 20 c.p.s. ordinarily require a fairly high intensity level for most individuals to hear them. Sounds with very high frequency, those approaching the level of 20,000 c.p.s. or greater, are difficult to hear or are not heard at all. An increase in loudness of these sounds does not improve the human ear's ability to hear them. Such high-frequency sounds are called ultrasonics.

EXTERNAL AND MIDDLE EAR

The ear receives sound energy and converts it to electrochemical impulses by a very complex mechanism. It begins with the external ear, which is designed to collect and funnel sound waves into the ear itself. The external ear functions as an auditory chamber. In some animals its direction can be changed to better localize sounds, or, as in the dog, it can be folded down like a tent to protect the ear from unwanted sounds. Unfortunately, the human external ear doesn't provide this facility. The external ear funnels into a small canal called the external ear canal. This is guarded by numerous fine hairs to protect it from foreign bodies and insects. Many glands in the skin in this area produce ear wax. The external auditory canal ends blindly, in an oval-shaped membrane—the eardrum. This pearly-white membrane is the limit to the portion of the ear designated as the external ear.

Beyond the eardrum is the middle ear, which may be thought of as the open cavity of a kettledrum, the eardrum itself representing the taut sheepskin of the kettledrum. The hollow cavity of the middle ear contains three very small bones, the malleus, the incus, and the stapes—sometimes called the hammer, anvil, and stirrup because they are shaped like these objects. The hammer is attached directly to the eardrum. Sound waves striking the eardrum cause the tiny hammer to move a small amount. Being connected directly to the anvil, the hammer makes the anvil vibrate. The anvil is connected to the stirrup and transmits the vibrations to it. The stirrup-shaped bone is anchored to another rounded membrane somewhat like the eardrum, only much smaller, called the oval window. Thus, the middle ear is really a hollow, irregular-shaped chamber with its external surface being the eardrum and its innermost point being the oval window. These two membranes are connected by the little bony chain of the hammer, anvil, and stirrup (Fig. 9).

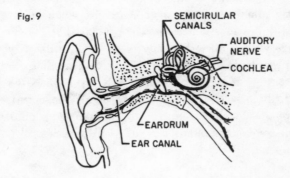

Fig. 9

SEMICIRULAR CANALS

AUDITORY NERVE

COCHLEA

EARDRUM

EAR CANAL

The middle ear is connected by a long narrow hollow tube (the eustachian tube) from the bottom of the chamber to an opening in the back of the throat. The purpose of this little canal is to maintain equal pressure between the inside of the middle ear and the external ear, in order to prevent the eardrum from being distorted by air pressure. It becomes important in air transportation. If you are flying and the air pressure outside the ear is decreased, the pressure inside the middle ear chamber will be too great and cause the eardrum to be pushed outward. Conversely, when you have been at altitude and start descending, if the pressure stays low in the middle ear chamber the increased air pressure as you come down will push the eardrum inward. The unequal pressure can be uncomfortable and can cause mechanical damage to the ear. The eustachian tube enables air to move in and out of the middle ear chamber to equalize the pressure. Chewing gum, yawning, and other mechanisms which help open this tube at the back of the throat prevent difficulties.

THE INNER EAR

Beyond the oval window is still another chamber, called the inner ear. The oval window is connected to a long tube which is curled on itself in the shape of a snail. Its shape is responsible for its name, the cochlea. The end of this tube also has a rounded membrane. The tube is a very complex structure and is filled with a clear fluid. As the membrane at the oval window vibrates when it is stimulated by the stirrup, it causes vibrations all along the fluid-filled spiral cochlea, and the tiny membrane at its end bulges in response to them. Inside the tube are many minute structures. From some of them, called hair cells, project hairs that are attached to a thin membrane-type structure, resembling a spiral staircase within the twisted cochlea. As the vibrations pass along this membrane and stimulate the membrane and hair cells, they cause mechanical movements which stimulate tiny nerve fibers. Nerve impulses then travel along these minute fibers through the auditory nerve and carry the electrochemical impulse to the brain.

The cochlea is very interesting in that it is already tuned to receive certain sounds. In general, the first part of the tube responds to sounds of high frequency, and farther along the tube the cells are tuned to progressively lower frequencies so that the sounds with the lowest frequency are detected at its end. The tuned spiral cochlea stimulates an endless variety of nerve fibers. These transmit impulses to an area at the surface of the brain which can be mapped to show the points where sounds of different frequency levels are detected. Naturally, both ears have this mechanism, and nerve fibers from the right and left ears cross over on their way to the brain, so that each area for hearing on the surface of the brain is represented by impulses from both ears. The mechanism of two ears with two hearing centers, the crossover of the nerve fibers, the response to different levels of intensity, and other aspects of this ingenious device provide man with stereophonic hearing. He can thus detect distances and location; i.e., he has auditory spatial orientation.

THE LABYRINTH

Connected to the cochlea tube for hearing is another part of the ear called the labyrinth. This is important to the sensation of balance. The mechanism is a set of three semicircular tubes, called the semicircular canals. They are interconnected, and all three are perpendicular to each other. Thus, the three canals have a three-dimensional shape. They are filled with fluid and act very much like a carpenter's level. If the position of the head is moved, there is movement of the fluid within the semicircular canals. Since the three canals are perpendicular to each other, it is clear that if the head is moved up, down, forward, backward, or from side to side one or more of the canals will be stimulated.

Since the fluid in the semicircular canals has its own inertia, if the head moves abruptly, the fluid will lag in its response to the movement. You can demonstrate this same inertia in a glass of water by jerking the glass suddenly. As the glass moves, the water appears to move, but actually the inertia of the water makes it lag in response to the movement of the glass. The lag of inertia stimulates specialized cells within the semicircular canals which are connected to tiny nerve fibers and relay the message to the brain. The sensation of balance is integrated with many complex inputs from the body, including the eyes and even a sense of position of the arms, the legs, and the rest of the body.

When the labyrinths are highly stimulated, as in spinning or whirling, they can provide so many impulses to the brain that a person may become ill. This is what motion sickness is. Stimulation by movement can cause abnormal movements of the eye, nausea, vomiting, and dizziness. Inflammation or disease of a labyrinth can produce similar reactions. Disease in the nerve which conducts impulses from the labyrinth to the brain or disease in circulation affecting the blood supply to the labyrinth mechanism can cause an individual to lose his normal sense of balance. This condition is quite common in older people because of increasing atherosclerosis.

Having an important bearing on ringing of the ears, loss of balance, and decreased hearing is circulation. The artery that goes out to the end organ can be impinged upon by abnormalities of the spine, particularly in the neck region. Disease in the major arteries that originate from the aortic arch near the heart also contributes to this impingement. Sudden movement of the head which applies pressure from an osteoarthritic spur on the artery can impede its blood flow to the ear, resulting in these problems. In addition, changes take place in the nerve and the ear itself. Alcohol and nutrition affect normal ear function too.

LOSS OF HEARING

There are many different causes of hearing loss. The simplest is the accumulation of wax in the external auditory canal which can easily be removed. Disease of the middle ear and disorders of the cochlea and the adjacent auditory nerve can cause deafness. So can central damage to the nerve pathways within the brain.

Damage to the eardrum may or may not cause significant deafness. If the eardrum is pierced and the hole is small and in the right location, the principal effect will be to decrease hearing for low-frequency sounds but usually not to interfere much with hearing normal conversation. Thickening and other changes in the eardrum have similar effects.

A very common cause of deafness is a disease of the middle ear called otosclerosis. This affects 4 percent of the total population and as many as 45 percent of those who are handicapped with loss of hearing. It can occur in younger as well as in older people. The most frequent times of occurrence are just after puberty, during pregnancy, or with the menopause. The primary problem is that the bone around the middle ear chamber is dissolved. This may begin as a small spot and is followed by gradual absorption of the bone. As the bone dissolves, new bone is formed, but it is not laid down in the normal fashion and usually appears in excess amounts. As the new bony process is developed, it may obliterate the oval window and the connecting stirrup. By immobilizing the stirrup bone, it destroys the ability of the middle ear to transmit sounds to the oval window.

One indication of the cause of the deafness can be found by simple examination with a tuning fork. The tuning fork is struck so that its tines begin to vibrate. Then its handle is placed on the bony mastoid process just behind the ear. The vibrations are transmitted by the bone directly to the inner ear—that is, to the cochlea and the auditory nerve, bypassing the middle ear chamber which is affected by otosclerosis. Individuals with otosclerosis can hear the vibrations quite well by bone conduction.

When the vibrations can no longer be heard, the tuning fork is removed from the mastoid process and the tines of the fork are held directly in front of the ear. With the tuning fork in this position, the individual with otosclerosis will hear nothing because the vibrations entering the ear and striking the middle ear chamber will not be transmitted by the bony chain. This sequence explains why a person with otosclerosis deafness can often hear over the telephone better than during normal conversation. The telephone receiver pressed against the ear provides a means of bone conduction.

A person listening to the vibrating fork in front of the ear hears the sound by air conduction. With the tuning fork placed directly over the mastoid bone, he hears the sound by bone conduction. In the normal ear, air conduction is better than bone conduction. When a vibrating tuning fork is taken off the mastoid process of a normal person, after he can no longer hear the sound of it, and held in front of the ear, he can still hear the vibrations.

People with otosclerosis experience a gradual loss of hearing. First they notice that they cannot hear people whispering; later on they begin to have trouble hearing conversation. A large number of people with this problem can be successfully treated with surgery. In an earlier day, the stirrup bone would be broken free from its fixation by a very delicate operation. However, often it became fixed again, and deafness recurred. At present, a popular operation is removal of the stirrup bone entirely, a pad of fat tissue or other material being used to replace it. The operation is often dramatically successful.

The hallmark of uncomplicated otosclerosis is an audiogram which shows that the hearing is normal through a range of frequencies by bone conduction but is decreased at all frequencies for air conduction. Unfortunately, many people suffer a combination of different forms of deafness and have a decrement in hearing by both air and bone conduction.

A second common type of hearing loss, seen in older people, is associated with defects in the internal ear, the coiled cochlea and conducting nerve tissue. These individuals cannot hear high-frequency sounds. Initially, the loss of hearing is for sounds with frequencies higher than those normally noted in conversation. The presence of the hearing deficit will be noted only by laboratory testing. Decrease in hearing will be approximately the same for both air and bone conduction. This is the tip-off that it involves more than just the middle ear and helps to localize the problem to the inner ear. As the disease progresses, the individual begins to have difficulty understanding speech, mainly because the consonants are higher pitched than the vowels and are less loudly spoken. A number of speech discrimination tests have been devised to assess this problem. The typical progressive loss of higher-frequency hearing with progressive age is called presbycusis.

Other causes for inner ear deafness are damage to the cochlea and nerve mechanisms by a variety of medicines (including some of the antibiotics and salicylates), and certain diseases (including virus infections, diabetes, syphilis, and even low thyroid function).

Along with the loss of hearing, there is frequently a ringing in the ear, technically called tinnitus.

Loud noises can injure the ear and result in a decrease in hearing very similar to that noted with presbycusis. Constant exposure to high levels of noise will gradually induce ear damage and deafness. If the noise level is extremely high, it will cause pain. Sound levels of approximately 130 to 140 decibels will be painful regardless of the frequency of the sound. Continued exposure to levels of noise approaching 100 decibels for periods of eight hours or more or for repeated shorter periods can cause loss of hearing. In industrial situations in which noise is a part of the environment, therefore, the noise level is constantly checked and devices such as earplugs and earmuffs are used to try to protect the ears from damage.

Another common disorder of the ear is Ménière's disease. This affects both the hearing and balance mechanisms of the ear. It is thought that a change in the fluid pressure in the semicircular canals takes place. Since these are connected to the cochlea, both hearing and balance may be disturbed. At least at the beginning, generally only one ear is involved. There is usually ringing in the ear like the surf, or sometimes a high-pitched whistling. The ringing of the ear, or tinnitus, is accompanied with dizziness, technically called vertigo. Nausea and vomiting may also occur, along with the other symptoms commonly associated with faintness such as pallor and sweating. The first attack is likely to be followed by evidence of hearing loss in the affected ear.

You can do a lot to protect your ears. Noise deafness and aging deafness are similar and cumulative. By avoiding noise, including loud music, you can delay hearing loss. Preventing atherosclerosis helps both the function of hearing and the balance mechanism. The proper amount of vitamins is also important. Hence diet is a valuable measure in preserving the functions of your ears. If possible, medicines with toxic side effects should be avoided, and all ear infections should be treated promptly.

seven

The Heart and Vascular System

The greatest single deterrent to reaching old age in the modern industrialized society is heart and vascular disease, which causes heart attacks, strokes, heart failure, and other circulatory disorders. These account for over half of all deaths in the United States, more than all the deaths caused by cancer, accidents, infections, infant mortality, and any other reason. Of the approximately 1.8 million deaths a year in this country 1.2 million are due to heart and vascular disease. About half are the result of heart attacks (myocardial infarction) or occur suddenly, in association with disease of the arteries to the heart muscle. Thus, nearly one out of three people dies from disease of the arteries to the heart muscle, and about half of these deaths are sudden.

Often the first warning that a person is ill is sudden death. This does not leave much time for diagnosis or preventive treatment. In most communities over half the individuals who die of heart disease do so before they can reach the hospital. Clearly, if you want to stay young and fit, you must avoid heart disease. One out of three deaths caused by coronary artery disease occurs in individuals before age 65. Aside from those whose lives are suddenly cut short because of coronary artery disease, many survivors remain disabled.

A NEW DISEASE

The enormous number of deaths from heart attacks occurring in the industrialized nations of the world is all the more impressive because death from atherosclerosis of the arteries to the heart was unknown until the beginning of the twentieth century. Spotty deposits and changes in the arteries had been observed, but they were infrequent and not sufficiently severe to be correlated with symptoms during life or to be accepted as a cause of death. The fact that coronary artery disease could bring chest pain and heart attacks was not even recognized until 1910 to 1912. Since that time, the incidence has gradually risen in industrialized societies to the shocking proportions observed today. Matched with this spectacular impact of atherosclerosis upon society is the almost certain knowledge that much of it can be prevented by proper living habits.

Clearly, the fatty deposits in the arteries (atherosclerosis) are not a manifestation of genetic aging. Atherosclerotic changes have been well documented in apparently healthy young men. Men in their early 20's have had serious heart attacks that were in no way different from the heart attacks observed in individuals past 65 years of age. In both instances there is an accumulation of the fatty deposits, or atherosclerotic plaques, in the walls of the coronary arteries. The deposits are particularly likely to occur in men. Studies of battle casualties of the Korean War showed that nearly 80 percent of young men of an average age of 22 already had gross evidence of fatty deposits in their coronary arteries. In 10 percent of these young men the changes could be classified as severe. With increasing age, the incidence and severity of the fatty deposits in the coronary artery increase. The atherosclerotic changes observed in the coronary arteries are no different from those seen in arteries elsewhere in the body. It is their critical location, interfering with the blood supply to the heart, that makes them so important and enables them to exact such a tremendous toll.

Many aspects of coronary artery disease point to its lack of correlation with simple aging. Caucasian females are usually spared severe atherosclerosis during their childbearing years, but after the menopause they too gradually accumulate atherosclerotic changes in their arteries. By age 65, the incidence of heart attacks is about equal in white men and women.

Worldwide studies over a period of several decades have shown that heart attacks and problems associated with coronary artery disease diminish when a population's food intake is significantly decreased. In countries occupied by foreign troops during World War II, the incidence of heart attacks fell drastically. This drop has been correlated with the decreased amount of food available for the populace, particularly food rich in saturated animal fats and foods like egg yolks that are rich in cholesterol. Foods such as sugar which are high in calories in proportion to their bulk were sharply restricted in these populations. After the war years when food again became plentiful, the incidence of atherosclerosis of the coronary arteries skyrocketed. Similarly men who were kept as prisoners of war and on reduced food rations lost large amounts of body fat and demonstrated a clearing of any evidence of atherosclerosis of the coronary arteries. Studies of prison populations and numerous other worldwide situations have all clearly pointed to the role of diet as one of the main factors in the development of atherosclerosis, whether it be of the coronary arteries or the arteries to the brain or elsewhere in the body.

Diet is only one of several factors in developing atherosclerosis, but it is an important one in the habit pattern of individuals. Parallel to the progressive rise in the frequency of heart attacks in the industrialized population has been the increased consumption of cigarettes since 1900. The decline in physical activity associated with an increasingly mechanized society, and in general the habit patterns which can be attributed to the soft living of the "good life" are additional important factors.

BLUE BLOOD FOR RED

To understand the heart and its role in circulation it is best to consider it in terms of its function in operating a very sophisticated four-chambered pump. To pump blood the heart must have two essential characteristics. Its chambers must have sufficient volume to accumulate blood and it must have enough muscle strength to eject the blood. Just as the amount of air you can breathe is dependent upon the volume of the lungs, so the amount of blood which can be pumped is dependent upon the volume of the chambers of the heart.

The lungs are more passive organs, and the air moves in and out by the muscular action of changes in the size of the chest (thorax). The heart has no such external mechanism; it must accumulate blood and eject it as a result of its own activity. It accumulates blood by relaxing and dilating, gradually filling itself to capacity. It ejects blood by contracting to obliterate its cavities, thereby squeezing blood out into the circulation.

A simple concept of the heart is one that envisions the right side of the heart as pumping blue blood (poor in oxygen) and the left side of the heart as pumping red blood (rich in oxygen). Hold your hand down and look at the veins on the back of your hand. The bluish color of the veins is the result of the low oxygen content. The veins in the hand join to form a smaller number of larger veins, and as the blue blood moves along the veins toward the heart it enters larger and larger veins. (One may think of small roads connecting into highways and finally into superhighways.) All of the blue blood in the arms, the head, and the lower parts of the body, abdomen and elsewhere, gradually returns to the right side of the heart, which consists of an upper saccular chamber (right atrium) and a lower muscular chamber (right ventricle).

After the muscular lower chamber is filled with blue blood, it begins to contract and squirts accumulated blue blood through one main artery (pulmonary artery) to the lungs. The artery soon divides into a right and left branch for the right and left lungs. The blue oxygen-poor blood is pumped through the lungs via smaller and smaller arteries until very fine blood vessels carry it past the small air sacs that contain oxygen. Here the blood discards the excess carbon dioxide it has brought from the cells in the body at the same time it takes on oxygen. The process of unloading excess carbon dioxide and picking up oxygen causes the blood to change to the bright red color of oxygenated blood. The bright red blood passes beyond the air sacs, and the small vessels gradually converge into the larger ones until finally there are four large veins carrying the oxygen-rich blood from the lungs to the left side of the heart. These four veins enter an upper saccular chamber (left atrium). The accumulated blood in the upper left atrium is squeezed into the lower left chamber of the heart (left ventricle). It is this heavy muscular chamber that must perform the major work of the heart.

As soon as the left lower chamber is filled, its muscular wall begins to contract, squeezing down on the blood in the chamber. As the pressure mounts, the blood is squirted out of the left ventricle into one huge artery (aorta) connected to the top of the left ventricular cavity. This main artery carries all of the blood for the entire body with the exception of the lungs. Rising from the heart it arches upward just underneath the top of the breastbone and then makes a U-turn backward and courses downward through the chest along the spine. It passes through the diaphragm and down along the abdomen, still riding next to the spine. As it approaches the pelvic area, it divides into two main branches, one for the right and one for the left leg.

The aorta is a long white elastic tube, or a giant artery. Smaller arteries branch off the aorta to provide blood to all the different regions of the body. The first two arteries that branch off the aorta are for the heart muscle itself. They are called the right and left coronary arteries. The small openings into the coronary arteries lie just outside the muscular pumping chamber of the heart. The right coronary artery extends over the surface of the back side of the heart. The left coronary artery extends over the top part of the heart and quickly divides, sending one main branch to the left side of the heart and another over the front surface of the heart. These arteries lie over the outer surface of the heart muscle. As they divide, the smaller branches penetrate into the heavy muscular wall of the right and left ventricles. The branching continues until tiny vessels are formed which enable the blood supply to be carried to the individual muscle fibers of the heart. These small branches have interconnections, and the small branches of both the right and left coronary arteries tend to connect with each other to form a network of multiple blood vessels to the entire heart. Thus it is theoretically possible for blood to pass through the left coronary artery to the entire heart muscle, or conversely, for blood to pass through the right coronary artery to the entire heart. This is an example of nature's redundancy in providing adequate blood supply for the heart muscle. In many people these interconnections are not well developed.

After the arteries to the heart muscle originate from the aorta, additional branches off the top of the U-shaped arch provide blood to the arms, head, and brain. The accumulation of fatty deposits, or atherosclerosis, at the origin of the branches that must send blood to the brain can result in poor circulation to the brain, leading to symptoms of brain dysfunction and even causing strokes.

As the aorta courses down along the spine, branches are given off to the muscles between the ribs, and finally to the digestive tract, the liver, the kidneys, the reproductive system, and indeed, all other portions of the body. The red oxygenated blood reaches the cells and unloads oxygen to make possible the cellular processes. Here carbon dioxide accumulated from previous cellular activity is picked up, and the blood changes from the bright red characteristic of oxygen-rich blood to the bluish color of oxygen-poor venous blood. The blue oxygen-poor blood courses through the veins until it is finally collected again in the right atrial chamber to start its journey once more.

Not only does the circulation provide for the transport of oxygen and carbon dioxide but it also transports vital food substances and important chemicals such as hormones. The food substances absorbed from the digestive tract enter the venous system and are then circulated to the entire body to give adequate amounts of food energy for bodily processes. The circulation, then, can be thought of as a transport mechanism.

A UNIQUE MUSCLE

The heart is not only a volume organ to accumulate blood but a muscle. The most unique thing about the heart muscle is that it is remarkably like the other muscles in the body. Heart muscle consists of long fibers of muscle tissue which contract to carry out their work, just as the muscle fibers in the calf of the leg must contract for the movement of the foot in walking. The forceful contraction of the heart muscle fibers enables the heart to pump blood. The contraction requires energy, which requires food substances and oxygen. The amount of energy expended by the heart muscle is directly related to how much work it must do. Again it is like the other muscles in the body. The more a muscle is required to work, the more energy it must expend. The work of the heart is measured by the amount of blood it must pump under pressure. Expressed simply, a heart that pumps 5 quarts of blood at a pressure of 120/70 is not working nearly as hard as a heart that must pump 30 quarts of blood at a pressure of 220/70.

Whenever the body requires more oxygen, the heart has to pump more blood, and normally the increased amount of blood pumped into the arteries causes the pressure to rise. Thus, increased work or effort of the body results in increased work of the heart muscle. Consider the distance runner. When he is resting quietly, his heart may not be working very hard, but when he is running, the amount of oxygen that his legs and body need is sharply increased. To provide this oxygen, more blood must be pumped to the lungs and eventually to his working body muscles. The heart must work harder.

For the heart to pump more blood it must maintain or increase the volume of blood it ejects each time it beats while the heart rate is increased. Well-trained endurance athletes are able to increase the volume per beat whereas untrained individuals are less likely to do so. One of the determining factors in how much blood the heart can pump is its volume size. The training of the endurance athlete increases the volume capacity of his heart. Its actual size and its maximum rate determine the amount of blood the heart can pump, technically called cardiac output. If the body muscles are well trained, the amount of physical work that can be done is limited by the maximum amount of blood the heart can pump to the working muscles. Thus the volume of the heart is the limiting factor in physical work for most young, healthy individuals. As a result of many studies of middle-aged American males in the Air Force population during maximum exertion, I also know that the limiting factor for most 35- to 45-year-old American men in apparently good health is the volume capacity of the heart. Healthy individuals, therefore, who exercise to their maximum capacity will experience no major difficulties except for the manifestations of heavy work.

THE VITAL ARTERIES

It is possible to limit the amount of work which the heart muscle can do by limiting its available blood supply. Just as the working leg muscles require more blood to provide necessary energy, when the work of the heart muscle increases, it too must receive more blood. The amount of blood it can receive depends upon the state of the coronary arteries originating from the great aorta. During exercise these arteries normally dilate, so that more blood flows to the heart muscle. As the work of the heart (the amount of blood it pumps under pressure) increases, the amount of blood flow to the heart muscle increases.

Individuals with atherosclerotic blockage of the coronary arteries may have their exercise capacity limited because the coronary blood flow to the heart muscle cannot be increased. In this event the working heart muscle may not get enough blood, and a condition called myocardial ischemia results (*myocardium* referring to the heart muscle and *ischemia* meaning insufficient blood flow). The accumulation of chemicals and waste products in the ischemic heart muscle causes chest pain. The chest pain brought on by exertion is one of the manifestations of atherosclerosis of the coronary arteries. Called angina pectoris, it literally means strangulation of the breastbone. Chest pain caused by atherosclerosis of the coronary arteries is characterized by a heavy pressure or squeezing sensation in the center of the chest, usually directly underneath the breastbone. It can also cause heavy oppressive pain in the pit of the stomach or up into the neck and jaw. The pain often radiates into either the left or right arm or both although it more often affects the left arm. The pain of angina pectoris is of short duration, usually less than 10 minutes. If it lasts much longer, the heart muscle has probably been damaged or myocardial infarction has occurred.

CHANGES THAT KILL

The atherosclerotic buildup in the coronary arteries is similar to that noted in other arteries. Its strategic location blocking blood flow to the heart muscle adds to its importance. The accumulation of the fatty yellowish plaque, gradually clogging the opening in the coronary arteries, partially obstructs blood flow and causes anginal pains when the work of the heart is increased—for example, during physical exertion. Eventually the plaque may rupture, as a pimple does, and extrude its material into the opening. This may occlude the coronary artery; hence the term *coronary occlusion*. At the site of rupture a small clot or thrombus may form which is the origin of the term *coronary thrombosis*. Because of the coronary occlusion the area of heart muscle supplied by this artery may not receive sufficient blood, particularly if the interconnecting small branches between the right and left coronary arteries are not well developed. This area of heart muscle may then die, just as any other muscle area or tissue in the body dies if its blood supply is shut off. An area of dead tissue is called an *infarct*, and an infarct in the heart or myocardium is called a *myocardial infarction*, known as a heart attack.

Thus the buildup of the atherosclerotic process within the coronary artery can be responsible for intermittent chest pain called angina pectoris or for a heart attack. If the area of dead heart muscle is replaced by scar tissue and the patient recovers, he may return to reasonably normal life depending upon how much disease is present in the rest of the coronary arteries and how much heart muscle has actually been damaged. Obviously the more heart muscle that is damaged, the less strength and work capacity the heart will have.

Not all patients with coronary artery disease who die suddenly have evidence of an actual myocardial infarction or even a coronary occlusion. The atherosclerotic process in some way causes an imbalance in circulation to the heart muscle and makes it begin to twitch irregularly rather than contracting in a smooth, normal manner. Rapid twitching of the ventricular muscle fibers is called ventricular fibrillation. When it develops, the heart muscle is no longer able to eject blood and effective circulation stops. Unless the circulation is restored within a few minutes, the brain is damaged and death ensues. A large number of the sudden deaths associated with coronary artery disease are on this basis.

Not all arrhythmia attacks can be definitely ascribed to coronary artery disease. Some of them may be related to changes in the heart muscle itself. The heart muscle may become irritable because of the accumulation of various chemicals and possibly even because of lack of exercise and conditioning of the heart. The heart muscle of the endurance athlete has long efficient fibers that are a result of training. The relatively inactive middle-aged sedentary individual tends to have a small heart with a rapid heartbeat and short heart muscle fibers. Short muscle fibers tend to cramp, just as muscle fibers in the calf of the leg may shorten and cramp, manifesting irritability. The small heart of the sedentary person with its necessarily short thick muscle fibers may be more susceptible to irregularities of the heart or ventricular fibrillation which can cause sudden death. Regardless of whether the irregularity is caused by the heart muscle fiber changes or the changes in the artery, the outcome is just as fatal unless immediate attention is available.

Coronary artery disease of long duration weakens the heart muscle. If sufficient muscle damage occurs, the pumping capacity of the heart is diminished to the point that heart failure ensues. The inability of the heart to pump adequate amounts of blood will allow fluid to accumulate in the lungs causing symptoms of shortness of breath, cough, and other difficulties. Eventually failure of the right ventricle muscle results in the accumulation of blood in other parts of the body so that fluid collects in the abdomen, and the liver, feet, and ankles swell. All of these events—sudden death, angina pectoris, heart attacks (myocardial infarction), and heart failure—can be caused by coronary artery disease from fatty deposits in the coronary arteries. These events are the major health problems of our society and the number one cause of death. The means to significantly reduce their occurrence is at hand for those who wish to use it. *Animal studies have shown that in many instances the athero-sclerotic changes in the coronary arteries can be reversed even after they have developed.* Similar studies in human populations in prison environments and during wartime suggest that the same is true of man. Thus, it is never too late to take measures against the atherosclerotic process.

The damage that has already occurred, such as brain damage from strokes or loss of muscle tissue from previous heart attacks, is not reversible, but much of the atherosclerotic process in the arteries can be notably reduced. There are a few individuals who cannot gain optimal benefits by the ordinary measures of changing their living habits, but the vast majority of persons afflicted with this disorder which leads to untimely death can achieve remarkable improvement with prospects for a longer and healthier life through sensible changes in their living patterns.

It should be pointed out that certain diseases contribute to the development of coronary artery disease in a unique way. Transplanted hearts, for example, tend to be subject to severe coronary artery disease as part of the heart rejection phenomenon. This is in no way a refutation of the evidence gathered over several decades showing that living patterns, particularly with regard to diet, exercise, and tobacco, are significant factors in the development of coronary atherosclerosis. The point is that additional factors can also contribute to the disease. This observation is important in heart transplants but it has very little application to the millions of people who suffer from coronary atherosclerosis as a consequence of their personal habits.

THE OTHER CHANGES

Almost all of the changes of the heart that are attributed to age are brought about by atherosclerosis and are really acquired aging. Elevated blood pressure can cause enlargement of the heart even if atherosclerosis is not present. Elevated blood pressure, however, contributes to the development of atherosclerosis affecting both heart and brain. It is often related to atherosclerosis in the kidneys, obesity, and factors having directly to do with living patterns. The heart enlarges in the presence of high blood pressure because of increased work; some of the same elements are observed as in the endurance athlete, whose heart work is increased in consequence of his physical activity. But the healthy enlargement of the athlete's heart is associated with an increased volume capacity, while enlargement of the heart from high blood pressure often means just thickening of the muscular chambers. The physical activity of the young athlete is beneficial and conducive to development of an optimally healthy cardiovascular system.

The diseases of the individual organs disabled by atherosclerotic disease of their vasculature are considered under their appropriate sections; thus, strokes caused by atherosclerosis of the arteries to the brain are dealt with in Chapter Four, "The Nervous System." It is important, however, to discuss changes noted in the aorta as a result of aging. Atherosclerotic deposits do develop in the aorta. Normally the young aorta is very elastic. As blood is ejected from the heart into the aorta, it balloons out, absorbing the volume of blood and making it unnecessary for the blood pressure to rise too high. A valve at the outlet of the heart closes to prevent the blood from flowing back into the heart when the elastic characteristic of the aorta causes it to contract. The contraction helps propel the blood along the aorta and out to the body. Thus, part of the work of the circulation in the younger individual is accomplished by the elasticity of the aorta. With age (perhaps from wear and tear and partly from atherosclerotic deposits) this elasticity is lost. The U-shaped arch of the aorta begins to lengthen, and the elongated aorta becomes prominent on x-ray examination. As the aorta becomes rigid, it no longer expands nicely when blood is ejected from the heart. Yet the same amount of blood is pumped into the stiff inelastic tube. Blood pressure therefore rises more sharply in the older individual than in the younger. The rise in blood pressure commonly noted in older people is usually related to changes in the aorta. Part of this problem can be prevented to the extent that the atherosclerotic deposits in the aorta can be prevented or delayed.

SIGNS OF CIRCULATORY FITNESS

The prevention of atherosclerosis is essential in averting death and aging. In light of our present knowledge, this means adjusting living habits in regard to diet, exercise, tobacco, coffee, alcohol, and other factors, to be discussed in the appropriate chapters in Part III.

You can get some idea about how healthy your heart and circulation really are. Unless you already have changes in the coronary arteries which can affect the heart rate and its normal beating mechanisms (heart block), a very good indicator is your resting heart rate. Individuals who have resting heart rates below 70 per minute have a much better outlook for life than those whose resting heart rate is over 80 per minute. Well-conditioned men without significant heart disease should have heart rates of approximately 60 beats per minute. Endurance athletes have rates much lower than that. A good example of the influence of physical conditioning on the heart is the case of Roger Bannister. Before he trained to break the four-minute mile, his resting heart rate was in the middle 70's. After he had completed his training to establish the new world record, his resting heart rate was below 40 beats per minute. Characteristically, the heart of the endurance athlete develops its maximum volume capacity and maximum ability to increase the amount of blood it can pump when called upon to do so.

Thus if your resting heart rate is rapid, you know that your circulatory system is not in optimal condition. Factors which contribute to the rapid heart rate include lack of physical activity, excess use of tobacco and coffee, obesity, and anxiety. More will be said about these factors in subsequent chapters.

Another good index of the state of your circulatory system is the degree of obesity you have. The presence of excess fat deposits under the skin usually is an indication of increased fatty deposits in the coronary arteries. If you're fat, you're not fit. If you're fit, you're not fat.

eight

The Lungs

Not too long ago diseases of the lungs were the major cause of death and a frequent cause of disability. The dramatic change in this situation is evidence of the progress that has been made in the medical sciences in the past century. In 1900, when atherosclerotic heart disease was a relatively unimportant medical problem, tuberculosis was the leading cause of death in the industrialized nations of the world. It is still an important factor in many overcrowded, disadvantaged regions. Before the advent of antibiotics, pneumonia was a frequent illness in the aged and responsible for many deaths. Although pneumonia is still a problem in the older group, its significance as a major threat to life has been markedly curtailed. The diseases of the lungs that are common in older people today are bronchitis, emphysema, lung cancer, and, even though it is less prevalent today, tuberculosis.

Aside from the diseases of the lung which can afflict the elderly, other changes in the lungs contribute to the picture of acquired aging. Some of these are preventable. The most significant changes are related to a decrease in functional capacity of the lungs which can limit a person's exercise capacity, strength, and endurance. Changes in the lung can reduce the amount of oxygen available to the blood and hence to the brain, which limitation in turn affects the brain's function. If the decrease in oxygen to the brain is sufficient, it aggravates the common mental confusion noted in aging. Because atherosclerotic changes normally limit the circulation to the brain anyway, any additional problem in oxygenation of the blood imposed by disorders of the lungs makes matters worse. For this reason it is important to maintain optimal function of the lungs as long as possible.

A CLUSTER OF BALLOONS

To appreciate how aging affects the lungs it is necessary to have some knowledge of how they work. Actually the function of the lungs in ventilating the body is relatively simple. The windpipe or trachea extends down the throat and divides in half to send a right and a left air tube (bronchus) to the right and left lung. These branch into a number of smaller air passages in a manner similar to the way a tree branches. The air passages get smaller and more numerous until eventually they end in tiny blind air sacs which resemble balloons. Each of these is called an alveolus. The baby has about 20 million alveoli or air sacs at birth. They increase in number during the early growth stages of the body and by the age of eight the child has 300 million, which is the normal number found in the adult.

Each time we breathe in new air, the old air that is in the windpipe and respiratory passages is sucked deeper into the air sacs. Only the last part of the air we breathe in actually reaches the tiny air sacs. Each time we exhale, only part of the old air is expelled, leaving a large amount of old air in the lungs. Consequently the air enclosed in the air sacs is not the same as the air in our external environment but a mixture of old and new air. It contains less oxygen, more carbon dioxide, and more moisture. If we breathe deeply and rapidly, we can expel a larger amount of old air and take in more new air. This larger exchange of air tends to increase the amount of oxygen in the air sacs. If we hold our breath for any reason, limiting the exchange of air, the oxygen in the air sacs is gradually used up, leaving old unused air with a lesser amount of oxygen in the lungs.

The mixed air within the alveoli is under the same pressure as our external environment, or approximately sea level pressure. The exchange of gas which includes oxygen and carbon dioxide in the body is really accomplished by changes in the pressure exerted by the gas itself. If there is a great deal of oxygen in the alveoli (for example, while breathing oxygen), the oxygen pressure is increased and there is more pressure for it to be pushed across the membrane of the tiny air sac into the nearby circulation of the blood stream. In fact, the difference in pressure created by the oxygen gas in the lungs and in the blood flowing through the lungs is responsible for normal respiration. The pressure of the oxygen gas in the normal alveoli is approximately 100 mm. (the pressure in millimeters of mercury). Since the pressure of oxygen gas dissolved in the circulating blood is much less, oxygen moves across the membrane of the air sac into the blood stream. Once in the liquid part of the blood, oxygen interacts with the hemoglobin in the red blood cells for additional storage.

Another factor which will influence how well the lungs function is the characteristic of the membrane forming the air sac (alveolar membrane) —or, if you compare it to a small rubber balloon, the characteristic of the wall of the balloon. If the membrane is thick and heavy, it is difficult for gases to diffuse freely across it. Problems of this sort are called errors in diffusion. A swollen, inflamed lung membrane, for example, may interfere with the normal diffusion of oxygen from the lungs into the circulation.

A third factor in determining how well the lungs work in accomplishing respiration is the actual flow of blood through the lungs. Even if the mixing of the air in the alveoli is perfectly normal and the lung membranes are healthy, permitting normal diffusion, if there is no blood flow to an area of the lung it cannot assist in respiration. The proper flow of blood to all the different air sacs is called perfusion. Any blood which is shunted through the lungs without coming in contact with any of the air sacs does not pick up a new supply of oxygen and causes a drop in the normal level of oxygen in the blood returning to the heart from the lungs.

Thus, there are three major aspects of respiration that are important. The first is the mixing principle that determines the amount of oxygen in the tiny air sacs. The second is the characteristic of the lung membranes which affects the diffusion of oxygen across them. The third is adequate circulation to the air sacs to enable oxygen to be picked up by the circulating blood.

THE BREATHING CYCLE

The lungs are strictly passive organs. Their contraction and expansion are totally dependent upon the muscular action of the thorax and diaphragm. The chest cavity is a closed semivacuum space, with a negative pressure inside. This negative pressure causes the inactive, elastic lungs to expand to fill the chest cavity. The muscles that move the ribs to increase the diameter of the chest, and the movement of the diaphragm at the bottom of the chest cavity, can change the size and dimension of the chest cavity. As the chest expands, there is a greater degree of negative pressure, and consequently the elastic lungs expand more to fill the space. This is what occurs during inspiration. During expiration the size of the chest cavity is diminished, again through the actions of the muscles of the chest cage and the action of the diaphragm. As the size of the chest cavity diminishes, so does its negative pressure, and the lungs therefore passively contract, expelling air through the trachea.

The concept that the lungs are entirely passive in terms of respiration is an important one because much of a person's capacity to ventilate the lungs is dependent upon the muscles of the chest and diaphragm. If these are weak or the chest cage is deformed, the ability of the lungs to ventilate the body is impaired. Indeed, this is a major factor in some of the changes in respiration noted with acquired aging.

CHANGES IN BREATHING WITH AGE

Many measurements are used to evaluate how the lungs function mechanically to ventilate the body. The amount of air breathed in and out of the lungs is only a small portion of the amount which can be ventilated with a maximum effort. One measurement of lung capacity is called the *vital capacity*. This is simply a measurement of the maximum amount of air which can be inhaled into and exhaled out of the lungs with one breath. Clearly a person with very large lung capacity is able to inhale and exhale a larger amount of air.

The amount of air moved with a single breath by a young healthy male is about 5 or 6 quarts. In studies of the space pilots, the astronauts, and the pentathletes competing for the Olympics, values of 5.7 to 6.4 quarts were average. Some individuals exceeded and others were slightly below this amount. The young athletes were in their early 20's, and most of the space pilots were in their early 30's. Thus there was about a decade of difference in their ages. All were average sized individuals. In an older group of men 62 to 92 years of age considered to be in good health, studied by the National Institutes of Health, the average vital capacity was only 3.6 quarts with a single respiratory effort. Comparison of the two groups reveals that the capacity of the lungs with a single breath is significantly decreased with advancing years.

A second measurement of the function of the lungs is the maximal breathing capacity. This shows how much air can be moved into and out of the lungs over a short span of time, usually 10 or 15 seconds; the values are converted in terms of a minute. Again there was a marked difference between young healthy men and older men who seemed to be in reasonably good health. Despite the differences in their age group, the young endurance athletes and the space pilot–astronaut group had almost identical capacities to move air in and out of the lungs. Their average value was about 180 quarts of air per minute. The older men, between 62 and 92 years of age, thought to be in optimal health were able to ventilate only 104 quarts a minute, again a significant decrease in the capacity of the lungs to ventilate the body.

Despite the decrease in the ability to ventilate the body as evidenced by these measurements the lungs were quite adequate in older individuals to provide the normal amount of ventilation needed for normal respiration under resting conditions or with activity requiring a minimum amount of effort. The respiratory system shows clearly what is often seen with acquired aging: no significant changes under resting, quiet circumstances, but a marked decrease in maximum functional capacity.

In both younger and older individuals the air flowed freely through the respiratory passages, indicating that age alone would not produce any obstruction to the flow of air in the lungs. Some older persons with lung disease do have obstruction to their respiratory passages. The best-known clinical example is the asthmatic, regardless of his age. The obstruction to the respiratory passages causes the characteristic wheezing and effort required to exhale air. Lesser degrees of blockage may not produce symptoms if they are minimal. Acquired age alone does not cause this type of change in the lungs.

Another characteristic change seen in the ventilation aspects of the lungs in older people is the increased amount of old air that is retained in the lungs. There is a change in the size and shape of the thorax, particularly if a buffalo hump has developed, caused by decalcification of the thoracic spine. The changes in the muscles and skeleton of the chest along with other changes result in the lungs' retaining a larger amount of old air, technically called an increase in residual volume. This is important because it affects the mixing function of the lungs and tends to decrease to some extent the amount of oxygen that is available to the circulating blood. Basically there is more old air to be mixed with the new air. The changes in the chest cavity and the chest wall, including its muscles and skeletal system, affect the work of breathing. It takes more effort to move the chest cage to cause the lungs to expand and contract with simple respiration. Since the muscles also are weaker, it is harder and harder to achieve maximum capacity in ventilating the lungs. The result is decreased vital capacity and decreased maximal breathing capacity in the older individual.

Although there are some changes in the lungs, the effects of acquired aging on the function of the lungs are largely due to the loss of muscle strength and degeneration of the spine. Preventive measures can help avert the deformity of the spine, and proper regular breathing exercises can help maintain the strength of the respiratory muscles. These measures are included in the discussion of the musculoskeletal system and of exercises (Chapters Thirteen and Sixteen). The prevention of these changes is another example of what can be done to help a person maintain good health in his later years. The failure to prevent them presents an excellent example of acquired aging from disuse.

With acquired age there are some changes in the ability of gases to move across the alveolar membrane to oxygenate the blood. These disturbances in gas diffusion and circulation coupled with changes in air mixing characteristically cause a slight decrease in the oxygenation of the blood. In young healthy people the oxygen pressure in the blood is usually about 100 mm. Hg. In many men 60 or 65 years of age or older the oxygen pressure may be only 75. Such a drop may not drastically lower the amount of oxygen that is carried by the blood in the red blood cells, but it does significantly affect the pressure to move oxygen into cells. This becomes particularly important in terms of the pressure of oxygen to cause oxygenation of the brain and the nervous system. The oxygen pressure within the cells of the neverous system cannot be any greater than the oxygen pressure in the circulating blood; in fact, it is usually lower. Thus, the drop in oxygen pressure associated with change in the lungs of many older people can be a significant factor in how well the nervous system functions. If atherosclerosis of the arteries to the brain is present, the amount of blood supplied to the brain may decrease by 20 percent. The decrease in circulation and in the amount of oxygen in the blood leads to lower oxygen use by the brain.

In general, the aging lung loses its volume capacity and undergoes changes which influence its ability to transfer oxygen to the blood stream. These changes can effect the oxygenation of the blood and the entire body.

CHANGES AFFECTING WORK CAPACITY

The amount of work a person can do if he has the muscular capacity is normally limited by the amount of oxygen which can be supplied to the working muscle by the lungs and circulation. In young healthy individuals the amount of air that the lungs are able to ventilate is far in excess of the amount of air required to accomplish heavy work. To illustrate the principle: If you put a young man on a treadmill and have him work as hard as he can, at the time he has achieved his maximum effort the amount of air he is breathing in and out of his lungs will be far below the maximum amount which he *can* inhale and exhale. This evaluation is determined simply by measuring how much air is ventilated during the maximum exertion and with a separate test measuring the maximum capacity of the lungs to move air in and out of the body. A young healthy astronaut, for example, may be capable of physical work on the treadmill which requires him to ventilate almost 100 quarts of air a minute to accomplish his task, whereas off the treadmill he could ventilate as much as 200 quarts of air a minute, as determined in a separate measurement of the ability of his lungs. His lungs, that is, are capable of ventilating twice as much air as he needed when he had reached his maximum level of physical effort.

These figures are not unusual in young, well-trained men, and the factor that limits their exercise capacity is the heart's capacity to pump blood. In the older individual not especially trained, average maximum ventilation capacity for his lungs may be only 100 quarts a minute, and with his decreased respiratory capacity he will not be able to perform nearly as much physical work as the younger person. The limiting factor in his case will usually be his lungs. These statements do not necessarily apply to individuals who have had training programs. They do illustrate, though, that in the older person there is a marked decrease in capacity for maximum physical exertion.

COMMON DISEASES IN AGE

Other than the decrease in function of the lungs which limits functional capacity as described above, there are some common diseases of the lungs in older people. They are not a major cause of death in comparison to heart attacks or strokes, but they can be extremely disabling. Chronic bronchitis and emphysema are good examples. Actually these two diseases often occur together and have features in common. The tiny alveolar air sacs become overinflated and cause the lungs to retain an excess amount of air. Frequently the air passages become constricted, as they do in the acute asthmatic attack, only usually not quite that dramatically or severely. This obstruction to air flow and overinflation of the lungs are the hallmarks of chronic bronchitis and emphysema. There may also be irritation of the lung passages and chronic infection. Although some occupations appear to contribute to these problems, the major culprit in modern society is cigarette smoking. Statistics in the state of California show that there were only 1.5 deaths per 100,000 people from emphysema in 1950. Ten years later deaths per 100,000 population had reached 9.5 —a sixfold increase—and in all instances these individuals had a previous smoking history.

Lung cancer has become more important in recent years. Deaths from cancer of the respiratory system now represent nearly 10 percent of total deaths from cancer in the United States and are five times as frequent in men as in women. Respiratory cancer is more often a disease of late adult life; it is seldom noticed before age 40, but after that the incidence markedly increases. The mortality from cancer of the lung is 28 percent higher in whites than in nonwhites. Almost all people who have lung cancer are smokers (90 percent or more). One problem in detecting lung cancer is that it has to obtain a size of nearly half an inch before it can be seen on a chest x-ray. By this time the cancer will contain over a billion cells, and some of them may already have spread to other parts of the body. The simple truth is that most cases of cancer of the lungs could be prevented by eliminating cigarette smoking. This assertion applies only to cancer which originates in the lungs. Cancer that begins elsewhere in the body—for example, in the uterus—commonly spreads to the lungs if not treated early. This is an entirely different problem.

It is somewhat surprising to note that tuberculosis is still an important disease in older people despite the tremendous advances which have been made in recent years in eliminating it as a major public health hazard. The influence of age on the development of tuberculosis can be seen from the number of cases per 100,000 population as noted in studies accomplished in 1966:

Age 15–24 years	13.4 cases
Age 25–44 years	28.0 cases
Age 45–64 years	39.6 cases
Age 65 or more	50.4 cases

The occurrence of tuberculosis in many older people is not a manifestation of a new infection. An individual who had what seemed to be an unimportant, harmless, primary infection in youth can suffer a reactivation of the process and have tuberculosis without additional exposure. This is one reason why repeated lung examinations are of particular importance in older people. Of course, the reactivated tuberculosis in lungs can then spread to other parts of the body.

Devastating as the various diseases of the lungs that occur in older age can be, it is still impressive to note that the diseases of the lungs that once were the major cause of death now represent only a small portion of the medical problems in the older population. What is more impressive is the decrease in functional capacity of the lungs that occurs with age and the likelihood that much of it could be avoided with a constructive preventive program carried out on a regular basis by the individual.

nine

The Digestive System

With the exception of cancer, disorders of the digestive system do not represent life-threatening situations for most people as age progresses. Nevertheless, symptoms and problems frequently arise in the digestive system. Like many other problems attributed to aging, they can often be minimized or avoided.

With the years appetite decreases and dietary patterns often change. Many disorders of the digestive tract, including such problems as spastic colon, irritable colon, constipation, sometimes diarrhea, and ulcerlike symptoms, are not directly related to any apparent structural change. The incidence of cancer of the digestive tract is significantly increased with advancing age, particularly cancer of the colon, rectum, stomach, liver, and pancreas. Several structural disorders of the digestive tract that occur in older people include diverticula or pockets, particularly of the colon, hiatal hernia (herniation of part of the stomach through the diaphragm), gallbladder disease, decrease in stomach acid and other factors necessary to prevent anemia, and hemorrhoids.

The loss of appetite is often associated with loss of teeth and dental problems. The ability to enjoy food depends upon the ability to chew it properly. Careful attention should be given to retaining the teeth in their optimal condition for as long as possible and then to replacement with adequate dentures. A change in appetite may also be caused by loss of taste and with it the loss of smell. One of the best stimuli to a good appetite is physical exercise. All too often the level of physical activity of older people is reduced.

Emotional and social aspects of living influence the appetite. Many older people live alone and thus lack the social aspects of eating which are conducive to a good appetite. Many older people become depressed and lose their appetite. The debility that accompanies weight loss from decreased appetite merely sets up a vicious circle, contributing further to depression and emotional factors which in turn aggravate the problem of loss of appetite.

In addition to loss of appetite, older people develop different and less desirable eating habits. There is a tendency to quit eating foods which provide adequate bulk and water in the diet. Vegetables, fruit, and cereal are particularly important, being rich sources of vitamins, and so are lean meat and other protein foods. Many older people prefer sweets and soft foods relatively lacking in bulk. Disturbances in the function of the digestive tract are likely to follow, including constipation.

Personality change in older people is manifested by greater self-concern and an inward orientation, often directed toward the status of their health and fear of impending death. Their introspection leads them to worry particularly about their digestive tract. In consequence, ulcerlike symptoms appear in some patients and problems of gastritis, diarrhea, spastic colon, and constipation in others. Sometimes medicines, including some of the agents used in treating high blood pressure, contribute to constipation.

CONSTIPATION

A frequent cause of concern in older people is constipation. There is some validity to the statement that there are three ages of man—the young man is interested in a good-looking woman, the middle-aged man in money, and the older man in his bowels. Individuals who have changes in personality and other manifestations of change in the function of the mind are particularly prone to have bowel problems. A major approach to managing problems of constipation is directed toward the well-being of the mind. Obviously, the symptoms of senility associated with atherosclerosis of the arteries to the brain contribute to these evidences of self-preoccupation and factors which aggravate constipation.

The problem of the bowel is not restricted to old age, but it is more prevalent with increasing years. The bowel seems to be a central issue in people's lives beginning with birth. Very soon the child learns that when he soils his diaper he gets attention. Already a means is available to him to start manipulating his parents, and the struggle begins. Shortly thereafter comes the phase of toilet training. The child instinctively recognizes that his mother is pleased when he "performs well," and as his mother stands beside him urging, "Do it for Mummy," whether he does it or not depends on whether he wishes to reward or punish her. Psychiatrists have long known that bowel habits and stool training are a significant part in the development of the human personality. Deeply ingrained in most people's psyche is the idea that excrement is unclean or evil. To rid oneself of excrement is in essence to rid oneself of evil; hence the beginning of the formation of ritualistic concepts related to bowel movements.

The colon, or large intestine, is a very sensitive organ. It pales or blushes in response to emotions. These changes reflect the alterations in blood flow to the highly vascular colon. Pain, thoughts of pain, fear, or unpleasant subjects will cause the arteries to the colon to constrict, resulting in blanching of the lining. The observation of food or eating and things relating to digestion, on the other hand, increases the blood flow to the colon, causing it to redden, since it is engorged with blood. Anger, hostility, and resentment stimulate contractions and motility of the colon, and there is an accompanying increase in the secretion of mucus by the many glands that line its inner aspect. Thus the person who is angry and hostile may have an overactive bowel, and his movements may contain considerable mucus.

Many people have a distorted concept of constipation. They are firmly convinced that they should have one bowel movement a day. This becomes increasingly difficult in the older person who stops eating food which contains an adequate amount of bulk and water. The diminished amount of food intake and lessened bulk naturally result in a smaller amount of waste material for a bowel movement. So it is important to understand that *constipation is not failure to have a daily bowel movement. No other single concept has contributed so much to the initiation of unhealthy bowel habits that lead to chronic constipation and colon difficulties.* The frequency of bowel movements is an entirely individual matter. It depends upon how much food is eaten and how much bulk the food contains as well as the person's physical activity.

Constipation really is the formation of hard stools that are difficult to pass. Prolonged failure to have bowel movements can cause gas and sometimes general lassitude. The symptoms of simple constipation are not dangerous. They are merely annoying.

All too often the individual who is not satisfied with the size of his bowel movements or their frequency begins taking laxatives. This practice ushers in a real bowel problem. Most chemical laxatives act to increase the motility of the small intestine, and their overall action is to propel undigested food from the small intestine into the large intestine. Normally food is completely digested in the small intestine before it even enters the colon. When undigested food is propelled into the colon, it then undergoes putrefaction, causing the formation of gas and distention. The colon, in response to the undigested food, slows down its normal activity. Segments of it even go into spasm. Thus, its entire normal rhythmic contraction is disturbed. The segments of the colon in contraction squeeze the intestinal contents and cause a lot of water to be absorbed from the remaining waste products. The result is a hard, dry piece of stool. The secretion of mucus is also greater, and in areas where the colon is not in spasm there may be softer stool material. Thus the typical response to use of chemical laxatives is the formation of small, hard, dry stools sometimes interspersed with more liquid stools and large amounts of mucus. The entire process results in the formation of excess gas. Dissatisfied with the bowel action, the individual continues to take more laxative, and the vicious cycle is perpetuated.

A contributing factor is the failure to form a good bowel habit. While it is not necessary to have a bowel movement every day, the person who has formed a regular bowel habit will have nature working for him instead of against him. Habits are in many ways useful servants. There is a normal reflex in the body that stimulates the call to stool whenever the stomach is filled. It is known as the gastrocolic reflex. This has a lot to do with why so many people feel the call to stool shortly after breakfast. As the contents of the colon are moved into the rectum, distention of the rectum also initiates the impulse. If the impulse is ignored, the reflex in this area becomes tired or literally resets its threshold, somewhat as a thermostat resets, and then a greater pressure is required to initiate the normal response.

Another habit contributing to colon problems is the excessive use of coffee, which can cause diarrhea and gas in many people and the rapid propulsion of food through the small intestine much like a chemical laxative. Coffee is definitely an irritant to the digestive tract. It is a frequent cause of ulcerogenic symptoms and problems commonly lumped into the group of troubles called irritable colon. Alcohol also irritates the lining of the digestive tract, as does an excess amount of highly seasoned foods.

The type of diet that is desirable to develop normal bowel function has many features in common with the prevention of atherosclerosis and its consequent senility, and also with the prevention of cancer of the bowel. The main emphasis should be on devising a diet which contains adequate fluid and lots of bulk. It is important to recognize that many foods contain a great deal of water. For example, almost 80 percent of the weight of most fish and 70 percent of lean round steak is water. Much of the weight of vegetables and fruit is water. Foods lacking in water are principally the sweets, such as sugar, which is almost totally devoid of water, and most fats, like lard, which contains no water at all.

Foods containing little or no water have a large number of calories per unit of weight. The way to increase the bulk in the diet and achieve normal bowel function is to avoid (1) foods that are made with sweets such as sugar and (2) foods that derive the major portion of their calories from fat. This automatically means that the necessary calories will be obtained from foods with the greater amount of bulk: the entire gamut of vegetables, including those used for salads, fruits, and natural cereals.

The person who wishes to prevent the development of bowel problems or to alleviate those that already exist might well begin a definite program of bowel training and proper dietary habits. To set up an automatic stool habit, it is a good idea to take advantage of the gastrocolic reflex which normally initiates a bowel movement. There is some tendency for this reflex to occur after each meal, but one can choose the meal that is most compatible with one's living patterns—usually breakfast.

If the bowel reflex is to be trained to respond to breakfast, the breakfast should contain an adequate amount of liquid. It should provide at least one glass of juice and a bowl of cereal with milk—either hot cereal like oatmeal or prepared cereal such as shredded wheat. If you are one of those rare individuals who cannot tolerate sugar, you may use honey for sweetening. If you cannot tolerate the milk sugar (lactose), you can use a soybean milk substitute. However, check the label carefully if you want to avoid saturated fats believed to be a factor in developing atherosclerosis. If the label says coconut oil or vegetable oil (often a code term for coconut oil), use a different brand. In the interest of preventing too much fat in the diet, it is well to use low-fat milk or fortified milk. At the end of breakfast you should have one glass of warm water. Additional fruits are acceptable. Avoid the high-calorie fatty breakfast that provides little bulk (exemplified in the eggs-and-bacon routine so common in the American diet) in order to keep the saturated fat level in your diet down. It is complete folly to limit breakfast to a cup of hot coffee sweetened with sugar with or without added cream. This offers no bulk and a limited amount of nutrients other than calories, and the coffee generally stimulates the stomach to produce acid pepsin juice, which irritates the digestive tract.

Immediately after breakfast develop a habit of going to the bathroom and sitting on the commode for a period of time, whether or not there is a bowel movement. This can be carried out daily. It is a good idea to take some reading material or something else to keep the mind off the bowels, and very soon a normal bowel pattern can be established.

Individuals who have had long-standing constipation and are used to the laxative habit will have to totally discontinue using any form of chemical laxative. It may take some time to retrain the bowel, during which period every two or three days a small warm-water enema may be necessary. Other individuals will intermittently need some type of agar or bulk-producing laxative. This is not a chemical laxative but is only for the purpose of increasing bulk. It too should be discontinued as soon as possible after a more normal diet pattern is established. Some people also recommend taking a small amount of mineral oil if needed to soften the stool and induce normal movement. This too should be discontinued as quickly as possible. It often takes four to six weeks to develop a normal bowel habit in a person who has had prolonged difficulty. Persistence is essential, and an absolute must is an adjustment of the diet so that it is based on lean meat, lean fish, lean fowl, vegetables, fruits, and cereals and avoids refined products such as cakes, refined flours, sugars, and fats. A daily exercise program is also useful if one has been lax in that department.

Individuals who have had persistent colon difficulties will notice that certain foods are gas producers and cause increasing trouble. Often these are foods which have a hull—for example, green peas. If they are mashed or pureed so that the hulls are broken, sometimes they can be tolerated. In other instances foods that are known to have this effect must simply be avoided. However, there are so many good vegetables, fruits, and cereals that most people can develop a diet which is quite satisfactory and still have enough food items to provide sufficient bulk.

DIARRHEA

The opposite problem, diarrhea, is less often noted in older people. Unless it is caused by an infection or a disease such as ulcerative colitis, it is usually a manifestation of nervous tension. Coffee and alcohol and highly spiced foods can contribute to this problem. A reasonable number of adults cannot tolerate milk because the digestive tract will not handle the lactose milk sugar. These people lack an enzyme that is necessary to split the milk sugar into simple sugars so that it can be absorbed. The unabsorbed sugar acts like a chemical laxative and may cause gas, bloating, intermittent diarrhea, and constipation. The solution is to stop using milk and milk products. It is easy to determine whether one has this problem by just eliminating all food products that contain milk or are prepared with milk in any form. Soybean milk can be used as a substitute, and there are fortified soybean milk products that contain calcium and approximately the same amount of other nutrients as normal milk. These products can also be substituted in most cooking that calls for milk.

DIVERTICULA

A common problem in older people is the presence of diverticula. These are small pockets most often located on the colon. Actually they are small ruptures or herniations of the inner lining of the colon. Like the rest of the digestive tract, the colon is a thick muscular tube. It has a layer of muscles that run lengthwise and another layer of circular muscles. Inside the colon is an inner lining, the mucosa, which contains glands and lubricating materials. In the small intestines the mucosa cells secrete enzymes and other chemicals necessary for normal digestion. The outer wall of the colon and small intestine is a tough fibrous coat.

Diverticula are produced by the separation of the muscular wall of the colon and herniation of the lining of the colon through the muscular layer and toward the tough outer layer. The resultant little pocket is called a diverticulum.

Diverticula are rarely seen in young people before the age of 35, but one out of five Americans over 40 has diverticula of the colon. Fortunately, only one out of 25 people over 40 years has symptoms from diverticula. These can be the sensation of fullness, gas formation, and nonspecific symptoms, or, more rarely, those of inflammation. The diverticula can act somewhat like an appendix, and if one of them becomes severely inflamed it may even rupture. Happily inflammation of a diverticulum creating a significant medical problem occurs in only about one out of 500 people over age 40. Diverticula can cause griping pain, often in the left lower portion of the abdomen. Rarely a diverticulum may result in rectal bleeding.

The exact cause of diverticula is not known, but it is thought that they are related to increased activity of the colon. That is, they occur in individuals who have areas of spasm and hypermotility in the colon, most often associated with poor dietary habits. Diverticula are particularly prevalent among people who have access to refined foods. They are 40 times as common in people in North America and northern Europe as they are in some of the native tribes of the so-called undeveloped countries. Individuals who are essentially free of diverticula are also relatively free of carcinoma of the colon. There is a strong suggestion that the difference in the dietary patterns is a major factor in the lower incidence of both cancer and diverticula in people leading a somewhat less affluent life and eating a more natural diet.

The treatment of diverticula is much the same as that used in the prevention or treatment of constipation unless, of course, there is an acute problem such as an inflamed diverticulum, which requires immediate medical attention. Proper treatment means the same kind of diet that has already been discussed in the prevention of constipation and the development of proper bowel habits.

HIATAL HERNIA

Another disorder of the digestive tract which is much more frequent in older people is hiatal hernia. In this condition the hole in the diaphragm is sufficiently large to allow part of the stomach to herniate or slide through into the chest cavity. Rarely there are individuals who have a birth defect in the diaphragm which may permit a major portion of the stomach to slide through into the chest. I have seen large hernias in individuals who have had no symptoms whatever. One of these was in a young space pilot who was a candidate in the final selection of the nation's astronauts. He had been flying jet aircraft for years and was a top-notch pilot. During the detailed examination for the astronaut program, an x-ray examination made while he was lying on his back showed the stomach sliding into the chest. Before that examination he had never had any difficulty with his digestive tract and had been a highly successful aviator.

The more common form of hiatal hernia is that which occurs in older people. One study has shown that more than 67 percent of individuals over 60 years of age have hiatal hernia, generally associated with a relaxation or an enlargement of the normal opening in the diaphragm where the esophagus passes through the diaphragm into the stomach. Many such hernias do not create any symptoms. A usual pattern is that a small portion of the stomach where it joins the esophagus is actually pushed through the hole in the diaphragm. The normal closure mechanism at the entrance to the stomach is thus prevented from working properly, and acid pepsin juice and materials from the stomach are regurgitated into the lower portion of the esophagus. In this event the lining of the lower esophagus is literally burned by the acid contents of the stomach, causing heartburn or indigestion. Often there is sour belching and a diffuse burning feeling in the pit of the stomach or near the lower portion of the breastbone.

Occasionally a hiatal hernia produces other symptoms, including a sensation of pressure and discomfort underneath the breastbone with pain radiating into the back or shoulder, up into the jaw, and sometimes down the inner aspects of the arm. The pain may resemble that of an acute heart attack, and differentiating between the two is sometimes difficult.

It is not clear why hiatal hernia develops so frequently in older people. Sometimes obesity is a factor. The increase in pressure of the abdominal contents may contribute by pushing a portion of the stomach through the normal opening in the diaphragm. Women are particularly prone to have hiatal hernia especially if they have had a number of pregnancies.

For those who have hiatal hernia with symptoms there are a number of practical things which can be done. The basis for management of hiatal hernia symptoms is reducing the possibility that acid pepsin juice from the stomach will be regurgitated into the lower esophagus. Of course high on the list is weight reduction to eliminate abdominal pressure. A second measure is to avoid large meals by eating six small meals a day. They should contain the kinds of foods previously discussed to provide adequate bulk in the diet and prevent constipation. There is no conflict between these two programs. One simply divides the menu into six portions instead of trying to eat it all in three meals.

A person with hiatal hernia should refrain from eating anything for at least two hours before lying down. When he is on his back, it is much easier for the contents of the stomach to regurgitate into the lower esophagus if the closure mechanism at the entrance to the stomach is faulty. One is also wise to avoid eating things which tend to slow emptying of the stomach. Cold foods, such as ice cream, delay the emptying of the stomach sometimes for hours. Fatty foods, too, slow the normal emptying of the stomach. If the last meal of the day before bedtime is relatively low in fat and does not include anything cold, the emptying of the stomach before bedtime will be speeded up.

The diet should be planned to avoid stimulation of acid pepsin juice by the stomach. A bland diet for this purpose definitely precludes coffee or any other drink which contains caffeine, such as tea. It also means avoiding alcohol.

There should be no tight garments around the waist, such as a tight girdle or belt which would cause pressure to squeeze the hernia through the diaphragm. Men are notorious for wearing a belt several inches smaller than their true measurement. There should be no stooping or bending, such as leaning over to tie the shoelaces or to mop the kitchen floor.

The head of the bed should be elevated about 10 inches either on blocks or on strong chairs. A similar mechanism of raising the head should be employed for couches or any other furniture used for recumbency or sleeping. These simple devices will go a long way toward preventing the discomfort of hiatal hernia.

PEPTIC ULCER

Peptic ulcers of the stomach or duodenum do occur in older people but they have no specific relationship to aging. Nervous tension and emotional factors in addition to dietary factors, such as the excess use of coffee or alcohol, and the cigarette habit are equally important in both young and old in the formation of peptic ulcers. The complicating factor in the older person is atherosclerosis of the arteries that supply the area of the ulcer. This often creates complications from a bleeding ulcer.

ACHLORHYDRIA

As people get older, the amount of hydrochloric acid normally formed by the stomach tends to decrease. This condition is called achlorhydria. There is considerable disagreement about what kinds of symptoms it produces, but the absence of hydrochloric acid, along with the absence of a substance formed by the stomach called intrinsic factor, is fundamental in causing pernicious anemia, a disorder that is almost never seen in individuals before the age of 35.

GALLSTONES

Gallstones occur more often in older individuals than in young people, although they are not specifically related to aging. As a matter of fact, the cause of gallstones is incompletely understood. It is thought that infections of the gallbladder contribute to their formation, and sluggish flow of bile may be a factor. Or perhaps some chemical balance is disturbed which normally maintains the solubility of bile. Most gallstones are really made up chemically of the cholesterol formed by the liver and secreted in the bile in combination with some portion of the bilirubin pigment (bile pigment) substance and calcium. Such stones are called mixed stones. Rarely, a stone consists of cholesterol alone. The bilirubin or bile pigment is formed from the hemoglobin of destroyed red blood cells. It gives the bile its characteristic greenish color.

In white females gallstones occur in about 6 percent of the population between ages 30 and 62, and the peak rate is 9 percent in females between 50 and 62 years of age. They occur somewhat less frequently in males, with a peak incidence of 5 percent in men aged 50 to 60. Racial differences contribute to the incidence of gallstones. Over 50 percent of the Navajo Indian women over age 40 have gallstones. This characteristic does not seem to be related to the Navajo woman's diet or how many children she has had or whether or not she is obese. Since the cause of gallstones is not completely understood, no constructive program can be offered at this time to help prevent their occurrence.

DISEASES OF LIVER AND PANCREAS

Disorders of the liver and pancreas do not seem to have any age relationship. The liver is capable of regenerating its own damaged cells, and it is such a redundant organ that the simple aging process as we know it has no significant effect upon the liver or its function. The disorders of the liver are associated with classic diseases and toxic or physical injuries. A similar statement can be made in reference to the pancreas.

HEMORRHOIDS

With progressive inactivity and poor bowel habits, it is not surprising that many older people suffer from hemorrhoids. Although they do occur in the young, they are more common in older people. Hemorrhoids may be thought of as dilated or varicose veins of the rectum and they are directly related to man's habit of walking upright. They are induced by gravity, as you can understand by a simple illustration. Hang your hand down by your side and look at the back of your hand. See how the veins pop out. The column of blood in the veins from the shoulder to the hand creates pressure because of the influence of gravity. Gravity causes the blood to have weight, and the higher the column of blood, the greater the pressure it will exert. Now, if you raise your hand up to your eye level and look at the back of the hand, you will see the veins collapse. They are now above the heart level, and the blood runs downhill to the heart.

The veins around the rectum are constantly distended when you are sitting upright or standing, because like the veins in the back of the hand they are subject to gravity. It is interesting to note that the four-footed animal simply doesn't have hemorrhoids. In the cow, for example, the heart rests at the lower part of the chest in the lower part of the body, and the rectum underneath the tail is actually above the heart. The veins around the rectum in the cow and other four-footed animals will be drained flat like those you observed in the back of your hand when you held it directly in front of your eyes. With long-standing continued pressure from gravity the dilated veins around the human rectum gradually become varicose veins, like the ones people are familiar with in the legs, but these are called hemorrhoids.

Factors which increase the pressure in the rectal veins can contribute to hemorrhoids. These include any tumor mass that might be in the rectum, constipation with obstruction of the rectum, the frequent moving of hard, dry stools, and childbirth with its increased pressure on the rectum.

One protection against the dilatation of the veins is good muscle tone around the rectal sphincter. You can see the veins in the legs collapse under normal circumstances during walking, and the reason is that the muscular contractions milk the veins and create external pressure against them, preventing distention. Similarly, muscle tone around the rectal area helps prevent venous distention there. Physical activity and exercises to tighten the seat muscles help to preclude serious hemorrhoids, although exercise alone cannot do so.

Hemorrhoids are divided into two groups, internal and external. The external hemorrhoids are directly underneath the skin at the anal region. This area is abundantly supplied with nerve fibers, and these are the hemorrhoids that produce symptoms—the sensation of sitting on a ball or the painful irritation common to external hemorrhoids. A clot may form in a small vein just below the skin, and the swelling and clotted area causes the irritation and pain. Sometimes these hemorrhoids need to be surgically excised to relieve the symptoms. Hot sitz baths and local application of anesthetic agents are often helpful.

The internal hemorrhoids are inside the sphincterlike valve of the rectum. Since there are no pain-sensitive nerve fibers here, internal hemorrhoids usually do not cause discomfort except when a thrombosed vein becomes so large that it protrudes through the opening of the rectal sphincter and is actually caught or strangulated. At this point the person will become aware of symptoms. The usual sign of internal hemorrhoids is rectal bleeding. Constant recurrent bleeding on a nearly daily basis, even if it is a small amount, can gradually contribute to the development of an anemia, just as menstruating can in the woman during her childbearing years. Internal hemorrhoids often require surgical correction, but some can be injected with sclerosing substances which cause the dilated veins to become scarred and fibrosed, thereby eliminating the hemorrhoid.

Obviously the important thing to do in preventing hemorrhoids is to maintain a good bowel habit along the lines described in the management of constipation problems and to maintain good muscle tone. *Bleeding from the rectum or simple hemorrhoids should not be ignored. A medical examination is indicated to determine the source of bleeding and to be certain that hemorrhoids are the cause. A common way for cancer of the rectum to manifest itself is by bleeding from the rectum or by creating enough pressure on the veins to cause hemorrhoids. This is why it is absolutely mandatory to have a rectal examination if you suspect you have hemorrhoids. Only in this way can an early malignancy of the rectum be found and corrected. It should be emphasized that early detection of cancer of the rectum usually means that it can be completely cured. Failure of early detection leads to a doubtful outcome.*

PROBLEMS COMMON IN YOUNG AND OLD

It is apparent that most of the disorders of the digestive system seen in older people are also seen in younger people, although some, such as diverticulosis, are rare except in middle-aged or older people. Most of the problems created by the digestive system in older people are major disturbances of function and do not really pose a threat to life. The digestive system has many built-in redundancies which enable it to operate adequately to maintain nutrition even when its function is seriously deranged. Nevertheless, its normal working is an important aspect of living better longer. The proper attention to diet and habits can contribute markedly toward that goal.

ten

The Sexual System

Of all the changes which occur in the human body with advancing years, probably none is more frightening than the loss of one's sexual capacity. Sexuality is closely related to self-image. The loss of sexual function alone is not the problem. The change signals aging and confronts the individual with the reality that youth is slipping away. It is natural that a woman would like to remain as young and attractive as she was before 30, and it is equally natural that the man would wish to remain as young, vigorous, and sexually potent as he was in his early years. Even the terms applied to the changes in sexuality in the middle and later years are indicative of the attitudes toward these changes. Women refer to the menopause as the "change of life," and a man's loss of sexual capacity is frequently called his "loss of manhood." The desperate search for a means to remain sexually active and sexually desirable is closely related to the search for continued youth.

OUR SEXY BRAIN

The sexual system is profoundly affected by the nervous and glandular (endocrine) systems of the body. The changes in these systems are at least related to acquired aging.

Not a single cell in the body escapes sexual identity. Every cell contains within it the genetic code identifying it as female (XX) or male (XY). The propagation of the species is such an essential aspect for the continuation of man that it is directly linked to the brain. The truth is, the brain is the most important sexual organ in the body—and not only of humans but of other species also. In lower forms of life the region of the brain, called the hypothalamus, which is directly related to temperature control, emotions, and control of the autonomic nervous system is the main switchboard for many of the sexual functions. In man the cortex of the brain is also important.

The hypothalamus connects anatomically with the master gland of the endocrine system, the pituitary gland. The pituitary has two parts, a front and a back lobe (anterior pituitary and posterior pituitary gland). They are really two different glands that are linked to the floor of the brain. The posterior pituitary is stimulated directly by nerve fibers which extend to the individual cells of this part of the gland. The anterior pituitary is stimulated by a chemical substance produced by the brain in or near the region of the hypothalamus.

The anterior pituitary gland exerts a major control over the sexual organs and hence the sexual functions of the body. The whole system is quite complex, but the basic principles are relatively simple. The chemical secretions in the anterior pituitary gland control the ovaries in the female and the testicles in the male. They influence the adrenal cortex (the outer shell of the small gland above the kidneys) and in the female influence lactation.

The human sexual system, then, is comprised of the brain with its hypothalamus, the anterior and posterior pituitary, the ovaries and testicles, and the adrenal cortex. In addition there are the sexual organs themselves, which include the breasts and genitalia. The hormones elaborated by the endocrine system control the secondary sexual characteristics, such as hair growth and distribution as well as fat deposition and other characteristics commonly referred to as being male or female. Other endocrine glands—the thyroid, for instance—also influence sexual function even though they do not form sex hormones.

The sex of an individual is determined genetically. At the time the male sperm and the female ovum unite, the sexual characteristics of the future baby are already decided under normal circumstances. If the male sperm is a Y sperm, the baby will be an XY baby, or male. If the male sperm is an X sperm, the baby will have an XX chromosome pattern and be female. Since every cell in the body carries this genetic code, it is clear that the earliest development of the nervous system and brain is genetically labeled as male or female. A genetic male brain is one with cells containing the XY chromosomes. A genetic female brain is one with cells containing XX chromosomes. This, however, is only the beginning of defining the sexual nature of the future person.

Regardless of the genetic sex of the brain and body, the subsequent secretion of hormones by the developing fetus will have a lot to do with determining the sexual appearance and sexual behavior. Very early in fetal life, a small area of the cells that will later become sexual organs must differentiate. The result will be the formation of the male glands or the female glands and, incidentally, the adrenal cortex, which may explain to some extent why the cortex of the adrenal gland also secretes sex hormones. If all goes well, the male fetus will have cells that will begin to form the future testicles. At this stage in the normal genetic male, the formation of male hormones will actually direct its development. The male hormones will cause the brain cells to be organized into a functionally male brain. If male hormone is not present, the brain will be organized as a female brain regardless of the genetic characteristics of the developing fetus.

Many experiments have been done that prove this point. Providing male hormone during the developmental phase of the female fetus will result in a male-type brain and male personality behavior pattern. Male hormone in early fetal life is responsible for the development of normal male genitals.

The functional aspect of the brain in terms of sexuality really refers to the subsequent cyclic sexual responses. The adult female has a menstrual cycle covering an average span of about 28 days. This cycle is directly keyed to the function of the brain. The male does not have a similar cycle, and his brain is organized differently. Since there are both male and female cells in the brain, which ones are developed depends upon the presence or absence of male hormone during development.

The distinct difference in organization within the brain suggests numerous possibilities for continued investigation into the differences in personality behaviors and variance between an individual who appears to be strictly male and one who appears to be strictly female. These demonstrated changes, which can be induced in animals, clearly reveal that maleness or femaleness extends beyond simple genetic sex and that the entire organization of the brain with consequent body rhythms can be affected during early fetal growth. This is not to say that the behavior of individuals sexually in terms of male or female qualities is limited to the period of development, but rather that influences which determine the ultimate sexual characteristics of the individual have their origins long before birth.

No distinction is made here between inherited, functional, anatomical responses of the body and environmental influences. The process of learning affects fundamental chemical patterns within the cellular structures. Thus life's learning process constantly affects the body regardless of what equipment one begins life with. The total effect of what one begins with genetically, what happens chemically in the developmental process, and what happens in contact with the environment after birth determines the individual—specifically including sexuality.

If you thought that individuals reached puberty and underwent sexual changes because their endocrine glands finally had grown enough, think again. It is the brain that controls the onset of puberty. Investigators have proved this point by taking the immature anterior pituitary gland from an animal before puberty and transplanting it into an adult animal. The immature pituitary gland now in place underneath the brain in the mature individual functions in a mature fashion, controlling and stimulating the rest of the sexual apparatus of the mature animal. Experiments like these, involving the transplanting of glands between mature and immature animals, have shown unequivocally that the onset of puberty is determined by the brain. There appears to be some genetic code within the brain at birth that decides when puberty will begin, all other things being equal. As with other aspects of what we inherit, the start of puberty can be influenced by other factors, probably including nutrition.

FROM PUBERTY TO MENOPAUSE

Puberty is one step along the calendar scale of aging. The brain triggers the response, and the anterior pituitary gland begins to secrete hormones which stimulate the sex glands. In the female the ovaries suddenly enlarge and begin to secrete female hormones responsible for the changes in the female sexual organs, including the development of the uterus, the vagina, and the labial folds of the vulva. The changes in the uterus include the cyclic changes of menstruation.

In the male, characteristic masculine changes take place, with a marked increase in the amount of well-defined musculature. There is growth of the external genitalia as well as development of the secondary sexual characteristics such as hair distribution. The testicles enlarge and begin to secrete increased amounts of testosterone, which is responsible for many of the masculine changes.

With sexual maturation then, if everything has gone according to plan, the individual will develop with a genetic male brain and a functional male brain with an anatomical male body, or with a genetic female brain and a functional female brain and personality with an anatomical female body. Because of the complexities that enter into this end point, it is little wonder that there are many variations in between and that individuals may have both male and female characteristics. The wonder should be how frequently the entire complex system follows a recognized plan.

At birth the human female has all the cells which will subsequently produce mature ova for pregnancies. Her ovaries contain 200,000 to 400,000 cells, each one capable of becoming a mature ovum and being fertilized to produce pregnancy under the appropriate circumstances. This is in considerable excess of the number that are ever matured during the woman's active sexual life since only about 400 will actually be used for normal ovulation during the childbearing years. It is true that each succeeding pregnancy uses cells which are progressively older than were those used for the preceding pregnancy. There has been some speculation that this circumstance may give rise to a higher number of birth defects in pregnancies occurring late in life.

The male's sperm cells are not analogous to the female's ovum cells at birth. The male is constantly generating new sperm cells. As sperm cells are lost in sexual activity, more are formed.

The female retains the capacity for pregnancy until about two years after menstrual periods have ceased. There is great variation in when the reproductive period of the female may end, but usually it terminates in the latter 40's or early 50's. It is generally believed that pregnancy does not occur after the early 50's although there may be some women who have had children at older ages.

THE MENSTRUAL CYCLE

The menstrual cycle is really fairly simple. Assume for a moment that the ovary and the uterus are in a resting phase. Under influences of the hypothalamus, the anterior pituitary gland liberates a hormone called follicle-stimulating hormone (FSH), to stimulate the ovary. This causes one of the small ovarian cells to ripen into an ovum (egg). The developing ovum is called a follicle. At the same time the ovary is producing a lot of *estrogen,* one of the main female hormones. The amount it forms increases steadily as the follicle enlarges like a giant blister on the ovary.

After the ovum has reached full maturation, there is a sudden switch in signals to the anterior pituitary gland. It stops producing FSH and releases a second hormone called the luteinizing hormone (LH). This stimulates the blisterlike follicle to rupture and the ovum to escape. The process is ovulation and normally occurs at about the midpoint between menstrual cycles. The usual average date is said to be 14 days before the first day of onset of the next menstrual period for women who are regular, with a 28-day cycle.

Under the influence of LH the ruptured follicle develops new yellow cells and becomes a small rounded yellow body called the corpus luteum. This pea-shaped body within the ovary produces the major portion of the second important female hormone from the ovary, *progesterone.* If the ovum is not fertilized, the corpus luteum lasts approximately 10 days before it begins to degenerate.

The anterior pituitary and the ovary enjoy a relationship in which the first half of the menstrual cycle is initiated by FSH stimulating the formation of estrogen. The second half of the cycle is dominated by the LH from the anterior pituitary which stimulates the formation of progesterone. The two hormones from the anterior pituitary, FSH and LH, do not have any feminizing influence in their own right. They only act to stimulate the ovary. High levels of estrogen and progesterone inhibit the anterior pituitary from releasing FSH, limiting the number of follicles stimulated at a time.

The amount of estrogen formed by the ovary increases until ovulation, when it drops suddenly. After a few days, with the development of the yellow corpus luteum, the amount of estrogen formed increases again, along with progesterone, to reach a peak level at about the 21st day of the average menstrual cycle. Thereafter the amount of both hormones produced falls rapidly. When the progesterone and estrogen levels fall, normal menstruation ensues.

The uterus responds to the two hormones released by the ovary. During the first part of the menstrual cycle the estrogen stimulates the growth of cells that line its cavity, literally preparing the uterus to receive the fertilized ovum. When the estrogen level drops at the time of ovulation, some women experience some bleeding. This midmenstrual bleeding pinpoints the time of ovulation. With the secretion of estrogen and resumption of estrogen formation the lining of the uterus undergoes further changes to improve its capacity to act as a bed for the implanting of the fertilized ovum. If the ovum is fertilized, the sperm cell and ovum meet in the fallopian tube. The fertilized ovum then migrates to the cavity of the uterus and under proper conditions embeds itself in the prepared lining.

At the end of the menstrual cycle, if pregnancy has not occurred, the blood supply to the uterus is markedly constricted and the specially developed lining degenerates, leading to the normal bleeding of menstruation.

If pregnancy occurs, the corpus luteum is maintained and the placenta begins to develop. With these changes both estrogen and progesterone continue to be secreted and prevent the release of more FSH so as to preclude the possibility of an additional pregnancy. This principle of the action of estrogen and progesterone to stop release of FSH from the anterior pituitary is the basis for the birth control pill.

A third anterior pituitary hormone, called the lactogenic or luteotropic hormone (LTH), affects the female sexual process. Its main function is to stimulate milk formation or lactation. The actual process of lactation, however, involves the action of estrogen, progesterone, and LTH. The early changes in the breasts noted in pregnancy are related to the combination of hormonal influences. LTH may have other functions. It appears, at least in some animals and possibly in man, to increase the contractility of the uterus. LTH is stimulated by the sucking actions and by the mating act. Stimulation of the breast and intercourse appear to trigger the release of LTH, which in turn increases the contractility of the uterus to help propel the sperm cells up the uterus to the fallopian tube for their rendezvous with the freshly released ovum.

Multiple changes occur in the course of the menstrual cycle, changes in mood, personality, and (in some women) fluid retention. Not only does the brain influence the hormonal system, but the hormones influence the function of the brain and nervous system as well.

THE MALE COUNTERPART

The function of the male sexual system parallels the control of the female system by the pituitary gland. The principal male endocrine gland is the testicle. The ovoid-shaped testicular body contains the long convoluted tubules called seminiferous tubules. These are folded back and forth on each other like a long hose and bound together in little clusters or sections within the body of the testis. Each tubule varies from 1 to 3 feet in length, the combined length of the entire group of tubules in each testicle being over 300 feet. The sperm cells, formed from the walls of these tubules, are comparable to the cells in the ovaries that form the ova. The main difference is that new cells to form new sperm are constantly generated whereas the cells that form the ova are all present at birth.

As the cells migrate to the center of the tubule, they ripen and develop into sperm. The tubules all coalesce to join into one main larger tube, the vas deferens. The vas deferens folds back upon itself outside the testicle in the cordlike area called the epididymis. The vas deferens then follows the course along the cord of the testicle until it empties into the male urethra at the region of the prostate gland.

Just before the vas deferens enters the prostate, it is joined by the drainage tube from the seminal vesicles. There is one on each side (right and left). These are little saclike structures (shaped like saddlebags) located at each side of the prostate. They are not a repository for sperm but form a liquid secretion which is part of the male orgasm. The prostate also secretes fluid daily and discharges into the urine. The male orgasm includes the sperm cells from the testicles and the secretions from the seminal vesicles and prostate gland. The sperm cells formed within the testicles actually ripen as they migrate up the long course of the tubules and through the vas deferens. At the time of orgasm most of the sperm cells are ejaculated first with some secretions from the prostate gland followed by the fluid from the seminal vesicles. About 75 percent of all the sperm cells are in the first one-third of the seminal discharge.

Within the body of the testicle between the seminal tubules are other cells, called interstitial cells, which form testosterone, the male hormone. Because there are several stages in the chemical synthesis of the male hormone, the chemicals involved are sometimes called androgens, meaning male hormones. The testicle is specialized in the sense that androgen formation can stimulate the seminiferous tubules to form sperm. There is no comparable action within the ovary. FSH from the anterior pituitary also stimulates the cells in the tubules to form sperm. LH stimulates the interstitial cells to form androgen. Obviously the prolonged cycle observed in the female does not occur, but both pituitary hormones are active in maintaining the normal functions of the testicles. The amount of hormones secreted by the anterior pituitary is influenced by the level of testosterone. Thus, the feedback mechanism between the target gland (testicle or ovary) and the anterior pituitary is operative in the male as well as in the female.

The male begins to form sperm with puberty—as soon as the hormonal influences have stimulated adequate development of the male organs. As with the female, the timing for the onset of puberty and the subsequent formation of sperm as well as the increased formation of testosterone is under the control of the brain. Pituitary hormones and other hormones similar in action can be used to stimulate testicular function, which in turn results in masculinizing an individual. They are sometimes used when the testicles have not properly developed. The masculinization of the body can be achieved by the administration of testosterone. However, it should be pointed out that large doses of testosterone can lead to atrophy of the testicles. The additional testosterone seems to suppress testicular activity, which can be permanently impaired. Large doses of estrogen can similarly affect the function of the testicles.

One unique feature of the testicles may have a significant influence on the decline of sexual activity in males noted with increasing years. This is the character of its blood supply. To form normal healthy sperm the temperature of the testicles must be carefully controlled. Thus, in man the testicles are in the scrotal sac outside the body. The arterial blood going to the testicles carrying oxygen and nutrition to them is cooled by its passage among surrounding veins in the cord of the testicle. Literally heat is lost from the arterial blood to the venous blood. By the time the arterial blood reaches the testicle it is 3° C. less than body temperature. Moreover, the arteries to the testicles spread out over the body of the testicle itself rather than entering at a central point. A further distribution of the arterial blood is therefore allowed before it enters the part of the testicle where sperm cells are formed.

The arteries lying over the outer shell of the testicle penetrate the shell to form a perpendicular or sharp angle as they enter the body of the testicle. Within the arterial system points of sharp angulation are ideal locations for the formation of fatty deposits. For this reason *the testicles are particularly susceptible to atherosclerosis*. As atherosclerosis increases, it effectively limits circulation to the testicle.

OUR SEXY ADRENAL GLANDS

In addition to the primary organs and glands that are thought of as having a sexual function, the adrenal gland also secretes sex hormones. The outer shell of the adrenal gland, called the adrenal cortex, starts out as a sex gland, originating with the same group of cells that eventually become differentiated into either ovaries or testicles. Even the chemical structure of the hormones formed by the adrenal cortex is similar to that of hormones formed by the ovary and testicle. All of these hormones, therefore, are classified as *steroids*, a term used to designate their general chemical structure. The cells of the adrenal cortex are able to change their nature and actual function, which ability determines what kind of hormones the adrenal cortex forms. It is capable of producing male hormones, or androgens, and the female hormones progesterone and estrogen. Estrogen is apparently produced in very small amounts.

During intrauterine life the adrenal cortex produces mostly androgens rather than the other adrenal hormones that have no specific sexual role. Shortly after birth androgen secretion is curtailed. At the onset of puberty, the adrenal gland again secretes greater amounts of androgen. This is the main sex hormone formed by the adrenal cortex, although under certain circumstances it is able to produce larger quantities of the female hormones.

The sex hormones secreted by the adrenal cortex have essentially the same functions as the same sex hormones secreted by the testicles and ovaries. To add to the complexity of the formation of hormones by males and females, the testicles also form estrogen as well as androgens. The balance of male and female hormones produced in either the male or the female of the species has a lot to do with the subsequent development and body characteristics. A tumor of the adrenal cortex, for example, which results in the formation of excess amounts of male hormones in infant boys, will result in early sexual maturity and a very masculine young boy with large genitals and the pubic hair of an adult male. Women with all the attributes of femininity who develop a tumor of the adrenal cortex will undergo bodily changes because of excess androgen formations. The beard grows, and other evidences of masculinization are seen.

THE MENOPAUSE

Many authorities consider the female menopause a clear indication of aging. This depends entirely on what one's concept of aging is. The menopause certainly represents a change in life, but so does puberty. In general, the American woman has 30 years of life or more still before her at the time of the menopause. Moreover, there are few or no signs of senility. Most women continue to be vigorous, active, happy people after the menopause, although they have some identifiable changes. The menopause really signals the end of reproductive capability. While it usually occurs between 45 and 50 years of age, it can take place as early as age 25 or in the late 50's. I know of some women in their 60's and even early 70's who claim to menstruate.

All evidence points to the fact that the menopause is a result of ovarian failure. The ovaries just plain quit. They do not usually do so all at once, but the functions of the ovaries gradually cease or sputter to a halt. During this period there is a slow decrease in the amount of estrogen produced by the ovaries. The loss of this feminizing hormone causes the bodily changes and symptoms associated with the menopause. In addition, with the decline in the number of maturing follicles, there is a decrease or absence in formation of the corpus luteum which normally follows ovulation; as a consequence, essentially no progesterone is produced from the ovaries. The ovaries themselves shrink until they are so small they are difficult to find on physical examination, whereas normally they are fairly easily palpable in the woman of childbearing age. The ovaries do continue to form some estrogen, apparently for many years, but experimental studies have suggested that the amount secreted after the menopausal period is really of little consequence. Removal of the ovaries during or after the menopause has no significant effect on the amount of estrogen that can be measured in the body.

The continued production of female hormone after the menopause is accomplished by the adrenal cortex. If it is removed, there is a sharp drop in the amount of estrogen in the body. The continued secretion of estrogen in older women is established by the observation that as many as 20 percent of women 70 years of age will show evidence of estrogen stimulation of the lining of their vagina. Progesterone, the other female hormone, is also secreted by the adrenal cortex. Of course, the adrenal cortex continues to produce the male hormone, or androgen, and the relative amounts of all these hormones have a significant influence on the changes which occur in the body in the menopausal or postmenopausal period. Interestingly, the normal adult male eliminates in the urine (and therefore produces) about twice as much estrogen as a 60-year-old woman.

With the relatively sharp decline in the amount of estrogen formed by the ovaries, the anterior pituitary starts producing a lot more FSH, trying to stimulate the failing ovary. But no amount of hormone from the anterior pituitary is capable of rejuvenating it. The low estrogen levels produced by the ovary are not enough to trigger the sequential events of the menstrual cycle.

One of the earliest signs of the female menopause is the decreased frequency and irregularity of the menstrual periods. As the ovary sputters to a stop, the menses occur sporadically. This is the source of a great deal of anxiety for the woman who has been depending upon the menstrual period as a guide to birth control. Sometimes, as the hormonal levels surge and wane, there are periods of excessive bleeding or spurting. If it continues very long, in large amount, a doctor should be consulted.

The absence of the menstrual period itself is no guarantee that ovulation has not occurred. The preparation of the uterus to receive the ovum is a result of the estrogen stimulation from the entire ovary, not just the one follicle which is ripening to release one ovum to become fertilized. If there is not sufficient stimulation of the uterus, menstruation may not occur, but even so, if an ovum is released at this time and fertilized, a pregnancy may ensue. For this reason *a woman should not assume that she cannot become pregnant simply because her menstrual periods have ceased.* Menstrual periods are a particularly capricious sign of ovarian function. Their normal presence and occurrence signals normal hormonal function, but they can be absent in young girls and during middle life and they can be affected by a variety of emotional factors, despite ovulation. As a general rule, although no exact rules can be established, a woman can get pregnant for as long as two years after her menstrual periods have ceased.

The other reminder a woman has of her change in reproductivity is the "hot flash." The frequency and severity of hot flashes can vary a great deal, but they can be extremely annoying. The hot flash begins at the top of the head and passes to the feet. Basically, there is marked dilatation of the arteries in the skin, increasing the blood flow to the skin itself and causing an obvious, beet-red flush accompanied by the sensation of heat. The body senses heat from nerve receptors in the skin. Similar nerve receptors do not exist inside the body. Thus, we do not have a sensation of hot or cold inside the heart, inside the lungs, or even inside the muscles. The skin acts like the car radiator, and the hot blood goes to the skin for cooling. This is exactly what happens with the hot flash. The large amount of hot blood suddenly coursing through the skin causes the flash and the sensation of heat. This sensation of heat is totally independent of the actual body temperature taken by thermometer inside the mouth, rectum, or otherwise in the internal region of the body.

Because sweating is related to the amount of blood flow through the skin, the hot flash is often accompanied by sweat. As the hot flash passes and the heat is lost, the blood drains away from the skin and the woman will feel cold or actually have a chill. The sequence of events is: hot flash from head to toe, sweating, then chill.

The heat regulatory mechanisms of the body are controlled by the body's own thermostat in the hypothalamus close to the areas of the brain affected by all of the changes that occur with the menopause. Remember that the release of FSH from the anterior pituitary gland is brought about through the action of the hypothalamus and that the decrease in estrogen level will stimulate the hypothalamus and anterior pituitary to release FSH. With the frantic efforts of the hypothalamus to induce the anterior pituitary to stimulate the flagging ovary, the overflow stimulation disturbs the body's thermostat. The tiny thermostat influences the mechanisms which regulate blood flow to the skin for control of body heat and sweating. Many factors affect the thermostat, including too much hot spicy food and emotions. The hot flashes may occur day and night until this phase of menopausal adjustment ends.

Along with the symptoms of irregular menstrual periods and hot flashes, the menopausal woman may feel fatigued and not infrequently becomes irritable. The level of estrogen has a great deal to do with mood and accounts for some of the cyclic variation in the woman's nature between the first half of her menstrual cycle (the estrogen phase) and the last half (the progesterone phase). In addition to the effect of decreased hormones on the woman's mood, there is the obvious adjustment required to the change in life which signals loss of sexuality and disturbs her self-image. Because of the important psychological influences involved, it is difficult to sort out which reactions are associated with an identity crisis and which ones are the direct result of hormonal changes. In any case irritability, fits of depression, and crying spells, plus other evidences of personality change, are common during the menopause.

As if these changes weren't enough, the loss of femininity is heralded by the change in body fat distribution. The desirable distribution of fat normally attributed to femininity disappears. Fat is lost in the breasts and accumulates in the waist, hips, and thighs. There is an overall tendency toward obesity. Since the storage of fat is directly related to the amount of energy expended as opposed to the amounts of calories eaten, clearly part of the obesity associated with the menopause is due to a disturbance in the balance between calories consumed and calories used. The change in life situation often results in decreased physical activity, and the frustrations may lead to excessive eating. Even so, what fat is present tends to take on a different and, in the woman's mind, an undesirable distribution.

The loss of female hormones causes the female sexual system literally to dry up or degenerate. Eventually even the vulva changes. There is a loss of the normal hair distribution over the vulva, and the fatty deposits underneath the skin around the vulva are lost. The labial folds disappear and are lost into the surrounding skin. The skin itself thins out and develops a shiny appearance. In association with the loss of the normal prominence of the vulva and the changes over the skin, there is also an enlargement of the clitoris. The degree will be dependent to some extent on how much androgen hormone is being formed by the adrenal cortex.

The surface of the thin, shiny skin is much more easily irritated and infected. Small white thickened spots known as leukoplakia, meaning white plaque, develop at the surface of the skin. These may crack and fissures may form in them, making them sensitive. About 5 percent of them progress to develop a skin cancer. Therefore, they deserve medical attention.

The vagina regresses. The normal lubricating cells lining the vaginal wall thin out, and the normal secretions diminish or disappear, so that the vaginal vault takes on a dry, shiny appearance. Excessive dryness of the vault causes intercourse to be painful. The actual size of the vaginal vault may diminish, both by shortening and by shrinking in caliber. The small, shrunken, dry vaginal vault is not conducive to regular sexual activity. In women who have had children, the vaginal walls may tend to roll out toward the vaginal orifice. This condition is related to problems of prolapse, which will be discussed later.

The drying vaginal vault loses its normal acidity and becomes more alkaline, allowing certain types of bacteria to grow within the vault that would normally not be present. In the woman who is much older, with senile changes of her vagina, the yeast infections so familiar to the child-bearing female are unusal. Trichomoniasis is still common but not as frequent as in the younger woman. The older woman is, however, more susceptible to other types of infections. Irritation of the vaginal vault, sometimes with inflammation, is called senile vaginitis.

The doughnut-shaped cervix shrinks in size until its normal protrusion at the apex of the vaginal vault is hardly apparent. In fact it may be flush with the wall of the vagina. The opening of the cervix which normally provides passage into the uterus is often closed. If the uterine activity is totally halted, and the uterus is essentially atrophied, this is of no great consequence. However, if there is an inflammation within the uterus, it can result in accumulation of pus in the uterus unless the cervix is opened and drainage is permitted. The uterus is a site for cancer, and occlusion of the cervical opening makes it difficult to obtain cancer cells with such normal procedures as the Papanicolaou (Pap) test.

The uterus becomes small in the postmenopausal woman, but it should never be forgotten that one of the most common cancers in the older female is cancer of the lining of the uterus, which is responsible for 15 to 50 percent of all postmenopausal bleeding. This is one reason why *any woman who has stopped menstruating for a significant period of time and then bleeds again should consult a physician without delay, even if she has had a recent examination.*

In addition to the more specific sexual changes that are noted as a result of the menopause, the body undergoes other changes directly related to this event. The skin changes, over the face particularly. Coarsening of the skin is often accompanied by an increased growth of hair. Actually the number of hairs is the same, but the hair becomes coarse and darker. There is no essential difference between the number of hairs on the face of men and women. The difference is whether it is fuzz or hair. With the change in balance between male and female hormones many women experience varied degrees of baldness, although certain "beauty treatments" also contribute to this problem.

As time progresses, the voice takes on a more masculine characteristic and deepens. One out of four women in the postmenopausal age develop degeneration of the spine, called osteoporosis. Specialists in this problem are of the opinion that much bone change can be prevented by adequate treatment of the menopause. Although part of the process can be arrested, whether it can be reversed is another matter. In particularly severe degeneration of the spine older women can lose several inches in height and develop marked deformity of the chest cage. This compromises ventilation of the lungs and decreases their normal function.

Finally, there is considerable evidence that loss of estrogen hormone is related to an increased rate of fatty deposits in the arteries or atherosclerosis. Heart attacks are much more common in women who have had their ovaries removed surgically and occur at an earlier age. The changes in the arteries that are suspected to be caused by loss of estrogen hormone are thought to be related to a change in the cholesterol and fat particles in the blood that are implicated in the atherosclerotic process.

Some women go through the menopause with a minimal amount of difficulty. It has been thought that these are the women whose ovaries continue to secrete a little more estrogen than is found in less fortunate women, or they are women whose adrenal cortex secretes enough estrogen and progesterone to prevent the gross and more disabling changes of the menopause. As mentioned earlier, about one out of five women even in their 70's still have evidence of estrogenic activity as indicated by the character of the vaginal vault.

There is considerable variation in the menopausal changes. The woman who develops marked evidence of masculine changes is probably the one who secretes appreciable amounts of male hormone from the adrenal cortex, and when this is no longer balanced by adequate amounts of estrogen, the masculinizing characteristics appear. Other women have a great deal of difficulty with hot flashes, nervousness, and irritability but do not necessarily show evidence of masculinization. The large number of women in the postmenopausal period who have skeletal changes and the vast array of degenerative sexual functions are strong arguments for active treatment to prevent these changes in middle life.

The best way to treat these problems is to prevent them. Therapy is dependent upon the administration of female hormones, including estrogen or the popular synthetic estrogen taken by mouth, stilbestrol. Even the sequential birth control pills are useful in treating or preventing the problems of menopause. The sequential birth control pills used for this purpose provide approximately two weeks of estrogen-type medicine followed by two weeks of estrogen and progesterone—type medication. Thus, the birth control pill simulates the ovaries' hormonal secretions of the first and last half of the normal menstrual cycle. The interruption of seven to eight days in the taking of the pill permits the normal menstrual period to occur. Any time estrogen and progesterone are administered in adequate doses and then stopped, menstrual flow occurs. There are several advantages to continuing birth control pills in middle life, well past the time of possible pregnancy. During the phase when the woman is not sure when ovulation is occurring and the periods are irregular or sporadic, the birth control pills provide insurance against an unwanted pregnancy late in life. Then, continuing the pill diminishes or obviates the symptoms of the menopause.

In addition to the female hormones that are given in the treatment of menopause, some physicians approve of giving small amounts of testosterone, or male hormone, in some instances. This is thought to improve the strength and vigor of the individual and increase sexual desire. Doctors who are aggressive in replacement therapy consider that a total replacement of hormones is necessary to prevent the "aging process" at this point in life. They often also prescribe small amounts of thyroid and sometimes small amounts of adrenal cortex hormones.

Besides hormone replacement to prevent menopause changes, maintaining physical health is most important. The middle-aged woman should make every effort to watch her diet and avoid obesity. Adequate amounts of hormones will not prevent obesity if exercise and diet habits are poor. The large number of young overweight females in the childbearing age is ample evidence of this truth. Obesity will speed the process of acquired aging. In addition to a proper diet and exercise program, an active interest in sex should be maintained. While hormones can help keep the vaginal vault in good condition, one factor which prevents shrinkage and atrophy is its use. Even when the vaginal vault has already shrunk and changes have occurred, hormonal replacement under proper medical supervision combined with the normal and appropriate amount of sexual activity with a vigorous male will go a long way toward retaining normal sexual function.

It is true that the best way to maintain the various functions of the body is to continue their use. An unused muscle atrophies, and a similar analogy applies to other parts of the body. If the bones are not put under stress but are allowed to rest, they decalcify. It is a common observation that if a cow is separated from her calf so that the udder is not stimulated or the milk is not taken, the udder will stop producing milk and the cow becomes "dry." Disuse results in loss of functional capacity. Because the sexual process involves developed and conditioned patterns, even at the cortical level of the brain, and follows through the entire sequence of hormonal control, repeated use reinforces the pattern and the capability of normal function.

A menopause can occur through surgical intervention—for example, removal of the ovaries. In such instances hormonal replacement is indicated just as much as for the usual degeneration of the ovaries, perhaps even more so.

Much can be done to prevent the menopausal changes that affect the entire body. These are aspects of aging which are preventable. There are still many unanswered questions, but the primary failure appears to be in the ovary. Why the ovary should degenerate long before the end of the normal female life span is not known. Whether strictly genetic aging related to time-sequential events is involved or there are some other hormonal influences not yet discovered, remains to be seen. At present, the remarkable universality of cessation of normal ovary function in women in different cultures and different societies with all types of different living habits strongly suggests that it is a genetic age change. But this merely signals the end of the span of ability for reproduction, not the onset of senility. If the problems of senility could be solved by hormonal replacement of estrogen in women and male hormone in men, they would be simple indeed.

GENITAL PROLAPSE

A common problem of the older woman is genital prolapse. This is usually a direct outgrowth of childbearing.

The uterus is suspended by ligaments in the pelvic outlet. The bottom of the bony pelvis or the outlet of the birth canal is actually laced with a series of muscles which provide support to the pelvic organs, including the rectum, bladder, uterus, and vagina. These muscles are stretched during childbearing and during delivery, as are the ligaments and structures that help support the uterus. With several pregnancies the overstretched muscles and ligaments may weaken so that the structures rupture into the vaginal opening. The cervix of the uterus may actually protrude from the vagina. More often the stretched and dilated walls of the vagina that form a partition between the rectum at the back and the bladder in front permit either bladder or rectum to rupture into the relaxed vaginal vault.

Because of the prolapse, the normal position of the urethral orifice draining the bladder may change. In this case urine sometimes collects in the vaginal vault and subsequently leaks out of the vagina. The retained urine can contribute to setting up an inflammation of the vagina. Moreover, urine may stagnate within the bladder itself in the part of the bladder that herniates through the relaxed wall of the vaginal vault. This protrusion is called a cystocele. The stagnant urine in the bladder can become infected and contribute to cystitis. Loss of normal control of the the bladder also occurs. The decrease in estrogen causes the cells lining the outlet of the bladder and urethra to degenerate, resulting in frequency of urination and burning. This change is reversible with hormone substitution therapy.

Where the back of the vaginal wall is weakened, the rectum may bulge forward into the vaginal space. Bowel movement then becomes difficult, and the woman may need to press upon the bulge in the vaginal vault, pushing the rectum back into place so that normal elimination can occur.

Of course the relaxed vaginal vault leaves a lot to be desired in normal sexual relations. Fortunately all of these conditions can be significantly improved if not corrected with appropriate surgical procedures. The goal is to replace the torn or overstretched supporting structures and reinforce the vaginal wall and the muscles to the outlet of the vagina. This rehabilitation will also do wonders for the woman's sex life, and it is much appreciated by her husband.

MALE MENOPAUSE

There is some doubt whether men undergo a change comparable to the menopause in women, although they usually have a decline in sexual capacity. The peak sexual activity of the male is in his teens and early

20's. However, he can be and often is sexually active past 70 years of age. I have letters from numerous men 80 to 90 years old who are still sexually active. History records a number of instances in which individuals past 100 have fathered children.

It is difficult to measure the amount of male hormone formed by the testicles because many common methods also measure other hormones formed by the adrenal cortex. One reasonably accurate study of men from 20 to 93 years of age showed that the levels of testosterone in the blood stream were about the same in all the age groups studied. Even so, there is a general impression that the amount of testosterone formed slightly decreases as the male grows older. In some men, perhaps because of atherosclerosis affecting the circulation to the testicles, the estrogen-testosterone ratio is reversed. The fact remains that in many men there is no change in the amount of hormones during middle or later life comparable to that noted in the female.

Nevertheless, some men apparently do have a bona fide hormonal change. They can be identified by demonstrating an increased amount of FSH formed to stimulate the testicles to produce testosterone. This finding is entirely analogous to that of increased amounts of FSH in the female formed to stimulate the lagging ovary. When there is an increase in FSH and a decrease in the amount of testosterone in the blood, combined with changes noted by examining a microscopic piece of tissue from the testicle, the diagnosis is established.

The hormone changes of testicular failure are part of the variations in the amounts of hormones formed in men of different age groups. One man's entire hormone and sexual system seems to be perfectly intact and functional into very late years, whereas another man may have difficulty much earlier in life.

At about 45 to 55 years of age some men experience symptoms which are similar to those noted in menopausal women. Perhaps the most prominent symptom identified with the so-called male menopause is fatigue and muscular weakness. Personality changes include anxiety reactions. Irritability, insomnia, generalized ill-defined muscle aches and pains, and difficulty in concentration can all be associated with a simple anxiety response. This is one reason why considerable debate exists about the actual occurrence of the male menopause and why it is necessary to establish changes on a basis of testicular failure.

Many men in our modern culture have an identity crisis as they approach 50 years of age. This is the point at which a person can no longer be a man of promise. Either he is a man of achievement or he thinks of himself as a failure. This is a point in life where one begins to look on the downhill side as opposed to the uphill side. There is less time left than has already elapsed. Goals for the future once sought so diligently now clearly are out of reach. The children have probably grown up and left home. The marriage may or may not be on a sound basis and frequently is not. Only so many individuals can become boss or head of the firm, or otherwise manifest success in a material way, and this fact becomes evident. Those who are not going to ascend to the pinnacle of success begin to see younger men passing them. All these changes in life situations represent a tremendous assault upon the individual's ego and self-image. It is little wonder when a man with such problems is faced with reality that he becomes anxious and depressed. Incidentally, anxiety and depression are frequent causes of fatigue and muscular aches.

Men in this age group, particularly those involved in office and executive positions, are often in poor physical condition. Lack of adequate, regular physical activity contributes to the general feeling of fatigue. Physical capacity is limited because they have not used their capabilities for years. Overeating has led to obesity and changes in body configuration. The lack of proper physical activity, excessive eating of the wrong kinds of food, excessive use of coffee, alcohol, and stimulants, cigarette smoking, and problems related to job progression, social position, and business achievement all begin to take their toll. Since social and environmental aspects influence the function of the body, resulting in poor health and changes commonly attributed to age, they are properly considered in the context of aging in our civilization. One major way to prevent aging is to maintain a healthy mental attitude, which includes a feeling of being needed and having long-range goals. The individual who finds himself a failure in his business or professional life clearly is short on long-term goals and a sense of being needed. To the extent that these are important in preventing the mental aspects of aging, he has already started down the road to acquired mental aging.

IMPOTENCE

One does not have to be old to experience impotence. It is a reasonably common problem, very often related to psychological factors. Nevertheless the life-styles of individuals in industrialized nations particularly contribute to this problem in middle age and later years. High on the list as a cause of impotence in the American male is the excessive use of alcohol.

The executive drinker frequently has repeated problems of impotence by the time he reaches 40 years of age. The means of preventing alcoholic impotence is obvious. One of the many reasons alcohol contributes to impotence when used continuously in sufficient quantities is its damaging effect on the liver. The liver is responsible for metabolizing and eliminating the accumulated estrogen formed by the body. As a result of liver damage, the normally produced estrogen accumulates in the body and has a feminizing effect, especially if it is not appropriately counterbalanced with sufficient formation of male hormones. This often leads to increased vascularity of the skin and no doubt contributes to the truncal obesity and other changes noted in the middle-aged excessive drinker.

Alcohol has other effects directly related to the nervous system which impair the normal nerve control mechanisms necessary for erection. An erection occurs only because nerves stimulate an increased arterial blood flow to the penis and restrict the normal outflow of blood. Blood trapped in the penis causes it to become erect and ready for action. Anything that interferes with the increase in the blood flow to the penis or the mechanisms for trapping the blood will cause impotence.

Testicular failure may contribute to the problem of impotence. This is very close to the true meaning of the male menopause. The individual may also have a lagging interest in sex. Atherosclerosis, the common problem in the industrialized society, is particularly prone to attack the arteries to the body of the testicles, diminishing their circulation. In the course of time it can reduce testicular size. The failure of testicular function affects the production of sperm and the overall level of sexual activity. This factor alone may not cause impotence. The mature male who has been castrated can often continue to have normal sexual relations. Of course, he is unable to generate sperm, but he can ejaculate fluid from the prostate and seminal vesicles, which really comprises a major portion of the emission during sexual activity anyway. Nevertheless the possible effects of atherosclerotic changes to the testicle cannot be overlooked, particularly if they are combined with liver damage from the excessive use of alcohol which allows estrogen to accumulate while testosterone production is curtailed.

Nutritional factors may also affect testicular function and in turn influence potency. Individuals on a starvation diet will lose normal testicular function; if the diet is continued for a prolonged period of time, testicular damage can occur. This is the logical outcome for men in starvation circumstances in prisoner-of-war camps. Although vitamin E is commonly referred to as a fertility vitamin, a more important one in man is vitamin A. Deficiency of vitamin A can cause degeneration of the seminiferous tubules and loss of their ability to form sperm. When adequate amounts of vitamin A are supplied in the diet, testicular function returns to normal. Starvation or an excessively low-calorie diet can lead to fatigue and generally decrease interest in sex and capacity to perform.

Atherosclerotic changes in arteries to the penis are another cause for impotence. This is just as effective as if the nerves to the penis which influence erection were damaged. The inflow of blood necessary to produce erection is mechanically blocked. A frequent accompaniment is blockage of the arteries that supply the legs. Afflicted individuals will complain of leg cramps when they walk very far or engage in physical activity. To the extent that atherosclerosis can be prevented its power to cause impotence can be nullified. This type of impotence is not intermittent; once it occurs it is fairly persistent unless correction of the arterial blockage can be achieved.

There are a number of diseases which act upon the nervous system and can induce impotence. Multiple sclerosis, a disease that has a generalized effect on the nervous system, is one. Diabetes is another—and all too common. A relatively young man, 40 years of age, for example, in seemingly good health except for mild diabetes may develop persistent impotence. This occurs because diabetes often affects the functions of the nerves throughout the body, a condition technically called diabetic neuropathy. It is important to recognize that diabetes can have such an outcome, and any young man complaining of persistent impotence should be checked carefully for diabetes. Otherwise he may be erroneously assumed to have a psychological problem. Unfortunately, only limited success can be achieved in correcting impotence by controlling the diabetes. This is specifically not a hormone problem, since testicular function in producing male hormones and sperm is normal.

It is less prevalent today, but at one time syphilis produced impotence in much the same way, by affecting the long nerves in the spinal cord that go to the penis to initiate erection.

A number of hormonal disturbances are capable of producing impotence, including failure of the anterior pituitary gland.

Impotence increases in the middle-aged and older male at the time when atherosclerotic problems are increasing. It is only reasonable to expect that it will often be part of the total picture of changes in health associated with our industrialized society. To the extent that this is the case, a number of the problems can be prevented. The influence of atherosclerosis on the testicle and the penis can certainly be minimized. Proper physical activity and the avoidance of excessive amounts of alcohol also help.

Many examples of impotence have a psychological basis. These problems can occur at any age and since they are not particularly related to acquired aging will not be discussed in detail here. Let it suffice to say that many middle-aged people find that their marriage has not improved through the years and after the woman's menopause the hostile marriage has become a major factor in producing impotence. The woman is not interested in sex if she dislikes her husband, and it is difficult for the man to perform in view of such obvious antagonism from his sexual partner. Finally, the problem may be compounded if when failure occurs the situation is used to taunt the already frightened male. Such behavior by the female sexual partner is one facet of the total picture of the "castrating female" that is identified within the hostile marriage. It is also one reason why a man is sometimes able to perform adequately with another woman but not with his wife. There are, of course, many other factors including boredom, lack of communication, and the whole range of marital problems that are often acutely aggravated when a couple has reached middle life.

Although sperm formation gradually declines in the male, there is still a sufficient number. A single discharge from the mating act may produce a little less than a teaspoonful of fluid and still contain over 250 million sperm. The ability to generate adequate amounts of normal sperm in older men has been documented. If atherosclerotic changes have already affected the testicles, normal sperm formation is less likely.

Interestingly, those areas of the world in which older men continue to be sexually active are also those areas that are relatively free from the atherosclerosis so often found in the younger men in the industrialized nations. The Abkhasians expect that a man's sexual activity will continue until he reaches 100 years of age. Among American men sexual activity often begins to decline significantly or actually stops before they reach the age of 60. One factor which decreases sperm formation is alcohol. The executive drinker who consumes six or seven cocktails a day or the frank alcoholic will have sharply reduced sperm formation as compared to other men in his age group with more healthy living habits.

THE BENT PENIS

The problem of the bent penis occurs most often in older men and is extremely distressing to the victim. When the penis becomes erect, it bends upward in the middle of the shaft, like an elbow joint. Technically, this is called Peyronie's disease. The main body of the penis has two barrels filled with blood. Between them on the top of the penis is a fibrouslike septum. When the barrels are distended with blood, the erection occurs. In the case of the bent penis, one or more scarlike plaques are formed in the septal area. This material will not stretch or expand when an erection occurs and causes the penis to bend upward. The principle is the same as if you stuck a piece of adhesive tape to the top side of a balloon. As the balloon inflates, the area attached to the adhesive tape does not expand, but the rest of the balloon does. The result is a bent balloon.

If the deformity is severe, the man will have trouble carrying out normal sexual relations. The cause of the plaque formation is not known, and plaques have been noted in young men although they are more common in older men. The treatment has not been entirely satisfactory. Radical approaches have been used, including surgery, but most specialists in male problems (urologists) prefer to either leave the condition alone or prescribe vitamin E. While some doctors have claimed good results with vitamin E for this purpose, others have been less enthusiastic. In any case it does no harm, so an individual with this problem could take vitamin E regularly (100 milligrams or 100 to 150 units three times a day) and if he is lucky, it might be helpful. Fortunately, the condition is not always permanent, and often the problem disappears spontaneously. Many a man can tolerate the period of frustration associated with his impairment if he at least has hope that there will be better days.

THAT OLD DEVIL PROSTATE

One of the most prevalent ailments of the aging male is prostate trouble. Inflammation of the prostate can occur at any age and is not necessarily due to venereal disease. The prostate is a good site for bacteria to implant and start inflammation, which can cause fever, chills, and a discharge. The tender, bulging prostate is a relatively frequent finding. In later life, enlargement of the prostate or changes in the prostate which tend to obstruct the urethra at the outlet of the bladder are common.

The prostate gland is a small hazelnut-shaped piece of tissue surrounding the urethra at the outlet of the bladder. Actually, the urethra passes through the center of the prostate gland. Because of its location just below the bladder and since the major portion of the gland is at the back of the urethra, it can be felt by sticking a finger in the rectum and pressing against the rectal wall. In this way, the outline of the shape of the prostate gland can be determined. The seminal vesicles, the saddlebag-shaped receptacles on each side of the prostate, can also be felt with an adequate examination. Simple enlargement of the prostate causes no problem. The difficulty occurs when it enlarges in such a way as to obstruct the opening of the urethral tube it surrounds—that is, when its central or inner lobe enlarges. The tough fibrous capsule around the prostate restricts its outward expansion and the pressure is exerted around the urethral tube, causing obstruction.

The progressive enlargement of the prostate is dependent upon male hormone. It begins to develop at puberty and finally matures under the influence of testosterone. Its size will be diminished if the testicles are removed before actual enlargement of the prostate has occurred. In fact, castration, if done early enough, can prevent prostate enlargement and the subsequent obstruction that follows. The prostate gland is not essential to sexual functions, but the fluid it forms contains nutrient material for the sperm. The sperm may remain viable up to 48 hours after discharge. The prostatic fluid also serves as a sexual lubricant for the male. During the excitement phase prior to the actual mating act the young male in particular may secrete reasonable amounts of it, but as years progress, it is less and less likely to be produced. The emission of prostatic fluid as a lubricant prior to the sex act is related also to the level of sexual arousal.

The exact reasons for enlargement of the prostate are not known. One theory is that recurrent inflammation of the prostate stimulates the enlargement. A variation of this theory is that if the prostate has been infected one or more times the inflammatory process itself sets up an autoimmune mechanism which stimulates the continued growth of the prostate. Another theory is that prostate enlargement is a direct result of male hormone. Incidentally, there is no evidence or proof that the frequency of sexual intercourse has anything at all to do with the subsequent enlargement of the prostate gland. Sexual abstinence will not prevent enlargement of the prostate.

Still another theory proposes that atherosclerosis is the cause of prostate enlargement. The basis of this theory is that the outer shell or the lobes of the prostate receive their blood from one artery while the central lobe, usually responsible for the obstructive phenomenon, receives its blood from another artery. According to the concept the artery to the outer lobes is frequently blocked with atherosclerosis and causes them to shrink. The central lobe then begins compensatory enlargement which results in obstruction. Whatever the truth of this theory, it is interesting to note that prostate enlargement and its obstructive symptoms are much more frequent in societies in which heart disease is common than where it is rare. A number of older native Africans are relatively free from prostate trouble—whether for genetic reasons or because of the low incidence of atherosclerosis and other problems is not known. In any case, it is difficult to see how atherosclerosis can be beneficial in any way to the prostate.

Simple enlargement of the prostate requires medical attention because it obstructs the flow of urine. The obstruction itself causes symptoms which are easily recognized and common in middle-aged males. As the bladder becomes overdistended and filled with urine, there is difficulty in starting urination and the stream may be small compared to that of a young man. Dribbling at the end of urination is a further problem. Because of the overdistended bladder the individual has to go to the bathroom frequently. Thus frequency, trouble in getting started, small stream, and dribbling are all signs of prostate trouble. The frequency can also disturb the victim at night.

The only satisfactory treatment to obstruction of the bladder with an enlarged prostate is surgical relief. There are basically three operations that are used to remove the obstructed prostate. One involves an incision in the skin at the side of the base of the penis in the scrotal area and an external surgical approach. This is called the perineal approach. In another open surgical procedure the incision is made just above the pubic bone to expose and remove the prostate. This operation is thought by many urological surgeons to be the simpler of the two open surgical techniques.

A current popular approach is the transurethral resection (TUR). It does not involve an open surgical incision through the skin any place. A rodlike instrument is introduced into the urethra through the penis and passed backward to the opening of the bladder at the very point where the prostate is squeezing down on the urethra. The rodlike structure has a small electrical cautery or knife on the end of it. This is used to bore a larger hole in the urethra where the enlarged prostate is causing the obstruction. Small chunks of the prostate are constantly bored out and removed until the hole is sufficiently large. Then the inner core of the central lobe of the prostate is bored out. With such an internal approach directly through the urethra open surgery is avoided. In very large prostates a considerable amount of tissue needs to be removed. Even in relatively small prostates, if an obstruction has occurred, the boring-out procedure is necessary to establish normal urinary drainage.

The TUR is the approach least likely to cause any disturbance in the sexual function after surgery. The perineal open surgical approach often affects the nerve to the area and more often results in postsurgical impotence than does the suprapubic open surgical approach. The doctor ordinarily tells a patient that, once he is fully recovered from a TUR, he should not have any problems with impotence. This, of course, is a correct assessment in one sense, but because of the age of the people involved and the many other factors which influence the occurrence of impotence, it may still occur in an individual after surgery whether or not it is related to the operation. Sometimes the patient takes a while after surgery to regain normal sexual function. It is important for him to realize, however, that, other things being normal, he should be able to return to a satisfactory sexual life.

A postoperative complication of the TUR and indeed the other operations is control of urination. The TUR bores out tissue in the area of the sphincter valves controlling the drainage of the bladder. The valves are damaged and time is necessary to reeducate their function and develop new functional nerve paths to control their action. The surgeon often advises certain training procedures such as trying to schedule the time of urination and holding the urine as long as possible to reeducate the reflex mechanisms for urination. In the course of time this problem also is alleviated.

Still another recent approach to prostatic surgery is to actually freeze the gland. The destroyed tissue then sloughs out. The process sometimes has to be completed with a TUR. This procedure can be used in selected cases in which surgery is too risky and may one day prove to have wider application.

There is hope that man will yet escape the surgeon's attack on his prostate. Hormone treatments used by various investigators have yielded promising early results. None of these treatments are yet approved for use in the United States. One of the hormones, Medrogestone, has been used by the Canadian physicians Drs. Robert E. Rangno, Peter J. McLeod, John Ruedy, and R. I. Ogilvie. They have reported good success in shrinking the prostate with hormone treatment in patients considered as poor surgical risks. The thought is that prostate enlargement is really the result of a hormone imbalance and eventually will yield to proper hormone therapy. Certainly there are many unanswered questions regarding the role of hormones in prostate enlargement. Some of the difficulties have been related to inability to measure the intact prostatic size and some to the inability to measure accurately specific hormones in the body. There may, for example, be an imbalance caused by increased production of FSH or other pituitary hormones when testosterone production declines. These are all theories but point the direction that research may take in solving prostate problems.

Some investigators have recommended using "antisex hormones," which neutralize the effects of testosterone. These may be beneficial in selected cases, but they present other complications that may make the cure worse than the disease—for example, the loss of masculinity. Clearly, if the prostate changes are associated with a hormone imbalance which develops in middle life and beyond, the better approach would be to adjust the underlying imbalance.

A more dreaded change in the prostate with aging is cancer. Since it can occur without producing any symptoms at all, a rectal examination that enables the physician to determine the nature of the prostate is essential. More than one "important individual" who has not had time for a medical examination has had cancer of the prostate spread to the extent that it was incurable. If found early enough, most cancers of the prostate can at least be controlled. Even if the cancer has spread outside of the prostate area to involve other regions of the body, there is still a good chance that it can be controlled for long periods of time. In some instances it is advisable to remove all cancerous tissue that is present; in others, depending upon the general state of the patient and other factors, it may be elected not to undertake such a major effort. In either case surgery, radiation, and hormonal therapy can all be used to control the problem. Radiation therapy has been reported to be successful in certain types of cases. In other instances it is necessary to remove the stimulating effect of the male hormone, which perpetuates the prostatic cancer and its eventual enlargement and extension.

Castration and the administration of the female hormones are used to eliminate the influence of testosterone in selected cases. Even if the cancer has spread, adequate treatment of this type will often control the cancer or even cause it to regress. If for any reason the patient obtains and takes testosterone, the beneficial effects of castration and estrogen treatment are lost.

SEX IN LATER YEARS

Aside from the various anatomical and physiological changes which occur with the decline in the sexual functions, there remains the question of the sexual habits of people in older years. This varies a great deal depending upon their health and sometimes upon their social and cultural attitudes, as well as their attitudes toward each other. In a hostile marriage the probability of continued sexual activities in the later years is greatly diminished. Where the sexual partners have been compatible through many years, have grown to have a mature love for each other, and have in the past enjoyed an active sex life, sex will probably continue to be an important aspect of their lives. I have received many letters from older women, 60 and 70 years of age, who still experience sexual desire and other women who enjoy regular sexual activity. On the other hand, some older women have no interest whatsoever in sex in later years and would rather not be bothered with it. These differences in attitude are likely to be more nearly related to the personality and psychological factors than to any actual chemical, hormonal, physiological, or anatomical aspect of the individuals involved.

Men frequently continue to be sexually active and interested over the years. Some, however, lose interest in sex life early. Unless they are stimulated by their sexual partner, their sexual interest will keep on declining until their sexual activity is minimal, if not absent. Just as there are variations in the level of sexual desire in different men and in different women at early ages, there are also variations in the later years. Obviously, the most satisfactory arrangement is for both sexual partners to have approximately the same level of sexual desire.

It should be pointed out that interest in sexual activity is influenced by medical and physical factors. The man who has Peyronie's disease, with the bent penis, is not likely to enjoy the situation and will have difficulty in performance, if he can perform at all. The woman who has senile vaginitis with a dry vaginal vault and an irritated vulva cannot possibly enjoy satisfactory sexual relations. Often the decline in sexual interest can be alleviated by proper medical treatment, and often proper medical treatment means eliminating infections when they are present and providing adequate hormone replacement, particularly in a woman. It also means, particularly for the man's interest, correction of prolapsed genitals and other complications that occur in women who have had several children. One thing is very clear in both males and females: Sexual desire does not necessarily stop in middle life but may continue at some level throughout the life span.

eleven

The Other Endocrine Glands

Aside from the endocrine glands and their hormones that influence the sexual system, there are other endocrine glands and hormones essential to the life process. They too undergo development and subsequent changes attributed to aging. Their change in function affects the sexual system as well as the rest of the body. Just as the sexual hormones are under the influence of the central nervous system and the pituitary gland, for the most part, so are the remainder of the endocrine glands.

THE ADRENAL GLANDS

The pituitary–adrenal cortex system has received enormous attention in the past few decades because of its generalized effect on the body and the exciting idea that hormones from this system could be used to cure a vast array of human ills including arthritis. Some of these early hopes have been disappointed.

The adrenal glands are essential to life. They are small amounts of glandular tissue resting above the upper pole of each kidney, a location that has given them their other name: suprarenal (above the kidney) glands. They actually have two parts. The central core is called the adrenal medulla and is where adrenaline is produced. The outer shell is called the adrenal cortex; it secretes the hormones that caused the excitement in recent years in the treatment of arthritis and many previously untreatable diseases. The hormones from the adrenal cortex and those formed by the sex glands are called steroids. All of the steroid hormones are formed chemically from cholesterol.

Although the intricacies of the chemistry of the cortical hormones are very complex, the basic nature of the hormones and their actions is relatively simple. Three types of hormones are formed by the cortex: (1) the glucocorticoids, (2) the mineral corticoids, and (3) the sex steroids. The most important of the glucocorticoids is called cortisol (this was believed to be the miracle substance that was going to cure all ills). It is sometimes called the stress hormone. The mineral corticoids influence the retention of sodium salt and potassium salt in the body. Their effects are exerted chiefly on the kidneys. The sex steroids include male hormone, or androgen, the female hormone progesterone, and smaller amounts of estrogen.

The secretion of the cortical hormones is under the control of a hormone from the anterior pituitary gland which is entirely analogous to the action of FSH and LH on the ovaries and testicles. The hormone from the anterior pituitary which stimulates the adrenal cortex is called adrenocorticotrophic hormone (ACTH). *Adrenocortico* refers to the adrenal cortex, and *trophic* refers to stimulation or growth. The abbreviation ACTH is commonly used to designate this hormone. When ACTH is produced, it stimulates the adrenal cortex to pour out hormones. The main effect of ACTH is to actuate the adrenal production of the glucocorticoids. If the level of cortisol in the body rises, the pituitary quits forming ACTH. On the other hand, if the amount of cortisol in the body decreases, the pituitary begins to goad the lagging adrenal cortex to produce more hormones. The effect of ACTH on the formation of the mineral corticoids or sex steroids is less important. Production of these substances is influenced by other factors as well.

The brain does affect the secretion of glucocorticoids. When a person is under psychic stress, a signal from the brain incites the anterior pituitary to pour out ACTH, which in turn stimulates the cortex to form cortisol and related hormones. This is the reason it has been related to stress. Other stressful conditions from the environment including being given a general anesthetic, exposure to toxins, the occurrence of shock, exposure to heat or cold, or major changes in the environment all activate this mechanism.

The cortical hormones affect the entire body. They cause changes in the cells that allow adaptation to a large variety of environments. The presence of the adrenal cortex in mammals enables them to live in different geographical regions with different climates and different environments and adapt to a wide range of circumstances. This is one reason cortical hormones have been called the adaptation hormones. The glucocorticoid hormones stimulate the release of glucose in the blood stream to raise the blood sugar. They thus provide foodstuffs for energy for physical activity and other body processes, but they also influence protein formation. Their continued use will actually cause destruction of protein from muscle and other areas of the body where protein is used as a building block. They influence fat metabolism too. One of the most striking effects is the redistribution of the fatty deposits to the trunk and face at the expense of fat deposits on the arms and legs. An individual with excessive secretion of glucocorticoids will have torso obesity with relatively skinny arms and legs. These hormones also stimulate the body to form more blood fats and cholesterol of the type that leads to atherosclerosis.

In proper amounts the glucocorticoids act to build muscle strength and capacity. One of the first complaints of an individual who has insufficient amounts of these hormones is loss of muscle strength and general weakness. The total mechanism of this condition is not understood. If excessive amounts of the hormones are present over a prolonged period of time, the destruction of muscle mass also leads to weakness. This again emphasizes the basic biological principle that there is an "optimal level" of almost everything in the body and of all activities related to the body. Too little or too much is not optimal, and either one may be damaging or may decrease the health potential of the individual.

The corticoid hormones stimulate blood formation. A deficiency of the adrenal glands can produce one type of anemia. The hormones influence the formation of white blood cells and other functions related to blood cell formation. They cause the stomach to pour out more acid pepsin. This factor and others can lead to a "stress ulcer" of the stomach or the small intestine which is a frequent complication of prolonged administration of cortical hormones.

Glucocorticoids affect bone metabolism. They impede the growth of cartilage in the body and hence can affect the growth in children if too much of the hormone is present. Through a series of complex mechanisms they interfere with the absorption of calcium from the digestive tract and increase the loss of calcium in the urine. The combination of these effects leads to the removal of calcium from bone, particularly the vertebrae, which contributes to degeneration of the spine or osteoporosis. This complication must be seriously considered if glucocorticoids are given over long periods of time in large amounts.

One of the exciting effects of the glucocorticoids is their action against infections and inflammation. As they change the body's reaction in terms of chemistry and cellular mechanism, fevers can disappear, shock can be reduced, inflammations and swellings vanish. These actions of the hormones have proved to be very useful in children with acute rheumatic fever involving the heart, which if it is severe presents a relatively desperate situation. There are numerous places in medicine where these hormones are extremely beneficial. In selected cases of rheumatoid arthritis they are useful in small doses. The problem of their use in individuals with long-term illnesses like rheumatoid arthritis is that the dose required to produce relief of symptoms is often quite large and when given over a long period of time can lead to complications. In addition, the underlying disease process may be continuing.

The action of these hormones against inflammatory processes is not always desirable. If given in too large doses over long periods of time, they can actually permit the spread of an infection such as tuberculosis. So once again the problem is raised of regulating the amount of hormone to an optimal level.

The glucocorticoids have a direct action upon the nervous system. When there are insufficient amounts, a person may have mental symptoms of depression, fatigue, and irritability. The presence of too much hormone may cause either depression or euphoria with excess amounts of energy. Such changes in the brain function correlate with the electrical activity from the brain. The changes in personality and frankly psychotic behavior which can occur with prolonged administration of these medicines are some of the undesirable complications that require caution in their use.

As seen from the above comments, the glucocorticoids affect the entire body. Their formation, and apparently the sex steroid formation, declines with age. However, the marked decrease of steroid hormones correlates directly with the decreased amount of muscle mass. The one exception is the drop in formation of the female hormone progesterone, which seems not to be related to changes in muscle mass. There is also a decrease in the amount of ACTH formed as years go by, which parallels the loss of total muscle mass.

The direct correlation between the amount of glucocorticoids formed and the muscle mass raises interesting questions: If measures are taken to maintain muscle mass during advancing years, will the production of ACTH and cortical hormones be maintained? In other words, is the right type of exercise one means of stimulating the continued biological activity of the body? Does exercise affect the master genes of the body which must control the signals of the body cells to produce various types and amounts of life substances? These intriguing questions cannot be answered at this time.

It is apparent that a great deal can be done to maintain the muscle mass with appropriate levels of physical activity. Even though knowledge is limited in this area, because of the direct correlation of muscle mass to the formation of ACTH and adrenal cortical hormones, it would seem logical to engage in physical activity directed toward keeping the muscle mass in optimum condition, to prevent if possible the hormonal changes observed with aging.

Many exercise enthusiasts have claimed that men placed on regular exercise programs which progressively improved their body condition and muscular capability underwent personality changes along the lines that were identified as masculine characteristics. If this observation is correct, one possible explanation is that the increase in muscle mass itself stimulates the elaboration of steroid hormones by the adrenal cortex and ACTH formation. Since the adrenal cortex produces a great deal of male androgen, such a correlation is not illogical.

Of course, conversely, the gradual decrease in the pituitary–adrenal cortical system may influence the ability of the individual to maintain muscle mass. Such practical problems deserve attention as they bear on the aging process. If indeed physical activity related to muscle mass is an important factor in preventing the decrease in steroid hormones and aging, it is one more example that disuse or improper use plays a major role in producing the changes of acquired aging.

The central portion of the adrenal gland, the adrenal medulla, functions separately from the cortex as if it were an entirely distinct gland. The medulla is directly connected to the nervous system. In this sense it is like the posterior pituitary gland. It produces the adrenaline hormones (epinephrine and norepinephrine). The adrenal hormones have been called the "fight or flight" hormones and are released during periods of acute stress that call upon the emergency resources of the body. The adrenaline mobilizes glucose sugar for energy and tends to raise the heart rate and blood pressure. Basically, it puts the body in the "go position" ready to use the maximum range of its capacity for the emergency at hand. As might be expected, since it is a response to acute situations, it must be quickly available. This is perhaps one reason that in its development the adrenal medulla is directly tied to the nervous system for its stimulation, unlike the adrenal cortex, which must depend on having ACTH circulated to it.

If a person is confronted with an emergency situation—for example, he sees a truck bearing down on him—the signal is rapidly relayed through the brain to the hypothalamus, which anatomically is connected to the sympathetic nervous system, its fibers going to the adrenal medulla. The impulses stimulate the medulla to release adrenaline quickly so that the body can mobilize its forces to outrun the truck or flee the danger. If the nerves to the adrenal gland are cut, the release of the adrenaline is not increased by such a crisis.

Excess pouring out of adrenaline causes a number of symptoms, including tremor, nervousness, and sweating. The adrenal gland may be properly thought of as part of the nervous system. Adrenaline substances are present for the transmission of nerve impulses at the places where there are connections between different nerve fibers in the sympathetic nervous system. This portion of the nervous system is therefore sometimes called the adrenergic (adrenaline) nervous system.

There is very little evidence of degeneration of either the sympathetic nervous system or the functions of the adrenal medulla with aging. It is important, however, to emphasize that the adrenaline hormones not completely destroyed by the body's metabolism are stored in the heart and brain and affect their function. They are thought to decrease the heart muscle's ability to use oxygen effectively, increase the resting heart rate and the heart muscle's irritability, and cause irregularities of the heartbeat. In this sense they have the opposite effect upon the heart from physical training. Bed rest and inactivity tend to permit the accumulation of these substances. Apparently exercise increases the metabolic destruction of the adrenaline products, thereby contributing to the slower resting heart rate and perhaps effecting other beneficial changes in the function of the heart muscle itself.

The exact role of the adrenaline products that are stored in the brain is not defined, but they are thought to contribute to the sense of fatigue and other aspects of mood which many people experience with inactivity. To the extent that the small-volume heart with its fast rate and the effects of the accumulated adrenaline products on the brain are related to changes associated with aging phenomena, the gradual accumulation of adrenaline products can be considered an acquired aging factor. To the extent that exercise eliminates the excess storage of these products in the body and creates optimal balance, it contributes to preventing these aspects of acquired aging.

THE THYROID GLAND

One of the earliest endocrine glands studied was the thyroid. It is located at the base of the neck just above the breastbone and just below the voice box. Its principal function is to form one hormone, thyroxine. Thyroxine undergoes some changes in the body's cells, but for simplicity's sake the thyroid hormone will be referred to here as thyroxine, the main output of the thyroid gland. Like the ovaries, the testicles, and the adrenal cortex, the thyroid is controlled by the brain and anterior pituitary gland.

The pituitary produces thyroid-stimulating hormone (TSH), which stimulates the thyroid to produce thyroxine. When sufficient thyroxine is on hand, its chemical presence inhibits the pituitary from forming any more TSH. By this mechanism the pituitary and thyroid control the amount of thyroxine in the body.

The pituitary can be induced to create more TSH by the brain's hypothalamus. Some stimuli have a direct action upon this mechanism. For example, cold stimulates the hypothalamus (remember, the thermostat of the body is the hypothalamus) to pour out chemicals, which stimulate the pituitary to form more TSH which stimulates the thyroid. The obvious purpose is to get the thyroid to increase the metabolism of the body, thereby generating heat and offsetting the influence of the cold. The cerebral cortex and other higher centers of the brain can influence the hypothalamus and its action in stimulating the pituitary. The whole system works very much like a simple thermostat mechanism.

Thyroxine is essential to the body's normal activities. It has two principal functions. At any age it tends to increase the metabolism in the cells by speeding up the chemical processing of nutrients. Metabolism generates heat and maintains heat. Thyroxine also increases the body's utilization of oxygen needed for metabolism. This last point is the basis for the common clinical metabolism test. By studying how much oxygen is used by the body, one can determine its level of metabolism. If the body is not using enough oxygen under quiet basal conditions, the function of the thyroid gland is said to be low. On the other hand, if the person is utilizing excess amounts of oxygen under properly controlled testing conditions, the function of the thyroid gland is said to be high— it is overactive. The latter state is called hyperthyroidism; the low-function state is called hypothyroidism. Because of its relationship to the metabolism of the cells throughout the body, thyroxine plays a fundamental part in all the functions of the body.

The second important function of thyroxine is to effect growth. Without adequate thyroxine, normal body growth does not occur. Babies born with grossly deficient thyroids will not mature normally and will be mentally defective dwarfs. Experiments have shown that if the young tadpole is given sufficient thyroxine it will rapidly go through its metamorphosis to become an adult small frog. If its thyroid is removed, the immature tadpole will merely progressively enlarge, becoming a large immature tadpole, never metamorphosing to the frog stage. Thyroxine is essential to the normal development and growth of the brain. Without it the usual number of brain cells will not appear and their characteristics will be abnormal. Hence the mental deficiency noted in children with untreated markedly low thyroid function. Thyroxine works with the growth hormone from the anterior pituitary gland to induce the normal growth process.

Either too much or not enough thyroxine will cause deficiencies in normal sexual function. Minor dysfunction of thyroid production is still compatible with the ability of a woman to become pregnant, but if the variations are too marked, reproduction is not possible. Many doctors are convinced that some problems of sterility are benefited by giving thyroid to the male. Obviously this will not solve all cases of sterility but it may be beneficial in selected individuals.

One action of thyroxine is to stimulate the absorption and utilization of the basic substance from carrots and other foodstuffs for formation of vitamin A. Insufficient thyroid can contribute to a vitamin A deficiency. Since vitamin A is essential in spermatogenesis, too little vitamin A leads to an inadequacy of the seminiferous tubules in forming sperm cells. One of the mechanisms of thyroxine in improving fertility in selected males may well be its relationship to improving available amounts of vitamin A. In any case it has been well established that thyroxine is essential to normal sexual functions in the production of sperm, sexual activity, and the maintenance of pregnancy.

Adequate amounts of thyroxine stimulate the development and size of the adrenal cortex and the production of adrenal cortical hormones. Through this mechanism thyroxine has far-reaching ramifications on the total body functions.

Individuals with abnormally low and abnormally high thyroid function actually present clinically opposite pictures. Low thyroid function causes one to become apathetic and show evidence of mental sluggishness. He may also tend to be physically inactive. His interest in life is significantly decreased. The skin may become thick and the hair oily and coarse. As the condition advances, the voice becomes lower and hoarser. Hypothyroid individuals have relatively little appetite, and since the metabolic level is not great, they are inclined toward obesity. With body sluggishness, constipation is a frequent problem.

Just as the other parts of the body function slow down, so does the blood-forming mechanism. Mild anemia, therefore, often accompanies low thyroid function. The heart rate slows since the metabolism is slowed and it is not necessary to pump as much blood to deliver as much oxygen as required in normal circumstances. The absence of sufficient thyroxine will lead to increased storage of body fat and a rise in cholesterol. Atherosclerosis is a frequent complication of long-standing severe hypothyroidism. The other changes in the body include a general slowing down that affects the entire body function from the brain to the bowel.

By contrast, the person who has an overactive thyroid gland will be nervous, overactive, and excitable. Characteristically, when the hand is held out there is a fine tremor. The skin is thin and dry and the hair is fine and dry. The appetite is frequently increased tremendously, and in spite of the higher caloric consumption, weight loss generally occurs. This of course is the direct result of the marked rise in metabolism with an increased need for oxygen. The greater need for oxygen plus the direct effect of thyroxine on the heart muscle speeds the heart rate. Sometimes an irregular heart action is observed. The blood fats tend to be low. Both extremely low and extremely high thyroid functions can affect the mental characteristics of the brain and can even cause frank psychosis.

The thyroid gland does change with age. The immature gland gradually grows to reach its adult size about the age of 20 to 25 years. After that, under normal circumstances, its size and function tend to decrease. Why thyroid activity slackens has not been established, but there is considerable evidence that the slowdown is related to a decrease in the amount of TSH formed by the anterior pituitary gland. TSH levels remain high until about age 35, then fall as thyroid function declines. At least, about 70 percent of older people with low thyroid function who are given TSH respond favorably and develop thyroid function to the level noted in younger people. Giving thyroid alone will not stop the aging process, but some authorities believe that giving thyroid to a person who shows definite evidence that his thyroid function is less than its previous optimal level, plus small amounts of sex hormones, will go a long way toward preventing many of the changes now attributed to aging. To the thyroid and gonadal steroid therapy other individuals would add small doses of adrenocortical steroids.

The fairly persistent demonstration of decreased thyroid function with increasing age is a good argument in favor of combining small amounts of thyroid with estrogen therapy to prevent the postmenopausal changes seen in aging women. Of course, selectivity for individual cases is a must since not every patient exhibits the same degree of change and certain abnormal functions of the body sometimes alter the picture completely from what would be expected under more usual circumstances. Thus a middle-aged woman who already has an overactive thyroid gland clearly doesn't need more thyroid hormone along with estrogen to treat the problems of the menopause or prevent postmenopausal changes.

THE PITUITARY GLAND

The major role of the anterior pituitary gland, as a master gland, is to regulate the functions of other glands, specifically the testicles or ovaries, breasts, adrenal cortex, and thyroid gland. The anterior pituitary gland produces five hormones (FSH, LH, LTH, ACTH, and TSH), which have been discussed in relationship to these functions. A sixth hormone produced by the anterior pituitary does not have this relationship with any other gland. It is the growth hormone (sometimes called the somatotrophic hormone, STH), and its production, like that of the other hormones of the anterior pituitary, is regulated or at least influenced by the brain. It stimulates the development of the muscle mass and the skeleton; it stimulates the growth of cartilage. (Without sufficient growth hormone the body is dwarfed.) It also stimulates the growth of the abdominal organs and the other endocrine glands, even though it does not call forth their specific secretions. Thus, indirectly, it affects the development of the sex glands, the adrenal cortex, and the thyroid gland.

When acting in normal fashion, STH causes the body to retain and utilize the amino acids of proteins, the building blocks for new cellular structure, which are so important in the growth phase of life. The need for large amounts of protein diminishes once full growth has been achieved. Just exactly how the brain controls the elaboration of the growth hormone from the pituitary is not known. Although the sex steroids do not have a reciprocal relationship to shut off the production of growth hormone, they do affect its action. This is particularly the case with estrogen. The growth hormone stimulates bone growth and height. When estrogen is given, it causes early calcification of the ends of the long bones and curtails growth in height by stopping growth of the long bones in the legs.

It is generally thought that the amount of growth hormone decreases once maturity is achieved and remains at a fairly constant level throughout the rest of life. This area deserves further investigation. Interestingly, the cartilage of the body continues to grow and sometimes seems to be accelerated in the middle and later years, producing larger ears and a larger nose. However, part of this aspect of age may also be related to decreased function of the adrenal cortex, since its hormones tend to inhibit the growth of cartilage.

The growth hormone has numerous other influences, including its effects on carbohydrate metabolism. But other than the points mentioned above, very little is known about its relationship to the processes attributed to aging.

Clearly, one way to affect almost all of the endocrine system is to affect the function of the anterior pituitary gland. This has been the basis of numerous endocrine experiments such as cutting the stalk between the pituitary gland and the hypothalamus, or actually removing the pituitary gland, transplanting it to a new location, or transplanting the gland from younger to older animals. In the total scheme of aging, one may note that the individual who has loss of function of the anterior pituitary gland presents many of the features attributed to aging. Such a condition is understandable since aging is associated with decreased formation of adrenocortical hormones, thyroid hormones, and sex hormones. This observation does not establish that decreased function of the anterior pituitary gland is the cause of aging, but merely identifies an area of importance to investigators of the process of aging.

When growth hormone continues to be elaborated in excessive amounts during the growth phase and is not adequately neutralized by sex steroids, the skeleton continues to grow until a human giant is created. This is the common cause of gigantism. It is also possible for excessive amounts of growth hormone to be formed after the long bones have calcified and stopped growing. In this instance the bones become heavier and thicker, muscle mass increases, the cartilage in the nose and ears enlarges, the hands and feet become larger, and the patient may complain of not being able to wear rings, shoes, gloves, hats, or other items. This is a fairly rare finding, but the picture is sufficiently distinct to be easily recognized. While such interesting manifestations demonstrate clearly the function of the growth hormone on the body, they really have no particular relationship to the aging process.

The posterior pituitary gland is mentioned here only for the sake of completeness, since very little is known about its relationship to the aging process, if it has any. One of its hormones is responsible for emptying the milk from the breast of the lactating female and for the contractions of the muscles in the uterus. It may play a role in labor. The other hormone is responsible for increasing blood pressure and also affects the kidney's mechanism in controlling water. Because of this latter function it has been given the name antidiuretic hormone, meaning it prevents urine formation by the kidney.

THE THYMUS GLAND

The thymus gland is located in the center of the chest between the lungs and in the region of the heart. The animal thymus is a common source of sweetbreads. Its hormonal functions remain in dispute. To some degree they are known to be similar to those of the lymph glands, which produce one type of white blood cells called lymphocytes. The thymus seems to be related to the body's immune mechanism and perhaps to the rejection reaction seen in organ transplants. It is believed to have an important part in providing the newborn baby with its own immune mechanism to help protect it against disease until the body acquires other defense mechanisms through progressive exposure to infections and consequent development of immunity.

The ratio of the size of the thymus gland to the size of the body is largest at the time of birth. In fact, it can be so large that examination of the actual size of the heart by x-ray is difficult. In the past, large thymus glands have been suggested as a cause for the mysterious crib deaths of young infants, a role which has never been proved or established. The gland continues to enlarge, reaching its maximum size at the time of puberty. Thereafter, it regresses in size, perhaps on account of the formation of steroid hormones. In fact, if young animals are castrated, the thymus gland will persist and not undergo its expected involution.

The thymus gland is influenced by the other endocrine glands. Growth hormones from the pituitary stimulate it to enlarge, as they do all other glands and organs. Similarly, TSH from the anterior pituitary, which stimulates the thyroid, also stimulates the thymus. If an individual has an overactive thyroid, therefore, he usually has an enlarged thymus gland. The hormones of the adrenal cortex tend to make the gland shrink. This action is very similar to the influence of the cortical hormones on the lymph glands. The role of the thymus in the immune and rejection mechanisms is shown by removing the thymus from newborn mice and demonstrating that skin grafts even from other animals will then "take" satisfactorily with no evidence of rejection.

The thymus remains small and atrophic in the later years. It is not degenerated, however, and can be stimulated to grow under proper hormonal influences. Whether the sudden decrease in thymic size at the time of puberty has any interrelationships in the endocrine system with regard to aging awaits further investigation.

THE PARATHYROID GLANDS

The parathyroid glands appear to be the only major endocrine glands in the body that are not influenced by the brain or under the control of the pituitary gland. Their function is directly related to calcium metabolism and bone formation. They are anatomically attached to either side of the thyroid gland, which position gives them their name. The hormone produced by them is simply called parathyroid hormone. If the amount of calcium in the blood increases, less parathyroid hormone is formed. If the blood calcium falls, more parathyroid hormone is formed to stimulate the release of calcium and maintain a proper mineral balance in the body fluids. The calcium level in the body is particularly important for the operation of muscles and nerves and even affects the action of the heart.

The parathyroid glands are affected by other endocrine glands only to the extent that other hormones influence the amount of calcium in the blood. Perhaps one of the most important examples of their response is seen in what happens when the sex glands begin to fail, which occurs in the postmenopausal period in women and usually later in men if their testicular activity decreases. The sex steroids stimulate the laying down of bony deposits. They stop body growth by calcifying the long bones in the legs. Quite naturally then, when there is a decrease in sex hormones, the opposite effect occurs. Parathyroid hormone's main action really is to mobilize calcium from the bones; if it is secreted in excess amounts, the result will be destruction of bone formation. When the stimulus from the sex hormones is gone or significantly diminished, the unopposed action of parathyroid hormone speeds up the dissolution of the bones. This leads to the osteoporosis type of degeneration of the spine seen in the postmenopausal period in one out of four women and in older white males.

Other than these interactions, which really reflect the changes with age in the other endocrine glands, there is no evidence of any change in function of the parathyroid glands with age.

twelve

The Urinary System

The urinary system includes the kidneys, the drainage tubes between the kidneys and the bladder (called the right and left ureters), the bladder, and the tube which drains the bladder to the outside (called the urethra). The kidneys are nature's blood filters. The bladder is a simple storage chamber for the urine. The right and left ureters and the urethra are just connecting tubes for the transport of urine. The kidney is affected by atherosclerosis and other aspects of acquired age. The functioning of the bladder, and of the entire urinary system, is affected by the state of the sexual system; for example, the prostate gland may obstruct the outflow of urine from the bladder, or genital prolapse in the female may cause difficulties with drainage of urine through the female urethra.

FILTERING THE BLOOD

Since the kidneys serve primarily to filter the blood, it has been possible to replace them with mechanical filters or artificial kidneys that have been developed in recent times. Without such a filtering process, or some substitute to accomplish the same purpose, life is not possible.

Normally one large artery carries blood to each kidney. As the blood circulates through the kidneys, it is filtered and emerges from the kidneys through one large vein, which then returns the purified blood to circulation. Over a quart of blood a minute filters through the kidneys, and since the heart pumps only about 5 quarts of blood a minute, this represents one-fifth of the circulation. Thus in an hour's time 15 gallons of blood will have circulated through the kidneys. The body contains a little less than 2 gallons of blood. Therefore, the kidneys have an opportunity to constantly filter and clean the blood for recirculation.

As the blood flows through the small blood vessels in the kidneys, its liquid part seeps out into the filtering mechanisms, which are a series of tubes in the kidney. The liquid part of the blood is the normal salt water in the blood stream plus various minerals, chemicals, and metabolic waste products. The blood cells and proteins in the circulating blood do not seep out into the tubes of the kidney but remain in the blood vessels.

Some of the liquid part of the blood seeps out of the arteries into the tubes of the kidneys. It is called the filtrate. It is a clear liquid substance, mostly salt water. Approximately half a cup of liquid filtrate leaves the blood stream and passes through the kidney each minute. Approximately 2 gallons of the watery filtrate, therefore, can be processed by the kidney every hour. Specialized cells that line the tubes of the kidney process the 2 gallons of filtrate to form urine. If the body needs to conserve water, the purified water is drawn out of the filtrate and returns to the blood stream. The urine then becomes more concentrated. If an individual has been drinking lots of water or has more water in the body than is needed, less water will be reabsorbed and the urine will be diluted. In addition, under the influence of various hormones including those in the adrenal gland and the pituitary gland, the filtering process regulates the minerals in the body, controlling how much salt or sodium, calcium, and other minerals will be eliminated in the urine. The basic mechanism always is to get rid of the excess but to conserve the essential.

There are optimal levels of almost all chemicals in the body, and when too much of any one is present it is normally removed one way or another. A simple example is blood sugar. It is absolutely essential to have sugar in the blood, but if the level gets too high the excess is eliminated through the filtering process that forms urine. This is the reason an uncontrolled diabetic has sugar in the urine. By regulating the amount of salt, minerals, and various chemicals eliminated from the body, the kidney also controls the acid-base balance of the body. These mechanisms are relatively complex.

The proteins that are digested and used by the body contain nitrogen, and when these substances are not used in building new tissues, the excess amount must be eliminated through the kidney. The nitrogen product that results from metabolism is urea. The function of excreting urea gives rise to the name urine. Everyone has urea in the urine, and it is increased in individuals who eat lots of protein. A different substance, but related to protein metabolism and various metabolic actions of the body, is uric acid. Uric acid is a normal product, but when the body has too much, it is eliminated through the kidney. If this excretion is not accomplished or if the body is overproducing uric acid, it builds up in the circulation and causes deposits in the bones and joints, resulting in gout.

Since the formation of urine by the kidney is the natural outcome of filtering and processing sterile blood, it is clear that under normal healthy circumstances the urine as formed by the kidneys is also sterile.

THE KIDNEYS' EFFECT ON BLOOD PRESSURE

The kidney is directly related to the mechanisms controlling blood pressure. For one thing, it interacts with hormones that regulate the salt and fluid retention of the body. Other mechanisms are more complicated. There are many causes of high blood pressure other than disorders of the kidney. A person who has persistent high blood pressure is more likely to develop fatty deposits in the arteries throughout the body. Thus when the kidney is at fault, it can accelerate the process of atherosclerosis and its multiple complications of senility, strokes, heart attacks, and abnormal function of almost any part of the body.

When atherosclerosis blocks the artery to the kidney or the small arteries within the kidney, the blood flow to the kidney is obstructed. The kidney apparently has ways to try to increase its blood flow by increasing blood pressure. This maneuver is often useful in life situations, but in the presence of atherosclerosis it merely aggravates the problem. Eventually a vicious cycle is created: The fatty deposits in the arteries to the kidney cause high blood pressure, and the high blood pressure accelerates the formation of more atherosclerotic plaques in the arteries to the kidney and elsewhere.

Any mechanical obstruction to the circulation of the kidneys can cause high blood pressure. If the obstruction, even if it is atherosclerosis, involves only the artery region outside the kidney, the plugged artery can be removed and replaced by a graft; when normal circulation to the kidney is restored, high blood pressure can often be relieved. Individuals with this type of problem have curable high blood pressure. However, this is not the most common cause for high blood pressure, and such an operation is not indicated in large numbers of people whose high blood pressure has quite a different basis.

If fatty deposits have also been made in the smaller arteries inside the kidney, these obstructed arteries cannot at this time be replaced and an operation is not feasible.

CHANGES WITH AGE

Although numerous studies have been done to show the changes which occur in the kidney in older age groups, it is important to point out that even with the prevalence of atherosclerosis in our society many older people retain reasonably normal kidney function. One report has it that over a third of patients 65 or older who were studied had normal kidney function. Most of the kidney disease seen is just that, disease and not genetic aging. Most disorders are the result of preceding infections, complications of atherosclerosis, or changes due to obstruction to the outflow of the urinary tract by the prostate or prolapsed female genitals or related to kidney stones. The identification of any change in the kidneys independent of actual disease which is responsible for shortening of the life span is not possible at this time. If infections or inflammations of the kidney, circulatory changes, and the obstructive problems could be prevented, there is no real evidence that the kidney could not function well for years beyond what we now expect.

Urinary tract infections are very common in older people. In fact, they are second only to pulmonary disease as the main cause of fever in people past 65. The vast majority of these infections stem from problems with emptying the bladder. In the female the decrease in female hormones associated with the menopause ultimately leads to degeneration of the cells that line the bladder and the urethral outlet, technically called atrophic urethritis. This change causes the bladder and urinary tract to be more susceptible to infections and injuries and possibly even to malignancies. The problem, of course, can be avoided by adequate replacement of the female hormones at the time of the menopause.

The second consideration in the female has already been mentioned in connection with prolapse of the genitals (see Chapter Ten, "The Sexual System"), particularly likely to occur in a woman who has had several children. The opening of the urethra may actually be in the vagina, causing urine to collect in the vaginal vault. This accumulated urine is subsequently lost during coughing, sneezing, and other such episodes which contribute to the female's problem of incontinence.

During the childbearing years a woman is constantly experiencing urinary tract infections partly because of her sex life. The bacteria that are normally present on the skin all around the vulva are introduced to the urethral outlet, and because the female urethra is short, they easily gain access to the bladder area. These conditions, associated with the mechanical effects of sexual activity, can easily set up inflammation of the bladder—cystitis. Childbearing itself produces pressure upon the bladder and the ureters which can sufficiently obstruct the outflow of urine from the kidneys to aid in the establishment of kidney infection, or pyelitis.

The male is less likely to have urinary tract infections in his earlier years; his primary problem is inflammation of the prostate (prostatism). Caused by bacteria, the vast majority of these acute inflammations are not venereal infections although certainly gonorrheal microorganisms can affect the prostate and produce inflammation of the prostate and urethra. Even bacteria that are found in the colon can invade the blood stream and eventually lodge in the urinary tract.

The older male frequently has enlargement of his prostate, or the central portion of it enlarges in such a way as to squeeze down on the urethral tube just as it leaves the bladder. The compression of the urethral tube, obstructing the outflow of urine, is the principal symptom of an enlarged prostate. This problem has been discussed in Chapter Ten.

thirteen

The Musculoskeletal System

We commonly think of youth as being associated with supple bodies with good muscles and strong bones capable of a wide range of physical activity and endurance. We think of age, by contrast, as being associated with loss of muscles, weak and brittle bones, and loss of body suppleness. Certainly within our framework of living patterns these concepts are true. Yet in many parts of the world older individuals continue to be physically vigorous with strong muscles, strong bones, and supple bodies. One need look no farther than the 70- and 80-year-old Africans who are tribal dancers. Many changes noted in the muscles and skeleton with age can definitely be prevented.

WHAT MUSCLES ARE

The musculoskeletal system is normally the largest organ system of the body. The muscles represent a major portion of the body weight except in the obese. There are three basic types of muscles. (1) The involuntary or smooth muscles are those found in the wall of the digestive tract, those which contract or relax the pupil of the eye, and those which control the opening and closing of numerous valves or sphincters. (2) The heart muscle has its own unique features but despite its involuntary autonomous activity still behaves essentially like muscle. (3) The voluntary muscles, under voluntary control, are also called the skeletal muscles. These are the muscle groups around the skeleton which control body movements and body position. They are the muscles we will be mostly concerned with here.

In the human body there are approximately 434 skeletal muscles. Each is divided into long fibers which, like a spring, are able to contract and relax. The lengthening and shortening of these muscle fibers are responsible for the contraction and relaxation of individual muscles. As the various muscles around a joint or body part contract and relax, they produce the smooth synchronous movement of the body. The individual muscle fibers are held together with fibrous material called connective tissue, and many of the muscles are encased in a fibrous sheath which looks very much like plastic wrapping material. The connective tissues in between the different fibers of the muscles and the sheaths of the muscles often join into long cordlike structures, principally of fibrous tissue, which are called tendons. Other fibrous sheaths attach directly to bony points and use the bones as levers in the movement process.

In the 434 skeletal muscles the human body contains approximately 250 million muscle fibers, and unless a person is grossly obese or has some other problem, these muscles represent 40 to 45 percent of the entire body weight. Loss of muscle fibers or changes in their size affect the body as a whole since they represent so much of the body.

The muscles should not be thought of simply as springs that contract and relax. They are the mechanical workhorses of the body. They do the work of locomotion and enable man to be a physical work animal. Consequently they must have fuel or energy sources. These are supplied by foods. In the physically active individual a good deal of the food energy consumed daily is used to support the work of the skeletal muscles. Within the muscle cells carbohydrate substances are metabolized by complex chemical systems to release energy used by the muscles for work. This process generates a great deal of heat. The muscles, therefore, are a major factor in producing body heat and influencing body temperature. Vigorous physical activity such as long-distance running has been demonstrated to raise the temperature of the body several degrees in normal healthy people.

The muscles contain a great deal of protein. If one excludes the stored fat which sometimes encases or surrounds muscles, it is correct to say that the muscles are comprised primarily of protein and water. If all the external fat is removed, about 70 percent of the muscle is actually water.

BONES AS MINERAL AND BLOOD BANKS

The muscles and skeleton work together and are indivisible in their development, function, and degeneration. The bony skeleton is not an inert mineral deposit but is actually comprised of many cells, laid down as an organized structure. The cells are mostly protein except for the marrow of long bones. The bony cells are impregnated with calcium and phosphorus, the deposition of which gives the bones their structure and rigidity. Throughout the active bony areas small arteries and veins provide nourishment to the bone cells which is just as essential to them as nourishment is to other parts of the body. The blood supply to a bone has a great deal to do with the process of calcium deposits or the removal of calcium from bone. The bone marrow serves entirely different functions and is important in the formation of blood cells. Outside the marrow is the more spongy bone, and finally come the outer layers of bone, which are the most dense, meaning that they are packed more tightly with calcium salts than other areas of the bone.

The calcium in the bones is constantly being exchanged with the calcium in the rest of the body, particularly that circulating in the blood stream. The bones represent a major calcium pool for the functions of the body. Calcium is essential to normal cell function. It even affects the contractility of the heart muscle and the time required for electrical events of heart muscle and other muscle. This mechanism can be demonstrated with the electrocardiogram.

Too much calcium in the blood stream can create problems, including deposits of calcium in the kidneys and other soft tissues of the body. There is an optimal level of calcium in the cells and in the blood, and as with so many other biological systems, too much or too little will cause difficulty.

In the formation of bones there is an intermediate or cartilage stage. Cartilage is the forerunner to bone formation. It contains most of the elements of bone, but the cartilage cells lack calcium salt and therefore remain soft like the cartilage in the ear or tip of the nose. In those parts of the body where bone is to be formed the early cartilage cells are gradually impregnated with calcium salts, and bone develops. In the areas which remain as cartilage this process doesn't occur. Once again we see evidence of a master blueprint for the development and function of the body. When the cartilaginous areas such as the tip of the nose and ears have been formed, in some way these cells are told not to accept calcium deposits and they do not progress to bone formation. By contrast, the original cartilaginous formation in the arms and legs is calcified and eventually becomes the firm, hard bones of the mature adult.

Throughout the growth stage of the body, many of the cartilaginous portions of the bones keep on growing. The cartilage in the nose and ears continues to grow with age; in fact, growth stimulated by changes in hormone formation may contribute to the gradually increased size of the nose and ears associated with increasing years.

The musculoskeletal system, then, provides rigidity and support for the body, the capacity for locomotion and work. In its optimal state, it is an elastic, supple system. At the bones' interconnections, or joints, there are cartilaginous caps. The joints are surrounded by membranes so that fluid may be retained in the joints to facilitate movement. Supporting structures are found around the joints and connect the muscles to the skeletal system. These are tendons and ligaments. The normal elasticity of the muscles, tendons, ligaments, and indeed the skeleton itself is essential for optimal musculoskeletal function.

A SYSTEM OF OPPOSING FORCES

One of the interesting things about the musculoskeletal system is the arrangement of the muscles and their attachment to the skeleton. For the most part there are opposing sets of muscles. This feature is very important in appreciating what happens to the musculoskeletal system with advancing years. Examples of opposing muscles are everywhere. The biceps in the upper arm contracts to bend the elbow. The triceps muscle on the back of the arm contracts to straighten the elbow. The actions of these two muscle groups oppose each other. Opposing muscles bend or straighten the joints in almost every region of the body, or rotate parts of the skeleton in opposite directions. Muscles along the back help us sit or stand upright. They are opposed by muscles from the other side of the trunk which allow us to bend the spine forward. There are muscles which help us rotate the spine to the right and other muscles which rotate the spine to the left. Large muscles in the front of the neck let us rotate the head to the right or to the left. Muscles between the shoulders help us keep our shoulders back in a normal position. Muscles across the front of the chest contract in an opposite direction and tend to roll the shoulders forward, producing the rounded-shoulder effect. The state of contraction and general position of all these muscles in relation to each other are responsible for optimal posture and movement.

THE ROLE OF HORMONES

The musculoskeletal system is significantly affected by hormones— even from the beginning of the developmental process. During the early years of life it is the growth hormone from the pituitary that stimulates the growth of new muscles and new bone. The growth hormone works together with the thyroid hormone in producing normal body growth. During the growth phase there is a great need for proteins, the building blocks for new tissue. At puberty a marked distinction in the character of the skeleton and muscles of the male and female occurs. Male hormones are responsible for the well-defined, strong, muscular characteristics of the male. Less male hormone and more female hormones result in the smaller musculoskeletal system of the female with its lesser amount of strength. While it is true that physical activity and training can affect this development in both the male and the female, the basic role of male and female hormones is to provide a degree of differentiation. All other things being equal, the human male is designed to have a larger, stronger musculoskeletal system than the female.

As the growth stage of puberty and adolescence gives way to the mature individual, hormonal influences again affect the musculoskeletal system. Sex hormones, male or female, stimulate the deposit of calcium in the cartilaginous regions at the ends of the shafts of the long bones. When the calcium is deposited and hard bone is formed, growth stops. If it did not, an individual could become a giant, as is clearly demonstrated in animals castrated in youth or in similar human examples. Absence of sex hormones results in continued growth of stature for some time before the growth hormone influences from the pituitary gland stop the stimulation. In general, animals castrated early in development have larger musculoskeletal systems than those that undergo normal sexual development. However, the muscles tend to lack strength, and a greater amount of fat is formed around the muscles themselves. While there remains some discussion about their actual role and how its effects are brought about, obviously the decline in sex hormones in later years is directly related to the subsequent loss of calcium from the bone, with degeneration of the spine and other bones. This period of life is also associated with a decrease in the size and number of muscle fibers.

The commonly observed decrease in the size of muscles with increasing age is not all time related. The muscle mass can be influenced by the amount and type of physical activity. A person with relatively small muscles can develop large muscles with a properly carried-out weight training program. Exercise which causes the muscles to have to contract firmly or against force will gradually increase the size of the muscles. Older individals who have continued forms of physical activity that constantly work the muscles often have retained a larger muscle mass than much younger individuals who follow no physical fitness program.

The range of possibility of development of muscle mass is so great that there is a very obvious overlap between the physically active older person and the inactive young person. Not that the very old person by physical activity alone can retain the maximum amount of muscular development that the human body is able to achieve. But physical activity is a major factor in maintaining muscle mass, and its absence is a major factor in failure to develop or maintain muscle mass.

Because physical activity progressively declines in individuals with increasing years or sometimes with material success, there is a tendency toward a gradual change in body composition so that a large portion of the muscle mass is replaced with fat tissue. This is a main reason for the change in body configuration attributed to aging. It is often said that as a person gets older his chest falls. The largest dimension is no longer around the chest but around the waist and buttocks.

It is intriguing to observe the decrease with age of steroid hormones generated by the adrenal gland and the sex glands that parallels the decrease in muscle mass. The measurable amounts of these eliminated in the urine decrease with age, but correlation with muscle mass shows that the same amount of the hormones is formed per pound of muscle in both the young and the old. While there is probably some inherent decrease, the question is whether or not the decrease in the hormones is associated with age or lack of physical activity. Since muscle size can be increased with exercise at almost any age, there remains the possibility that physical activity which increases size and function of the muscular system can in turn influence the master genes of the body that control the time sequence of the various cells and in so doing be a youth factor.

THE WAR WITH GRAVITY

The commonly observed loss of muscle mass in advancing years affects some muscle groups more than others. Muscle tissue is typically lost between the bones in the hand, leading to the development of the "bony hand" of older individuals. By appropriate hand exercises these muscle groups can be at least partially maintained. Similarly, the muscle fibers in the arms and legs tend to shrink, so that the size of the muscles in the extremities is decreased. The loss in size and strength of the abdominal muscle results in the relaxed abdomen which is a major factor in the familiar "bay window."

The muscles along the entire spine are likely to weaken, as are those between the shoulders. These and other changes are responsible for the posture and physical appearance of the body of older people. There is a constant battle against gravity to maintain upright posture. As the muscles weaken, the battle is lost and the body begins to sag. Just as an old tree gradually bends to the earth, the human body bends more and more; its muscles can no longer keep the skeleton in its optimal, upright position.

As the muscles become less and less able to maintain the constant state of semicontraction necessary for proper alignment of the spine, the spine bends forward, decreasing the normal tension on the abdominal muscles. Visualize a bow and its string. The bow is the spine; the taut string, the abdominal muscles. If you seize the bow by both ends and bend it or curl it, the tension on the string is released and the string becomes slack. So it is with the abdominal muscles. As the spine inclines forward, it relieves the tension on these muscles and they become slack.

Abdominal muscles that remain strong add support to the spine and reduce a great deal of the wear and tear of weight on the spine and spinal muscles. Thus in this sense they work together.

As the weak muscles between the shoulders lose their tone, they remain stretched even in the resting state. The muscles across the front of the chest (pectoral muscles) then contract or their fibers shorten, so that the shoulders roll forward. The end result is a combination of muscles in the front of the chest which are contracted, unable to stretch to their usual length, and muscles across the back of the shoulders which are weakened and overstretched. Clearly, correction of this type of problem involves treatment of both muscle groups, the relaxation and lengthening of those across the chest and the strengthening of those between the shoulders to provide normal shoulder position.

In addition to the changes observed in the spine, the joints begin to bend at hip and knee just as if they were giving slightly under the constant load of carrying the weight of the body. The flexed positions of the hips and knees contributes to the loss in height associated with increasing years. Maintaining the optimal range of capacity of the muscles will go a long way toward maintaining proper positioning of the hips and knees for optimal body posture. The tendons at the joints also shorten as the muscles remain contracted. The Achilles tendon in the ankle, for example, shortens, decreasing the mobility of the ankle. Regular stretching of a joint helps retain normal tendon length.

The elbows and wrists also tend to be slightly bent, and keeping their full range of motion is likewise an important aspect of preserving youthful vigor. The body makes constant adjustments to maintain balance as it loses the battle against gravity. Factors which influence the legs and spine gradually reach up to affect the neck and head, since the head must balance on top of the spinal column. The changes in the musculoskeletal system just described cause the head and neck to thrust forward a little. The face itself changes. If the muscles are not used frequently, the face may become impassive, and there is likely to be frequent blinking of the eyes.

The changes in body posture are not solely muscular. Degeneration of the spine, associated with the degeneration of the disks between vertebrae and actual dissolving of the bones, causes fractures of the spine, deformities of the vertebrae, and other derangements which magnify the problem. It cannot be emphasized too strongly that once these changes have become extensive it is impossible to reverse them. Therefore a preventive program for the musculoskeletal system must be established early in life. Since the formation of bone—and, indeed, its destruction—is frequently a long-term process, such a program should be initiated early and followed vigorously.

As skeletal changes occur, underlying medical problems often become more important. These include such things as having one leg shorter than the other (which causes the pelvis to tilt and the entire spine to be canted out of position) and old injuries of any type which have affected the skeletal system. The loss of normal muscle strength alone is a major factor in the frequent occurrence of backaches, and these of course are common even in young people, who also may have weak muscles. The overall preventive program for the musculoskeletal system is invaluable even in the early years in preventing backache. Appropriate exercise to achieve this goal is discussed fully in Chapter Sixteen.

MUSCLE CRAMPS

A frequent problem in advancing years in our society deserves special mention—muscle cramps. These occur particularly in the legs and feet. They have multiple causes, including unusual amounts or unusual types of physical exercise and certain neurological diseases. A common factor, however, is our old friend atherosclerosis. The muscles, like all other organs of the body, must have an adequate blood supply. Indeed, the amount of work that the normal, healthy, fit muscle can do is frequently limited by how much blood can be delivered to it. If a muscle gets insufficient blood, which in turn provides insufficient oxygen and fails to carry away the accumulation of carbon dioxide and other metabolic products, it will become fatigued or irritable and its chances of cramping are much greater.

In the extreme example, the person with severe atherosclerosis in the arteries to his legs will have muscle cramps after a minimal amount of walking. Characteristically, stopping walking and resting for a few minutes permits the circulation to catch up with the metabolism in the muscles, causing the muscle cramp to go away so that the person can walk again. Obviously, the desirable approach is to prevent atherosclerosis and the consequent decrease in function of the muscles. Sometimes the problem can be corrected by surgical procedures which provide improved circulation to the legs.

A large number of individuals have leg cramps at night and are not severely handicapped during the days. There are several reasons for nighttime cramps. Circulation is often a major factor. The calf of the leg and the feet particularly are the regions farthest from the heart, and when a person is lying down they are the least likely to get enough blood. As a result the muscles tend to cool during the long night hours. I have been repeatedly impressed by the many people who have obtained relief from night cramps of the feet and ankles by wearing warm heavy socks pulled up to the knees or using a heated blanket or other means to keep the feet and legs warm. Maintaining adequate temperature of the feet and legs in some way decreases their inclination to cramp.

Many muscle cramps, wherever they occur, can be relieved by stretching of the muscle. A muscle which is cramped is actually shortened and is weak and unable to function normally. Quite often simple stretching helps it gain its normal elasticity and hence its normal functional relationship to the musculoskeletal system. In essence this is what a well-designed, active exercise program does. It contracts and then stretches the individual muscles. While one group of muscles is contracting, the opposing group is being stretched or lengthened. By a balanced exercise system the muscles are stretched and shortened, stretched and shortened, and thereby hold their full range of capacity. When illness or injury interferes with this function, sometimes passive aid in either maintaining or regaining the stretching and contracting ability of the muscle is necessary. This is one of the important roles of physical medicine and physiotherapy or any of the other measures that are directed toward regaining or improving muscle function.

ARTHRITIS

An almost inescapable change in the skeleton with age is osteoarthritis, sometimes called wear and tear arthritis. It may represent true genetic aging in the sense that damaged or worn-out cells have been replaced so many times that they have reached their maximum number of reproduction as determined by genetic factors. Usually osteoarthritis affects the weight-bearing joints, particularly the hips and spine. Within the joint the cartilage cap at the end of the bones gradually wears smooth until the bony surfaces themselves begin to rub against each other. The entire process leads to damage or destruction of bone tissue in the joints. In response to the destruction, there is an overgrowth of new bone which takes on a different formation from that of the old. Some of the new bone grows out in the form of spurs or in lipping of the vertebrae, and this change in the architecture of the bony structure may cause trouble. The bony spurs, technically called ostephytes, can create pressure on other structures including nerves which cause pain.

Overuse of any joint can induce an arthritic change like osteoarthritis. It can be seen in the ankles of a ballet dancer or in the elbow of a baseball pitcher. It is more likely to occur in people who are overweight. The heavier the body, the greater the wear and tear. Most of the osteoarthritic changes in joints are caused by gravity. If the body were weightless, there would be no wear and tear on the weight-bearing joints and this form of arthritis would be almost nonexistent.

Despite the implication that it is a wear and tear disease, the fact that osteoarthritis occurs in some families more than in others suggests once again that a basic genetic factor at least influences the development of the disease. A common place for the manifestation of osteoarthritis is in the spine, particularly in the neck region because it must support the weight of the head. X-rays reveal osteoarthritis in the vast majority of men over 60 years of age; in people who live long enough, over 90 percent will show evidence of it.

A variant of this type of arthritis is the little nodular formations or osteophytes in the last joint of the fingers of the hand. This can occur without significant arthritic changes in the rest of the body and is more prevalent in women than in men.

The most frequent characteristic of osteoarthritis is that it causes pain. Of course, it can and does exist in many individuals without producing any symptoms at all, but when it limits motion and creates pressure on bodily structures, it is painful. In this type of arthritis the pain will go away if the part is rested. Thus, pain in the hip from osteoarthritis will be relieved by simple bed rest, removing the necessity for weight bearing. Small doses of aspirin are usually adequate for controlling the discomfort, but nothing is quite so useful in relieving the pain of osteoarthritis as rest. The joints that are involved are usually not swollen or red and hot unless there is an advanced stage of the disease with associated complications.

The degenerative process of the skeleton often affects the little spongy disks between vertebrae. These disks are poorly supplied with blood and deteriorate easily, sometimes even in teenagers. If the outer shell of a disk degenerates, its nodular center ruptures and can cause pressure on the spinal cord or nerves. Furthermore, bony spines can grow out from the edges of the involved vertebrae causing pressure on nerves. Many of these problems can be prevented or minimized with good exercise and other measures, but if pressure on a nerve has already occurred, frequently surgical intervention is required. Failure to treat the condition promptly, particularly if an area in the spinal cord is involved, can result in permanent, irreversible damage.

While it is not possible with our present state of knowledge to prevent osteoarthritis, some measures can be taken which will decrease the likelihood of being significantly disabled by it. Number one on this list is weight control. Avoidance of obesity is extremely important to avert overloading of the weight-bearing joints and subsequent arthritis. A second measure is maintaining the full range of mobility of all the joints and keeping up muscle strength to retain the proper relationship of joints to each other. Any joint not properly aligned is more likely to be put under abnormal stress, leading to degeneration and deformity from improper use. The ballet dancer and the baseball pitcher who develop a form of wear and tear arthritis engage in activities which involve positions of strain upon joints. The ankle structures were not designed for toe dancing, nor was the elbow meant to be subjected to the peculiar movements required of the highly skilled professional baseball pitcher. Activity and use are helpful, but they can also be harmful if overdone or carried out in an unusual or unhealthy fashion. The key words are *optimal* and *proper* in almost all of the biological functions.

To reduce the jar and shock of body weight other simple precautions are important. Sensible shoes enable an individual to maintain optimal posture and optimal walking action. One could raise some serious questions about the persistent use of high heels. This permits shortening of the Achilles tendon and distortion of the normal functional relationships of the lower extremity, which in turn can affect the balance mechanism of the entire body. Spongy innersoles in the shoes can absorb a portion of the shock of locomotion and weight bearing. Although the same may be said of spongy soles for shoes, consideration must be given to the traction provided by the shoe. Walking areas or areas where prolonged standing occurs should have some give; wood floors or suitable carpets and paddings will cushion the shock of standing and walking.

Weight bearing is not limited to standing or walking but is also a feature of sitting. The greatest pressure on the spinal column usually occurs in the seated position. One reason is the failure to maintain contraction of the abdominal muscles which along with the abdominal content help splint the spinal column and bear some of the stress. Seats that do not provide proper support contribute to the strain on the spine and eventually the mechanical aspects of wear and tear arthritis.

Perhaps the two worst kinds of seats are overstuffed furniture and swivel chairs. Furniture is a personal item and should be tailored to the size and contour of the individual. For optimal body support the seat of the chair should be firm, and its height should be such that the hips and the knees are at about the same level when the feet are placed comfortably flat on the floor. If anything, the seat of the chair should be tilted slightly so that the back of the seat is a little higher than the front edge. The depth of the seat should not be too great, so that the back of the chair can offer adequate support to the spine. The back should be either firm and straight or curved in such a way that the lower part of the chair fits the normal forward curvature of the spine. Many chairs can be improved if a small pillow is placed behind the lower spine, although excessive or unnatural forward curvature of the spine should be avoided.

As any traveler knows, most seats in public conveyances, including airplanes, are not designed for comfort. The seats are improper in size, the back of the seat is curved in the wrong direction, and no wonder the traveler is tired and frequently has a backache after a long trip. In summary, furniture for sitting should provide a firm base of the right height and depth and a firm back support correctly shaped or else straight. The use of proper furniture can minimize years of stress and strain on the vertebrae and skeletal system.

While osteoarthritis is the common form of arthritis and appears to be related to wear and tear and hence time of living, there is another well-known arthritis called rheumatoid arthritis. Being inflammatory in type, it is not to be associated with the aging process. This is the arthritis that is responsible for the red, swollen joints. The pain accompanying it is not relieved by simple rest, and it usually requires medicine and long-term supervision. This disorder ordinarily occurs in young women.

OSTEOPOROSIS

Of the different disorders associated with age that affect the musculo-skeletal system perhaps the most important is osteoporosis, and significantly, much of it can be prevented. *Osteo* means bone, and *porosis* means porous. Literally osteoporosis is porous bones or dissolving of bones. It is related to the loss of calcium from the bones throughout the body. This in turn results in shrinking of the bony tissue and, in areas where bone is placed under stress, is the underlying cause of bone fractures. Osteoporosis is a major contributor to the frequency of broken hips in older people and increases susceptibility to fractures with minor injuries. The loss of calcium from the bones particularly affects the spine. The individual vertebrae decrease in height. Some are actually fractured or dissolved completely. The decrease in the height of the vertebrae and the loss of vertebral structures are responsible in part for the decrease in height with age. With destruction and deformity of the vertebral bodies there is a loss of the normal support structures to combat the forces of gravity. The upper spine between the shoulders is particularly affected and may bend forward, causing the hunched back or buffalo hump so common in older people. Similar spinal changes in the small of the back also are observed.

This problem occurs earlier in women. Although the figures are highly variable, one out of four postmenopausal white women about the age of 60 is said to have obvious evidence of osteoporosis. It occurs in men (as a group) as much as 20 years later than in women. Since it is related to loss of calcium from the skeleton, it is more often seen in individuals with a smaller skeleton. This has been cited as one reason why it is less commonly observed in the older black female and almost never in the black male. The theory is that the more calcium that is deposited in the basic calcium pool in the bones, the longer it takes for it to be withdrawn and evidence of bone erosion to be apparent. *The cause of osteoporosis is clearly connected to a deficiency or defect in calcium supply for the body,* along with hormonal changes.

Diet is the cornerstone in the prevention of osteoporosis. *Women who are on calcium-deficient diets are five times as likely to develop severe osteoporosis as women who are getting adequate amounts of calcium in their diet.* The same observation probably applies to older men. Directly related to the diet is the problem of absorbing calcium from the digestive tract. Certain medical disorders interfere with absorption of calcium, exerting the same effect as a calcium-deficient diet. Most of them are specific medical abnormalities and are not a major factor in the vast number of people who develop osteoporosis. The amount of calcium stored in the body is a constant balance between how much is absorbed from the digestive tract and how much is lost. The main location for the loss of calcium from the body is the kidneys. Excess loss of calcium in the urine draws calcium out of the blood. Since the blood level must be maintained, calcium is then withdrawn from the bone. The function of the kidneys in eliminating calcium, other minerals, and water is regulated by hormones in the body, and in some medical conditions this can be a significant factor in causing osteoporosis.

The hormones that are normally implicated in the loss of calcium are the steroid hormones produced by the adrenal cortex and the gonads. These are the male and female sex hormones. Osteoporosis in women after the menopause is related to the decrease in sex hormones. The observation that decalcification occurs some 20 years later in men is consistent with the observation that the sex hormones in men do decrease in age but not precipitously as they do in women with the menopause. Characteristically, the decline of sex hormones in men is very gradual and extends over a longer period of time. For this reason, advanced osteoporosis in white men is more often seen in the 80- and 90-year-old group.

Other hormones have their influence. The stress hormones released from the adrenal cortex and commonly used in treating inflammations (sometimes correctly and sometimes incorrectly in treating arthritis) lead to a loss of calcium from the bone and the gradual development of osteoporosis.

Still another factor related to the speed of osteoporosis is the level of physical activity. There is abundant evidence that optimal levels of physical activity are important in maintaining bone strength and calcium deposits. If a leg is placed in a cast so that it can't be used, not only is there muscular wasting, but the bone in the leg tends to decalcify. Concerned with the problem of weightlessness in space, I have studied many young healthy men placed at bed rest. Invariably they lost calcium from the body after three weeks of bed rest. Under normal environmental circumstances, gravity definitely influences calcification of the skeleton, as was also demonstrated in space flights when men were in a relatively weightless environment for extended periods of time. Whenever the body is prone, as in bed rest, the effect of gravity on the weight of the body is essentially negated. The gravity forces are distributed along the entire long axis of the body. The normal weight-bearing parts of the skeleton are no longer required to serve their antigravity action. With the loss of gravity stimulation or stress, calcium is mobilized from the bone and osteoporosis ensues. The Man-in-Space program pointed out dramatically the crucial aspect of activity and gravity in maintaining the strength and integrity of the skeletal system. Clearly, individuals who have osteoporosis already need to pay strict attention to all of these measures, including avoiding excessive bed rest.

An individual's calcium loss associated with bed rest can often be minimized or reversed by having him sit up or stand. It is difficult to prevent decalcification even with reasonably high levels of exercise carried on while lying at bed rest. Experiments using bicycle-pedaling-type exercises and other physical activities have demonstrated that exercise alone while lying in bed is not enough to prevent osteoporosis— perhaps because it is impossible to achieve the level of exercise necessary to provide the same degree of stress or work on the bone required by the normal forces of gravity in an individual who is up and active.

The effects of osteoporosis can be devastating. Fortunately it is not often painful except in extreme form. Most of the pain associated with the disorder comes from muscle spasms and pressure upon nerves caused by abnormal positions of the spine or vertebrae. The loss of normal musculoskeletal function, however, associated with osteoporosis is only part of the picture. The compression of the chest cage because of the buffalo hump formation can significantly affect the lungs. There is already a problem with getting air to the lower parts of the lungs in older people anyway. If the deformity of the chest is sufficiently severe to compress major portions of the lung tissue, some areas of the lung will not receive fresh air and even though the circulation is adequate they cannot serve effectively in respiration. As a result, older individuals with severe chest deformity causing lung compression are most likely to have a drop in the oxygen pressure in their arterial blood. The circulation is then no longer able to deliver the amount of high-pressure oxygen to the brain and nervous system that it usually does. As discussed in Chapter Four, "The Nervous System," the level of oxygenation of the brain is an important factor in the function of the brain in terms of its thinking process, memory, and personality responses. So it is clear that osteoporosis not only causes musculoskeletal changes and is the underlying mechanism for many fractures but can, depending on its severity, affect respiratory function, circulatory function, and the function of the brain.

Treating osteoporosis that has already developed is relatively unsatisfactory. Sometimes the disease can be arrested, but the real benefits are derived from a preventive program. This should be structured along the lines of diet, exercise, hormone replacement, and avoiding any medicines or factors which can contribute to dissolving bones. Preferably the diet should contain 1 to 1½ grams of calcium a day, approximately the amount found in something over a quart of milk. The use of one quart of milk either in food preparation or as a beverage each day is perhaps the easiest and most practical way to provide the necessary amount of calcium for the body. Any amount of calcium less than that over a long period will result in a deficiency in the calcium stores and gradual loss of bone. Calcium deficiency is perhaps one of the most common findings in the modern-day diet.

Since many scientists believe it is not desirable to drink large quantities of whole milk because of its saturated fat content and its role in producing atherosclerosis, one can use fortified skim milk and still obtain the calcium. The calcium content in milk and in cottage cheese is not dependent upon the fat content in these products. The truth is, fortified skim milk contains more calcium per glass than ordinary whole milk because it has had nonfat milk solids added. Calcium is abundant in only a few foods in our diet. The best sources generally available are listed below:

	Grams
Whole milk, 1 quart	1.150
Skim milk, 1 quart	1.200
2% fat milk, fortified, 1 quart	1.500
Fortified skim milk, 1 quart	over 1.500
Nonfat dry milk powder, instant, 1⅓ cups	1.200
Uncreamed cottage cheese	
1 cup curd, pressed down	0.180
1 12-ounce package	0.300
Bread, white enriched, 1 pound	0.380
1 slice (18-slice loaf)	0.020
1 1½-pound loaf	0.571
1 slice, (24-slice loaf)	0.024
Bread, whole wheat (use values for white enriched above)	

Collards, 3½ ounces (100 grams)	0.250
Sardines, 3½ ounces (100 grams)	
Atlantic (solids and liquids)	0.354
Drained solids	0.437
Pacific, in tomato sauce	
(solids and liquids)	0.449
Salmon, canned (solids and liquid)	
Chum	0.249
Coho (silver)	0.244
Pink	0.196
Red (sockeye)	0.259
Beans,* mature dry seeds, raw	
White, 1 pound	0.653

* Red beans are similar, but lima beans have only half as much calcium. Soybeans contain 1.025 grams per pound raw.

Of course, when using nonfat dry milk powder, one can increase the amount of powder used in proportion to liquid. If a recipe calls for a cup of milk, it can be made with one-half cup dry milk powder to one cup of water rather than one-third. In this way additional calcium can be included in the diet.

Some people are unable to tolerate milk. Often these are adults who cannot absorb the milk sugar, lactose, from the digestive tract. A suitable substitute for whole milk is one of the enriched soybean milks or fortified soybean milks. The label on the can should clearly state that its calcium content is the same or similar to that of whole milk. Such products usually have to be obtained at a health food store, but when a fortified milk made from soybean is available, it can be used as a substitute for a calcium source. Read the label carefully, however. Soybean oil is low in saturated fat, but coconut oil (often listed as "vegetable oil") is mostly saturated fat. To avoid saturated fat, avoid products that contain "vegetable oil" and coconut oil. Some individuals will need to take calcium tablets prescribed by their doctor to meet their calcium needs. In middle-aged and older people one of the calcium salts, calcium carbonate, is not well absorbed if there is a low production of acid by the stomach. Many older people do have this problem, and for them the tablets are not a good choice as a source of calcium.

A proper exercise program is important in preventing osteoporosis. This does not mean overdoing it or going in for unusual or unnatural forms of physical activity. As with almost all other aspects of body function and maintenance, there is an optimal amount done in a correct way. Such a program should be directed toward helping to retain muscle mass and the strength of the muscles and their full range of motion. The exercise should strengthen the muscles that prevent bending or stooping and should stretch those muscles which tend to contract. A further discussion of preventive exercise programs is included in Chapter Sixteen.

The preventive program for osteoporosis is highly concerned with the maintenance of normal hormonal levels in the body. This may well be an individual matter but the weight of evidence is in favor of replacing hormones when they are deficient and thereby preventing osteoporosis in the future. For example, particularly at the time of menopause, unless there is clear evidence of sufficient sex hormones in the body, hormone replacement should be undertaken in preference to waiting until after the bones have already shown degeneration. Probably a similar program should be developed for men who show definite evidences of decreased sex hormone production unless the problem can be reversed by suitable exercise. The high death rate in men in the industrial societies (as in the United States) and the somewhat later development of osteoporosis in men as opposed to women have caused this problem to receive less consideration in men. If some of the other diseases that are responsible for the early senility and death of men can be eliminated, prevention of osteoporosis will become more important to the male.

Of course, the preventive program should include avoiding medicines which contribute to removing calcium from the bone and osteoporosis. The indiscriminate use of cortisone and related medicines is the chief culprit.

fourteen

The Skin, Hair, and Teeth

Although the skin shows changes over the years, these are not necessarily time dependent. The skin is a classic example of an organ which can constantly replace its older cells with young cells. Most skin changes are related to environmental factors and living habits.

There are certain alterations associated with different stages of life. The small baby has a smooth, clear, often pink skin. Women aspire to keep their babylike skin as a mark of beauty. With puberty and maturity the skin thickens and pores become more prominent. In many areas the fine hair over the surface of the skin becomes coarse and longer. The skin glands responsible for forming oily secretions become more active, particularly at puberty, setting the stage for the acne problems of the teenager. There are changing patterns of hair distribution from fetal development to the age of significant loss of hair over various parts of the body. Changes commonly ascribed to age occur mainly where the skin is constantly exposed, being most striking in the face, neck, and hands and least marked in areas not exposed. Microscopic studies of the skin of the buttocks, for example, may show few of the changes observed in the skin over the face or the back of the hands. This is one of the obvious indicators that environmental influences and living patterns play a major role in the differences in the skin seen with advancing years.

IMPORTANCE OF MOISTURE

The outer layer of the skin is called the epidermis. This is a layer of cells packed on top of each other like a pile of leaves. The larger cells are at the bottom, and as they move outward to the surface they are older and older. The older cells tend to dry out so that the outer layer of the epidermis is composed of flattened, dried cells, interlocked to form a tough, dry surface. They contain just enough moisture to be pliable. These older cells are constantly being shed from the surface of the skin. As the old cells are lost, new cells migrate outward to replace them.

The epidermal layer helps to retain moisture in the deeper layers. Part of the youthful appearance of the skin has to do with the amount of moisture it contains. If the skin loses its moisture, it becomes thin and dry, taking on the appearance attributed to age. The exposed surfaces dry out more easily than the unexposed surfaces. To prevent drying of the skin the humidity should be about 60 percent or more. The water in the skin is constantly being replaced by the flow of blood and lymph (the clear fluid) through the skin, water being lost at the surface by evaporation. Sweating is an active process which helps prevent drying of the skin.

The unexposed areas are more moist because the clothing traps the natural moisture at the surface of the skin. There is a constant loss of water from the skin which is not visible and for this reason is called insensible perspiration. When it is trapped by a garment, the air at the surface of the skin is more moist or humid. This is a factor in retaining the more youthful characteristics of the skin over unexposed regions of the body.

One of the important factors in the aging of the skin is the dry air in a heated house. In winter the humidity of many homes is less than that of the Sahara Desert. The heating dries out the air, and if the moisture is not replaced, remarkably low humidity results. This is undesirable for the normal function of the respiratory tract, and it is equally undesirable as far as maintaining the normal moisture of the skin is concerned. Coating the skin with any of the simple oils or petroleum products such as Vaseline creates an oily film and prevents the evaporation of moisture from the deeper cells. In this sense the oils and lubricants are moisturizers. An effective skin moisturizer does not add water to the skin but prevents the loss of the natural water that should be in the skin.

In the deep layers of the epidermis are special cells which release a dark pigment called melanin. It is this pigment that gives the skin its color. There are about the same number of pigment cells in black people as in white people and in those with all gradations of color in between. The difference is in how much pigment is produced by these cells. When the pigment is diffused out smoothly in the different cells of the skin, it provides a smooth even tan or darker color. If the pigment is grouped in clumps, the skin is freckled. In older people the clumping of pigment causes large dark spots, and since the pigment is not diffused to the nearby cells, the skin tends to be lighter around the spots. Total absence of pigment causes white patches or vitiligo, a problem which is particularly distressing to individuals with brown or darker skin. The large brownish spots are commonly called "liver spots."

Wind, sun, and lack of moisture in the air tend to dry out the skin. The exposed surfaces of the skin are normally protected by nature's devices. The man, usually exposed to more environmental factors, develops a heavy beard to protect his face during the most active phase of his life against the ravages of wind and sun. Over the forehead, nose, and areas of the face not normally covered by abundant hair are small glands in the deeper layers of the skin that provide an oily film for the surface. Both the hair (which is fine) and the oily secretions are also present in the female, but usually not in such an abundant amount.

Another common cause of drying is excessive washing, particularly with harsh soaps. Soaps and cleansing agents that remove the oil from the surface of the skin remove nature's lubricant, which was intended to serve as a moisturizer. The lack of oil, combined with the irritating chemicals found in many soaps and cleansers, causes the skin to lose moisture. Women often follow washing by the application of some form of moisturizer which helps to negate this problem. Men are less inclined to use a moisturizer.

SPOTS AND CANCER

A common problem with advancing years and exposed skin is the development of small, raised gray spots. These are the accumulations of superficial cells into plaques. Often observed in older people, they were originally called senile keratoses, but since they are seen also in younger people, they are now more properly called just keratoses. They occur on the exposed areas of the skin, most often over the face and hands. They are more common in men than women and can follow an injury such as a nick with the razor while shaving. They will not disappear spontaneously. They should be removed by a doctor, usually by chemicals, scraping, or surgical procedures. A significant number may progress to become cancer. Therefore none should be neglected.

The most prevalent form of cancer in men is skin cancer. This accounts for 21 percent of all the cancers in men, and 90 percent of the skin cancers are on the face. While some individuals may be more susceptible to cancer than others, it is clear that the exposure to sun, wind, and drying is a major factor in the development of skin cancer. *All skin cancers can be cured if they are treated adequately early enough.* More serious problems are the result of neglect.

THE ELASTIC LAYER

Beneath the epidermis is the inner layer of the skin, or dermis, sometimes called the glandular layer because it contains the various skin glands. These include the sweat glands, which produce normal odorless sweat, and the specialized sweat glands, really sex glands, which form sweat that emits an odor. Neither form of sweat gland is particularly important as far as the aging process is concerned. The hair follicles are located in the dermal layer, as are the oil-producing sebaceous glands. The skin is nature's radiator. It serves to cool the body. The hot blood inside the body is circulated to the skin where it interfaces with the external environment and has a chance to cool off. To achieve cooling, the external environment must be cooler than the body temperature. The loss of moisture from the surface of the skin, even if it is insensible perspiration, is evaporative cooling, not greatly different from what takes place in the water-cooled air conditioner.

The dermal layer also contains many elastic fibers. These provide the normal stretch mechanism of the skin and make it return to normal size after being stretched. The dermal layer gradually fades into loose fibrous connective tissue and attaches itself to the fibrous and membranous linings of the underlying muscles and other structures. Beneath the dermal layer where it merges with the connective tissues are areas for fat desposits. In some regions of the body there may be relatively little or no fat, as underneath the palm or over the upper eyelid. In other areas—over the cheeks or the buttocks, for example—there is likely to be more fat tissue. The fat tissue provides padding for the underlying structures and to the overlying skin.

It is the dermal layer with its elastic fibers that undergoes many of the changes of aging. Sun and exposure, as well as other factors, act on the elastic fibers in such a way that the skin loses its normal elasticity. It begins to behave like an overstretched balloon. Then, as underlying fat is lost too, the skin hangs in folds and wrinkles, about the face and neck particularly, and gives the characteristic appearance of the older face. The changes in the elastic tissue in the dermal layer, commonly noted over the face, do not occur in unexposed regions of the body.

Still another factor contributing to the folds in the skin is loss of muscle mass in the face and neck and perhaps loss of tone of muscles directly under the skin. Superficial muscles are attached to the inner surface of the skin. You can see their loose fibers along the neck if you will stick out your jaw and tense it; the strands of the muscle directly beneath the skin will then stand out. Segments of the superficial muscles extend under the skin of the lower face and neck. The distribution of muscle fibers varies considerably from one person to another. Family characteristics also often have a lot to do with the rapidity of changes in the skin. It is not unusual for a woman to have skin very much like her mother's.

SMOKER'S WRINKLES

Recent studies have shown that in addition to the exposure factors of sun, soap, chemicals, and wind, cigarette smoking helps cause skin wrinkles. A heavy smoker of 40 may have skin wrinkling similar to that of an individual 10 or 20 years older. Look at the skin of people in their 40's who are heavy cigarette smokers and compare it to that of your acquaintances in the same age group who are nonsmokers. The wrinkles at the corners of the eyes, or crow's-feet, are often especially deep and evident in heavy cigarette smokers. In one recent study by physicans it was claimed that the physicians could separate the heavy smokers from the nonsmokers merely by examining their face wrinkles. Heavy smokers also tend to develop prominent wrinkles around the edges of the mouth. These are particularly difficult to correct, even with cosmetic surgery.

THE FURROWED BROW

Contraction of the facial muscles also contributes to wrinkling. This is perhaps best seen in the forehead. The muscle directly underlying the skin over the forehead is the frontalis muscle. When it is contracted, the vertical wrinkles at the root of the nose and the other wrinkles across the brow occur. These wrinkles are secondary to the contraction of the frontalis muscle and are unrelated to aging processes. This is one reason why they are less evident in the morning on first arising. They can usually be abolished, at least temporarily, by preventing contraction of the muscle, as follows: A piece of ordinary brown wrapping paper tape, dampened on the gummed side, is attached to the skin while the skin is smoothed out and the muscle relaxed. When the tape dries it forms a splint, making it difficult for the underlying muscle to contract. In a very short time the wrinkles will no longer be seen. Using paper tape in this way trains the individual out of the habit of overcontraction of the frontalis muscle, helping to prevent the wrinkles over the brow and at the root of the nose. The tape should be torn roughly so that there will be no markings at the edge of the tape; for large pieces the edges of the tape can be notched or torn so that a hard firm line of attachment to the skin is not evident.

PROTECTING THE SKIN

When one understands the mechanisms that contribute to "aging" of the skin, it is clear that much can be done to prevent these problems. And once more a preventive program is often more effective than a remedial effort. High on the list of preventive measures is avoidance of overexposing the skin to sun and wind. Individuals with very dark skin are a little better protected because of the heavy pigment layer which tends to screen out the sun's harmful rays and the damaging effects that the ultraviolet radiation can have on the elastic tissue in the dermal layer. But regardless of the color of the skin, drying effects of weather can cause loss of skin moisture. An old-fashioned girl who thought that beauty was a soft, pale skin and avoided the sun did indeed maintain the youthfulness of her skin better than her modern sun-worshiping counterpart. The individual who wants that outdoorsy suntanned look should acquire it carefully, always remembering that ultraviolet light, essential to the tanning process, itself causes early wrinkling of the skin, and that a single excessive exposure which results in sunburn can irreparably damage the skin. Obtain a suntan gradually. Expose the skin to the sun only 15 minutes at a time for a number of days until a healthy tan is achieved. The best time to take the sun is in the early morning hours and late afternoon, thus avoiding peak exposure. Individuals who must work outside or be exposed to the sun should do so if possible in either the mornings or late afternoons, again avoiding the peak intensity of sun radiation. Even though gradual tanning is better than a burn, it is still a protective reaction of the skin to injury and contributes to drying and wrinkling of the skin.

The second rule in preventing changes of the skin is to maintain the skin's moisture. Avoid excessive washing and overuse of chemical cleaning agents and soaps which tend to irritate the skin and remove its natural oils. Cleanliness may be next to godliness, but overdoing it removes the oily protection over the surface of the skin man was created with. Indeed, overdoing it can even undo God's work. When the cleaning process is over, rather than adding other chemical irritants to the surface of the skin, it is wise to cover the skin with a thin oily layer—unless, of course, the skin is excessively oily to begin with. The application of a superficial skin oil is particularly important for individuals who tend to have dry skins. Almost any oil is suitable—olive oil, corn oils, safflower oil, or any of the petroleum-base lubricants or creams. It can be wiped off immediately with a dry cloth, and a thin layer of oil will remain to cover the outer portion of the skin and act as a moisturizer.

To retain skin moisture one must avoid exposure to low-humidity environments. The most common and practical area for concern is the house in the winter months. To prevent drying of the skin adequate humidity in the house should be maintained. A heated house without any means of adding moisture to the air often has an unacceptably low humidity. Avoid cigarettes since they are clearly linked to premature wrinkling of the skin. Do not become overweight. Obesity leads to fat deposits and overstretching of the skin. In the young skin its elasticity will bring it back into place without excessive wrinkling, but prolonged overstretching, as occurs in long-term obesity, or overstretching as a result of repeated cycles of gaining and losing weight contributes to loss of elasticity of the skin. There is no more clear evidence of this than the stretch marks over the abdomen that many women experience following pregnancy.

A program designed to maintain the muscles in the face and neck is important, though good studies of the effectiveness of such programs have really not been undertaken. Many enthusiastic claims are made for various facial exercises but there are far fewer well-documented studies. Even so, common sense and the physiology of the face and underlying muscles suggest that exercise can and does play a vital role. The size of the muscles in the face needs to be retained by special exercises, discussed in Chapter Sixteen.

FACE LIFTS

For those who have not been successful in fending off the ravages of time and exposure there is always the face lift. It does not restore youth to the skin but it can make the face look a lot better. It is a cosmetic procedure, not a youth treatment. Nevertheless, it has a place in treating problems of aging. The appearance has a tremendous impact upon the personality and self-image. If a person thinks he looks old, he will feel old. Once the idea is implanted firmly in the brain that one is old, one begins to act old and indeed becomes old. The psychological factors have far-reaching consequences in the process of aging. To the extent that cosmetic surgery makes a person look young, it is "instant psychotherapy." Not all people can expect to have a successful outcome from cosmetic surgery, and each case must be carefully evaluated by a competent and reliable plastic surgeon who regularly performs cosmetic surgery. There are a number of quacks in this field, so the best approach is to obtain a recommendation from the county medical society or the state medical society before going to see a doctor you have heard friends talk about or one you have read about in a magazine.

There are varied techniques for face lifts. You should select one that does not distort the facial features—does not, that is, alter the distances between the normal hairline and the rest of the face. If the hairline is pulled back too far it will make the face look large, which is not always the desired outcome.

A face lift is not as simple a procedure as many popular accounts would suggest. It takes months for the face to heal completely. There are numerous parts to a complete job, which includes work on the "bags" under the eyes and on excess skin above the eyes, correcting crow's-feet wrinkles, and lifting the sagging skin around the jaw and neck. Before contemplating any of these procedures the individual should improve the general health as much as possible, including eliminating all excess body fat, building up the facial muscles, correcting the habit of frowning that contributes to the furrowed brow, improving the moisturizing of the skin, and then evaluating the need for surgical correction.

THE HAIR PROBLEM

Although advanced old age is associated with a certain amount of loss of hair, it is erroneous to assume that gray hair or loss of hair necessarily means aging of the body. Both are strongly influenced by inherited characteristics unrelated to aging of the body. Man's evolutionary process is marked by progressive loss of hair. Both males and females of future generations may have to reconcile themselves to a relatively hairless existence. Actually it is not correct to say "hairless." There are about the same number of hairs in the adult male and female, even on the face. In the male the facial hair becomes coarse and long. In the female each individual hair may be so fine that it is not visible to the naked eye or is just fuzz. Distribution of hair changes even during fetal life. While the baby is developing, it may have hair over much of its face, particularly the forehead. Before delivery, the hair between the eyebrows and on the forehead is usually lost. In some instances, however, a large amount of hair is still present on the forehead. Before birth or shortly after a lot of the excess hair on the baby's body is replaced by finer adult hair.

Loss of hair, or balding, is really an extension of the process that begins with the baby's development. The loss of hair over the forehead merely proceeds backward, producing a progressively receding hairline.

In adult life there may be as many as 150,000 hairs on the head. Each hair has a long shaft that terminates in a little bulb somewhat like an onion. If a hair is pulled out, the bulb or follicle region generates a new hair. There is a constant loss and replacement of hair in normal people. About 10 percent of the individual hair follicles are usually resting, but they are not dead and soon they take their turn in generating new hair. A hair can be lost from a follicle because a new hair is ready to replace it. A single hair may mature, stop growing, and then wait to be lost and replaced by a new one. When the rate of producing new hairs is equal to the rate of losing old ones, no hair thinning or baldness will be evident.

In some animals all the new hairs are ready to be produced at the same time the old hairs have reached their maturity and stopped growing. At this point all of the old hair is lost almost simultaneously to be replaced by a new coat. It is during the so-called molting season that this exchange takes place.

Loss of hair or early baldness can occur in the teens, but it increases in frequency with age.

There are numerous factors related to loss of hair. A severe illness, particularly if it has been associated with a high fever, can cause the hair follicles to stop producing new hair and can bring about loss of the old hair. It is, however, a temporary loss, and the bald areas will eventually be replaced with new hair. Nervousness can sometimes make a person lose large patches of hair, but the hair will be replaced. Women may become greatly concerned about the loss of hair immediately after pregnancy. It is temporary, and after a few months new hair will grow.

A contributing factor in baldness is beauty treatment. Hair dyes and tints are likely to be very damaging to the hair follicles, especially if they are used too frequently. Part of the harmful effect is induced by bleaches. Tinting or coloring treatments should not be done more often than is recommended by the manufacturer of the product used. When the scalp shows signs of irritation and there is excess falling of hair, it is time to stop the beauty treatment. Otherwise, there may be little or no hair to beautify.

Straightening the hair or pulling it back tight in a ponytail or curling or any procedure that puts it under tension contributes to hair loss. Anyone who has a problem of increased hair loss should immediately stop all forms of styling which involve putting the hair under stress, leave the hair loose, and avoid chemicals, tints, and other treatments. The best course of action is to use only mild shampoos, not too frequently, allow the hair to hang loose, and use a soft brush sparingly. Once the hair follicle is actually dead, it is not rejuvenated. Sometimes it is difficult to tell whether a hair follicle is dead or resting, but time will provide the answer.

Hair transplants have been used in treating baldness. The hair follicles along the sides and back of the head are more sturdy and are less likely to cease functioning. Small plugs of hair follicles are taken from these areas and transplanted in rows across the bald areas. As these follicles take and grow out, they provide new hair for the bald areas. This is a long, expensive, difficult procedure, and the redistribution of the living hair follicles does not produce a full, thick head of hair, but it is a partial answer for individuals who would like to have some hair on top of their head.

Hair salves and many preparations have been advertised as helping cure or prevent baldness. To this date no really satisfactory treatment of this type has been devised. Specifically, there are no shampoos that will prevent or cure baldness. Such claims are purely fradulent. Because of the human desire to have hair, undoubtedly if and when a means of growing hair satisfactorily on bald heads or a means of preventing baldness is achieved, it will be a widely known fact and a very popular procedure.

Gray hair is simply hair which has lost its pigment. Pigment cells inside the hair shaft instill the color. Gray hair can occur very early in life, particularly as a familial characteristic. Rarely, gray hair, particularly in spots, will follow an illness and the pigment be regained. These are exceptional instances. Areas of gray hair next to a surgical incision may regain pigment. For the most part, hair that has once lost its pigment will not regain it. New hair that replaces old gray hair will be without pigment. If the hair does not lose its pigment, becoming gray or white, it will tend to darken with age.

There are a number of misconceptions about hair. Puberty, for example, does not cause a new hair growth on the face. It merely converts "peach fuzz" or even less obvious hairs to the coarse, rapid-growing hair of the male beard. This change is directly due to male hormone, and if male hormone is given to females, the hair on their faces too will become prominent.

Another common misconception is that cutting off hair will cause it to become stiff or larger or more prominent. Shaving does not increase the stiffness or toughness of the beard in either men or women. Cutting off the hair at its base leaves the hard, tough stubble at the surface of the skin. As the hair grows out longer, it loses some of its material and becomes more flexible. Thus, shaving or cutting merely allows one to feel the tough, original base of the hair itself.

TEETH AND AGE

The general appearance of the face is greatly influenced by the teeth. The older, toothless person is a classic picture of senility as we now think of it. However, there is an increased awareness that loss of teeth is not always necessary, and if they are lost, replacement with appropriate appliances can go a long way toward maintaining normal facial structure.

Any of the disorders that lead to loss of teeth are not the effects of age alone but more often the result of neglect. With the knowledge that has been gained in recent times a new generation in the United States and some other industrial regions will have better, firmer teeth, in part because of the widespread fluoridation of drinking water. This, along with improved dentifrices, has significantly decreased the number of cavities and poor dental structure so common in the past. It is possible that succeeding generations will arrive at old age with functionally good teeth and without the dental problems typical of many older people today.

If the tooth itself escapes cavitation and survives as it enters old age, there is an increased fluoride deposit in the enamel. This is responsible for the yellowing characteristic of older teeth. With time more calcium is also deposited in the teeth, which makes them harder. Thus, the older tooth is hard and yellow. The constant grinding process of the teeth gradually wears down the cusp and there is some loss of cusp height.

Aside from the preservation of the teeth themselves, there is the problem of maintaining the jawbone and sockets for the teeth, as well as the tissue around the teeth, called the periodontal tissue. Inflammation of these areas is the common problem of periodontal disease (pyorrhea). Inflammation of the soft tissues around the teeth, causing bone resorption, can even cause loss of the teeth. Proper dental hygiene, scaling of the teeth to remove plaque formation, and proper stimulation of the gingiva (gum) help prevent such an occurrence. If too much resorption of the jawbone has taken place, a dentureless mouth is a certainty, and the only course then is false dentures.

The jawbone can be affected in older people by osteoporosis. Just as the bony tissues can dissolve in the vertebrae and other bones in the body, the jawbone can lose calcium and its strength. This weakening can contribute to the development of dental problems in later years. As discussed previously, osteoporosis can be prevented.

Exercise of jaw muscles helps prevent degeneration of the jaw. This is one reason chewing is good for the teeth. When dogs chew bones they strengthen their jaws and clean their teeth in addition to obtaining needed calcium and phosphorus. The exercise program recommended to help prevent facial wrinkling also helps maintain the jaw structures.

A frequent difficulty in old age is maintaining oral hygiene. If an older person has lost the ability to use the hands properly, as with strokes and diseases of the brain, he is going to have more trouble in attending to oral hygiene. The result may be inflammations of the gingiva and soft tissues around the teeth.

In summary, a major share of the dental problems attributed to old age can be at least minimized or even prevented by proper programs beginning in childhood with the development of the teeth and an appropriate preventive dental program extended throughout life.

PART III

What Can Be Done Now

fifteen

Diet

One of the major differences between societies in which people live to vigorous old age and societies in which longevity is a rarity is the people's eating habits. Diet is an important factor in atherosclerosis, which in turn is responsible for many of the bodily changes of acquired aging. The diets of different groups of people vary greatly both in amount and in type of food eaten. In general, in the affluent nations, where excess calories are consumed, the incidence of atherosclerosis and senility is much higher than in the less affluent nations.

Animal studies suggest that the effects of diet on longevity begin with infant feeding. According to Dr. Roy L. Walford at UCLA Medical Center, decreasing the caloric intake by one-third in rats and mice extended their life span from 50 to 100 percent longer than that of the animals eating the higher caloric diet. The underfed mice and rats also had far fewer cancers than their fat friends. Apparently, for the best effect, the caloric restriction should begin with youth, although some benefit can still be obtained in the adult animals. Stretching out the developmental phase or slowing the growth cycle is related to increased longevity. There is every reason to think that these same principles would apply to humans. The type of foods as well as the total amount of calories is important. The effects of the type of diet on various animals have been studied for years. Recently Dr. Robert Wissler, of the University of Chicago, reported that Rhesus monkeys eating the typical American (affluent) diet developed artery-clogging atherosclerosis of the type responsible for heart disease, strokes, and many other aspects of acquired aging. The monkeys liked the rich American diet, just as people do, and they gained weight on it while they were clogging their arteries. When the monkeys' diet was changed to one containing less calories, less fat, and less sugar, the fatty deposits disappeared from the arteries, suggesting that changing the diet enables one to reverse the clogging process to some extent.

While consuming their normal diet, monkeys almost never develop atherosclerosis. These and countless other studies strongly imply that even in mature individuals a significant change in the diet can do much to arrest or even reverse the process of atherosclerosis. These observations, coupled with knowledge of the role of the diet in providing abundant vitamins and minerals, suggest that what we eat really is a major factor in what we are and how long we'll be that way. To favorably influence health and longevity, it's never too early or too late to begin a proper diet.

OBESITY

It is generally true that there are a lot more old skinny people than there are old fat people, although everyone knows many exceptions. Obesity may well be the most important medical problem of modern civilization. It is an obvious indicator of adverse habits that lead to early acquired aging and the numerous diseases associated with atherosclerosis. Obesity can cause increased blood pressure and increased blood fat particles and cholesterol, accelerating atherosclerosis. In addition, obesity brings a higher incidence of diabetes, and it often indicates less than optimal levels of physical activity. Any middle-aged American male and sometimes younger men who have significant obesity will almost always have early fatty deposits starting the process of clogging the arteries to the heart muscle.

Much of the confusion about the effects of obesity upon health has been caused by failure to understand what obesity is. There is not much difference in acquired aging and associated diseases between groups who are 30 pounds overweight and groups who are 50 pounds overweight. Many studies evaluating the influence of obesity have made the mistake of investigating diseases in two groups of fat people rather than diseases in optimally lean individuals and fat ones. For individuals who need to lose 50 pounds and lose only 10, their effort is somewhat akin to Rockefeller's losing a dime.

We are culturally habituated to the idea that a certain amount of fat padding is an indication of health. This is a residual from the fact that tuberculosis was the leading cause of death in 1900, when heart disease and many of the problems of atherosclerosis were relatively unknown. In those days, when tuberculosis and cancer were the big killers, weight loss was an indication of ill health. The health picture has changed dramatically since 1900, and now just the opposite is true Even many doctors' ideas of how much a person should weigh have been strongly influenced by social concepts rather than based on sound scientific observations. Young individuals in optimal health really carry very little fat on their body.

I studied a group of pentathletes over a period of several years and was always impressed with the physical evidence of their lack of fat. These young men were endurance athletes competing in the five events of distance running, swimming, pistol shooting, horseback riding, and fencing. One way of expressing the degree of obesity is to measure the percentage of body weight composed of fat. In over half of these men fat comprised less than 11 percent of their body weight. It was a rare individual who had a value of 15 percent or more, and individuals whose percentage of body fat was only 7 or 8 percent were not unusual. Yet they were in peak physical condition, representing optimal health by all standards. Similar measurements of Swedish gymnasts and other endurance athletes have provided comparable data. In persons this lean you can pick up the skin around the small of the back and elsewhere without finding any evidence of fat deposits. The fat stores so common in most people are simply nonexistent.

It is generally accepted that having 17 percent of the body weight in fat is normal. Many young American men who are considered lean by most standards have this much fat, and in countless others approximately 20 percent of the body weight is fat. With increasing age, the percentage of body fat rises in most affluent societies in both men and women. To illustrate in terms of cholesterol level: In the young pentathletes whom I studied, the highest cholesterol value in a battery of 16 subjects was 220. Three-fourths of these individuals had values below 200, and over half of them had values of 155 or below. In other words, the cholesterol levels were all below those we normally associate with atherosclerosis. The 50 percent with cholesterol levels below 155 would have a body chemistry very conducive to avoiding atherosclerosis. The problem, of course, is that most athletes do not continue their program throughout life and lose their advantage with the years. In an older group, approximately 30 years of age, the Gemini and Apollo astronauts were slightly heavier, but still over half of them had cholesterol values of 175 or below. A majority were in optimal condition (but not all) and as a group exhibited better health characteristics than their same age counterparts in the regular flying population of the U.S. Air Force. In a controlled study group of pilots of the same age which I used to compare to the astronauts, over one-fourth had cholesterol values of 250 or higher, values in the range that would significantly increase the likelihood of artery blockage by atherosclerosis, leading to heart attacks, strokes, and subsequent senility. As a group, these individuals were fatter than the astronauts while the astronauts were a bit fatter than the pentathletes. In my opinion, from the total available information from the literature and personal studies, obesity is a crucial factor in the development of atherosclerosis. It is frequently an indicator of disturbed body chemistry which leads to atherosclerosis. It is an indicator of either eating too much or having too low a level of physical activity and usually both.

To illustrate the important difference between "normal" weight in pounds and being "lean," I cite one of the astronauts. At age 30, he was 6 feet tall and weighed 158 pounds. Only 17 percent of his body weight was fat, but his cholesterol level was 300. By physical measurement he was slender. His body weight at ages 20 and 25 had been 154 pounds, and the most he had ever weighed was 164 pounds. Nevertheless, with a change in diet and a suitable exercise program, he was able to change his body composition, converting fat to muscle and in general decreasing the fat stores in his body. Two years later he weighed 155 pounds, but only 9 percent of his body weight was fat and at that time his cholesterol level was 167, well within the range of that noted in many of the endurance athletes, representing a decrease to almost half of its previous value. At this low value, his cholesterol level would no longer be a significant factor in causing atherosclerosis. At the previous high level of 300, his chance of developing atherosclerosis was much enhanced. This is not an isolated example, and it shows that the important factor is not so much the pounds on the scale but the body composition. This man actually increased his muscle weight while he was decreasing his fat deposits.

Another young man was studied over a period of years and showed what can be done to reverse an undesirable pattern. He was 5 feet 10 inches tall and at ages 20 and 25 weighed 175 pounds, being on the chubby side. The most he had ever weighed was 183 pounds. At age 32 he weighed 180 pounds, and 21 percent of his body weight was fat. His cholesterol level was 220. One year later, after physical conditioning and a dietary program, he had decreased his weight to 161 pounds, and only 8 percent of his body weight was fat. His cholesterol level had fallen to 162. Here again is a remarkable example of what can be done to lower the cholesterol level and the fatty particles in the blood, which in turn should reduce the likelihood of developing atherosclerotic clogging of the arteries.

CALORIC BALANCE

We have all heard people insist that they just don't eat a thing and still gain weight. That's about as logical as assuming that the balance of a person's checking account is growing even though he is not depositing any money. Fat deposits in the body depend on two simple facts, *calories in* and *calories out*, just like money in and money out. If there are more calories in than calories out, the deposit is in ugly fat deposits, which can damage health. True, certain factors may alter how many of the calories are available for energy and how many are used to cause fat deposits. A person may indeed be tired and lacking in energy, even though he is eating enough calories to form fat deposits. Moreover, a person can eat little and still gain weight, but he is obviously using very few calories, usually because of limited physical activity.

In some individuals with various medical disorders food is never really absorbed by the body through the circulation to the digestive tract but instead is rapidly propelled through the bowel. Clearly, then, the caloric balance of the body is really dependent upon two things: how many calories are absorbed and how many are used. Since it takes a lot of physical energy to use many calories, diet is often the main factor in causing obesity. One of the first dietary goals in maintaining optimal health is control of the caloric intake. To achieve it one needs to be "calorie conscious" and have some idea of the caloric values of foods.

There is much confusion in evaluating foods, most of which can be swept away merely by expressing the caloric values of foods, including the calorie value of the food constituents: proteins, carbohydrates, and fats. This obviates the problems associated with expressing foods in terms of weight (grams or ounces) or volume. Much of the confusion about food values stems from the fact that they can be expressed three different ways: by weight, volume, and calorie content. A cup of whole wheat contains more calories and nutrients than a cup of puffed wheat, not because puffing the wheat causes it to lose any of its calories or nutrients, but rather because the measurement is done by volume and the puffed wheat has been blown up by air. In terms of weight, 4 ounces of puffed wheat contains about the same food value as 4 ounces of whole wheat. These problems can be obviated by stating the calories for a serving of a given food.

Another important point is that foods contain far more than just calories. Water content is a major factor in determining how many calories any food has. Indigestible cellulose and a small amount of minerals and vitamins will be present, but it is chiefly water that dilutes the calorie content of many of the foods we eat. We can appreciate this point from the caloric difference between lard and lean round steak with all the fat removed. Three and one-half ounces (100 grams) of lard will contain a little over 900 calories. The same weight of the separable lean of round steak will contain only 135 calories. It is not just that there are more calories in fat than in protein; about 30 percent of the calories of the separable lean of round steak are from fat. The difference is that over 70 percent of the 3½ ounces of raw round steak is water, whereas pure lard contains no water. This is an important consideration in diets based on so-called high-protein foods, many of which really contain lots of water providing bulk to the diet and very few calories.

Sugar, a refined food, contains only 0.5 percent water for its weight. Thus 3½ ounces (100 grams) of sugar contains 385 calories, far more than would be found in a similar weight of the separable lean of round steak, but considerably less than is found in pure lard. The difference between the calories in sugar and those in lard is the difference between the caloric values of carbohydrates and fat. Carbohydrates usually contain a little less than 4 calories per gram whereas pure fats like lard contain approximately 9 calories per gram. Protein foods, like egg white, contain a little less than 4 calories per gram of protein. Egg white, incidentally, is over 87 percent water. A general idea of the influence of water content on the caloric value of various foods is provided from the following list:

	Percent water	Calories
Egg white	87.6	51
Drum, redfish	80.2	80
Potatoes	79.8	76
Shrimp	78.2	91
Fryer chicken, light meat without skin	77.2	101
Bananas	75.7	85
Round steak, separable lean	72.7	135
Butter	15.5	716
Wheat flour, all-purpose enriched	12.0	364
Sugar	0.5	385
Lard	0.0	902

You can plan your eating habits better if you understand which foods contain lots of calories per weight or bulk. These foods are the refined sweets, such as sugar, or foods made from sugar, syrups, or honey, like candies, cakes, and cookies; the fats (both vegetable and animal) which occur in food such as nuts, lard, butter, and margarine; fat meats of all kinds, fat fish (fat salmon), and fat poultry (like fat hens); refined cereals (like flour); and alcohol. Incidentally, since alcohol contains 7 calories per gram, individuals who consume large amounts of alcohol are ingesting an appreciable number of calories from that source. By contrast, foods which are low in calories are lean meats, fish, and poultry, skim milk, egg white, most fruits and vegetables, and many of the natural cooked cereals like oatmeal and rice.

REDUCING PLAN

If you have any evidence of fat deposits, you need to get rid of them. For most people with this problem a significant reduction in calorie intake is in order, best undertaken through a sensible, long-term project. Crash programs don't work, for either diet or exercise. You need to avoid fad diets; most of them are not balanced diets and cannot be continued for any length of time without the possibility of injuring your health because of vitamin and mineral deficiencies.

Many fad diets are based on the use of foods containing a great deal of bulk, and since protein is satisfying, some of them are based on "high-protein" food, which means lean meat. As previously mentioned, 70 percent of lean meat is water. Not all "high-protein" diets are low in fat, however. Even with all of the visible fat cut away, about one-third of the calories in lean round steak are from fat. Many other cuts of meat, as well as some fish and poultry, contain far more fat.

A gimmick which is often added to the high-protein diet is the elimination of carbohydrates, whether they occur in the form of sugar or in milk or in vegetables, fruits, or cereals. Carbohydrates influence the kidneys to retain a certain amount of water, but this is a healthy action. Cutting out carbohydrates causes a sudden loss of normal amounts of body water, which will decrease the pounds of weight as measured by the scale but will not do anything to eliminate fat deposits, unless the diet makes you sick.

The only way to reduce fat deposits is to restrict calorie intake and increase calorie use. Pills are sometimes taken to curb the appetite but they stimulate the nervous system and have many adverse effects on the body. They should never be used except under a reputable physician's supervision. Starvation diets can upset the chemistry of the body and cause serious health hazards.

An important part of reducing is learning proper dietary habits so the problem won't recur. This means learning to eat foods that contain less calories per unit of food bulk—for example, leafy vegetables, lean meats, and skim milk—and avoiding adding large quantities of fat during food preparation.

For most people who are reasonably active, a 1500-calorie-a-day diet will gradually induce weight reduction. Some individuals who are exceptionally inactive will lose weight very slowly on this program. Women between the ages of 35 and 55 often use an average of only 1850 calories a day, and those over 55 may use as little as 1700 a day. Since there are 3500 calories in a pound of fat, it would take a long time to lose much fat on such a program. However, this is a good place to start because it provides a means of establishing a well-balanced diet suitable for the reducing plans of many people. Foods chosen from the following list will comprise approximately a 1500-calorie well-balanced diet, including all the essential vitamins and minerals necessary for health (these measurements are all for the edible portion of food).

All of these each day (List A)	Calories
1 glass of orange juice	110
1 quart of fortified skim milk	600
2 slices of bread (1 slice 1 oz.)	
or 2 dinner rolls	150

Plus one of the following (List B)	
Bran flakes 40% (2 cups)	200
Corn flakes (2 cups)	200
Wheat flakes (2 cups)	200
Wheat, puffed (2½ cups)	140
Wheat, shredded (2 biscuits)	180
Oatmeal, cooked (1 cup)	130
Rice, cooked (1 cup)	225

Plus any two of the following (List C)	
Beef, separable lean only,	
raw weight 3½ oz.	150

Chicken, fryer, ½ lb. raw weight
  with bone and skin (remove skin
  before serving)   150–200
Fish, lean, 6 oz. raw weight   150

Plus any two of the following (List D)

Asparagus, cooked, drained, 1 cup   30
Broccoli, cooked (⅔ cup, 3½ oz.)   27
Brussels sprouts, cooked (⅔ cup, 3½ oz.)   37
Cabbage, cooked (1 cup)   30
Carrots, cooked (1 cup)   30
Cauliflower, cooked (1 cup)   25
Green peas, cooked (½ cup)   58
Squash, cooked (½ cup)
  Acorn   55
  Butternut   68
  Hubbard   50
  Winter   63
Tomato, raw, 1 (7 oz.)   40
Apricot, raw (3½ oz.)   51
Muskmelon or cantaloupe, netted (3½ oz.)   30
Nectarine, raw (3½ oz.)   64
Papaya, raw (3½ oz.)   36
Peaches, raw (3½ oz.)   38
Strawberries, raw (3½ oz.)   37

Plus any two of the following (List E)

Chard, Swiss, cooked, drained (3½ oz.)   20
Collards, cooked (1 cup)   55
Dandelion greens, cooked (1 cup)   60
Mustard greens, cooked (⅔ cup)   23
Spinach, cooked (⅔ cup)   27
Turnip greens, cooked (1 cup)   30

Individuals who use a small number of calories a day and wish to lose weight faster can safely eliminate the two slices of bread from List A and, if an even faster weight reduction is desired, can use only one of the items in List C. Otherwise, the number of items indicated should all be eaten to provide a balanced diet.

It is important to get protein from more than one source, since different kinds of proteins are necessary to include all of the essential amino acids. This objective can be met following the above diet, as various types of protein are provided by the milk, the cereals, and the meat. The diet ought to include some cereal, and one should therefore not neglect to use one of the items from List B.

If for any reason a person needs to restrict the caloric intake below the level suggested, it is wise to do so under a doctor's supervision. Vitamin supplements and possibly mineral supplements are usually necessary if anyone stays on a diet with fewer than 1500 calories for any length of time. Some of the commercial liquid diet preparations have been fortified with additional vitamins and minerals to make up for this lack.

You will note that sugar is not included in the diet. Individuals who can afford a few extra calories and still achieve their reducing goal should remember that 1 level teaspoonful of sugar has 16 calories. Most reasonably active people will find that 2 or 3 level teaspoonfuls of sugar per day in the diet does not cause any major difficulty. To use the amount of calories in 4 level teaspoonfuls of sugar, someone weighing 150 pounds will need to walk approximately one mile. Individuals who wish to be on a reducing program and use sugar should consider adding an appreciable amount of walking to their daily routine.

To judge how well one is doing in terms of calories in and calories out with any reducing diet program, with or without exercise, one should examine the change in the fat deposits underneath the skin. As long as significant residual fat deposits remain below the skin, additional fat reduction is indicated. Ideally, one should be able to trace the muscle patterns under the skin on the abdomen. To achieve this level of reduction of fat deposits usually requires a combined diet and exercise program.

FATS

One good reason for restricting fats in the diet is that all kinds of fats contain large numbers of calories. In addition, individuals who eat a high-calorie, high-fat diet are more prone to develop fatty particles and cholesterol in the blood, leading to fatty deposits in the arteries. Most scientists studying this problem therefore feel that the fat intake should be limited to less than 35 percent of all the calories ingested. Some authorities believe the level should be lower. In man's early development, he often ate diets much lower in fat since he depended heavily upon cereals, vegetables, fruits, seafoods, and lean meats.

In most societies in which individuals are relatively free from atherosclerosis for many years, the diet is limited in fat. The exceptions are those, like the Masai in Africa, whose diet is high in fat and high in cholesterol but whose total calorie intake is very low and daily level of physical activity is very high. They not uncommonly walk or trot 60 miles in a day. No doubt it would be possible to forego the limitation on fat ingestion if we markedly limited our total calorie intake and regularly engaged in levels of physical activity of that degree, but this drastic change is not likely or practical in most affluent societies.

There is also some evidence that the type of fat one uses in the diet is important. Fat is composed of a long chain of carbon atoms containing many hydrogen atoms. When the carbon chain holds as many hydrogen atoms as is chemically possible, it is called a *saturated* fat. Solid animal fats such as lard are saturated fats. Coconut oil is the main "vegetable oil" that is mostly saturated fat. Because it is often used in commercial products, if you choose to avoid saturated fats, you should avoid all foods labeled as containing coconut oil or unspecified "vegetable oil." The shorter-chain saturated fats—for example, butter—may not be solid.

Fats that have room to hold more hydrogen atoms are called *unsaturated* fats. If there is just one place on the carbon chain where hydrogen atoms can be added, the fat is called a *monounsaturated fat*. If there is more than one location along the carbon chain where hydrogen atoms can be added, it is called a *polyunsaturated fat*. Many animal fats contain both saturated and monounsaturated fats but scarcely any polyunsaturated fats—for example, beef. The polyunsaturated fats are found principally in vegetables, fish, and poultry. It is generally believed that the saturated fats are more likely to make the body produce an increased number of fatty particles in the blood and cause atherosclerosis. There is some experimental evidence that polyunsaturated fats actually reduce the cholesterol level in some people. Small amounts of certain polyunsaturated fats are essential for health. Recognition of this fact has given rise to the concept that it is better for a major portion of the fat ingested to come from polyunsaturated fats found in vegetables, fish, and poultry.

In 1970 the Inter-Society Commission on Heart Disease, after reviewing all the data available at that time on diet and heart disease, concluded that it was wise to limit the fat intake to 35 percent or less of the total calories and limit the saturated fat to 10 percent or less of the ingested calories. These recommendations can be achieved with minimal adjustments in dietary patterns. The Commission also recommended that the cholesterol intake should be limited to 300 milligrams a day. The amount of cholesterol in the diet appears to be of importance at least in some individuals as a factor in developing atherosclerosis.

As explained previously, the cholesterol levels in the body are often an index of the number of fatty particles in the blood and hence related to the development of atherosclerosis. If an individual is eating a high-calorie, high-fat diet, and the diet is not altered sufficiently, decreasing the cholesterol intake has very little effect. However, in individuals who do adequately control their calorie intake, their total fat intake, and their saturated fat intake, controlling the cholesterol intake as well is often beneficial. This goal, too, can be achieved with sensible dietary management.

There is no cholesterol in any foods except animal products. Thus,. from the standpoint of cholesterol intake, there need be no limitation on fruits, vegetables, nuts, or cereals. There is some cholesterol in most animal products, including lean beef, fish, and chicken, and small amounts even in skim milk, but only a few foods that are commonly eaten contain large amounts. The main one is the egg yolk. An egg yolk contains from 225 to 275 milligrams of cholesterol or nearly as much as the maximum daily amount recommended by the Inter-Society Commission on Heart Disease. Since one needs other foods, such as meat and at least skim milk, which have important nutrients but which also contain cholesterol, it is not possible to eat many egg yolks and still stay within the limitations recommended. The American Heart Association, in *The Way to a Man's Heart*, has long advocated limiting the ingestion of egg yolks to less than three a week, including those used in cooking.

Organ meats, particularly brains, also contain large amounts of cholesterol. Brains are not a very common food. Liver is a bit more common, and if one wishes to control cholesterol intake, liver and other organ meats should be used sparingly.

One can gain an appreciation of the relative cholesterol, fat, and saturated fat content of food by looking at the food classification list below:

I. **Low total fat—low saturated fat (calories less than 35 percent fat, less than 10 percent saturated fat)**

    A. No cholesterol   0 mg./3½ oz. (100 g.)

        Sugars, syrups, jellies, and jams
        Cereals
        Vegetables
        Berries, fruits, and melons
        Egg whites
        Beverages without dairy products or egg yolks
        Angel food cake

Some candies
Gelatin

B. Low cholesterol   0–100 mg./3½ oz. (100 g.)

Skim milk
Fortified skim milk
Fortified 1% skim milk
Nonfat dry milk powder
Buttermilk
Cheese, uncreamed cottage
Eggstra
Breads, rolls, and pastries, made without egg yolks
Bouillon
Most soups
Fish, lean
Shellfish, most
Chicken—fryer, without skin or breast with skin
                roaster, without skin
Turkey—young (24 weeks or less) without skin
              medium fat (less than 32 weeks) without skin
Cakes—few commercial; special home recipes

C. Moderate cholesterol   100–300 mg./3½ oz. (100 g.)

Lobster
Liver (chicken and hog)
Sweetbreads
Sponge cake

II. Low total fat—high saturated fat (calories less than 35 percent fat, more than 10 percent saturated fat)

A. Low cholesterol   0–100 mg./3½ oz. (100 g.)

2% low-fat milk
Canned milk (condensed, sweetened)
Ice milk, commercial
Cheese, creamed cottage
Some soups
Beef, separable lean only
Leg of lamb, separable lean only
Cornstarch pudding (no eggs)
Some candy

   B. Moderate cholesterol   100–300 mg./3½ oz. (100 g.)

   Heart
   Liver (beef, calf, lamb)
   Spleen

III. High fat—low saturated fat (calories more than 35 percent fat, less
than 10 percent saturated fat)

   A. No cholesterol

   Corn oil
   Safflower oil
   Salad dressings, commercial (some)
   Nuts
   Nut products

   B. Low cholesterol   0–100 mg./3½ oz. (100 g.)

   Fish (fat)
   Soups (some)
   Doughnuts

   C. Moderate cholesterol   100–300 mg./3½ oz. (100 g.)

   Cakes, commercial

   D. High cholesterol   300 mg./3½ oz. (100 g.)

   Caviar

IV. High fat—high saturated fat (calories more than 35 percent fat, more
than 10 percent saturated fat)

   A. No cholesterol

   Margarine (from vegetable oils)
   Cream, imitation (powdered or whipped)
   Coconut oil
   Cottonseed oil
   Olive oil
   Peanut oil
   Sesame oil
   Soybean oil
   Avocados
   Olives
   Brazil nuts

Coconuts
Potato chips
Salad dressing, commercial
Baking chocolate
Cocoa
Some candy

B. Low cholesterol   0–100 mg./3½ oz. (100 g.)

Lard
Cheese, processed
Milk, whole or canned evaporated
Breads, rolls, pastries (made without saturated fat or egg yolks)
Soups (usually cream soups)
Chicken—fryer with skin
             dark meat with skin
Turkey with skin
Meats with natural fat
Cold cuts
Fish (fat)
Cakes, cookies, pies
Ice cream
Some candy

C. Moderate cholesterol   100–300 mg/3½ oz. (100 g.)

Butter
Whipping cream
Heart with fat
Sweetbreads
Tongue

D. High cholesterol   300 mg./3½ oz. (100 g.)

Egg yolks
Brain
Kidney

MEAL PLANNING AND FOOD PREPARATION

Individuals who need to significantly limit their fat and saturated fat intake should plan their meals principally on items from Group I. Using a variety of foods from Groups I and II can easily provide a diet low in total fat and reasonably low in saturated fat. In meal planning it is a good idea, if you're going to use a dessert that falls in Group IV containing lots of fat and saturated fat (for example, ice cream), to have an entree from Group I, add no fat to your vegetables, and include a salad with no fats, being certain not to use eggs, avocados, or other fatty substances in preparation of the salad. Similarly, if the entree is going to contain a bit more fat, a dessert should be chosen which is low in total fat and low in saturated fat—for example, angel food cake served with sherbet.

A more detailed listing of the actual calories in specific food items which facilitates exact menu planning can be obtained by using the tabulated data in *What You Need to know About Food and Cooking for Health*.* The entire problem of food preparation and planning meals which can be restricted in calories, fats, saturated fats, and cholesterol, or any combination of these, can be solved with the food values available in tabular form in that publication.

Suffice it to say here that in preparing foods it is important to eliminate the addition of fat—for example, margarine or butter to the preparation of green peas or mashed potatoes. The addition of fats converts many vegetables from low-fat to high-fat items.

LOW-SALT DIET

The amount of salt in the diet may not be important to people who use salt sparingly. In those who use it in large quantities it can contribute to high blood pressure. One of the reasons for so many strokes in the Japanese has been identified as the liberal use of highly salted soy sauce. Even in normal people salt restriction leads to a modest decrease in normal blood pressure, in some instances to the point of being "low blood pressure," which is not harmful.

In people with high blood pressure restriction of salt, or more exactly sodium intake, is a valuable means of treatment. Dr. Walter Kempner of Durham, North Carolina, established that he could significantly lower the blood pressure and correct excess fluid accumulation by using a strict rice diet. His famous diet consisted of rice and fruit, both foods that contain very little sodium. A diet of fruit and rice alone is deficient in proteins and other essential items. It is not something you should try on your own.

* New York: The Viking Press, 1972.

Since the lower the blood pressure, the less likely the fatty deposits in the arteries, there is something to be said for salt restriction. The obvious place to begin is with eliminating the addition of salt for seasoning. A help here is the use of spices, common to the Orient. Small amounts of spices can replace the need for salt. Less salt will be required in conjunction with some household condiments, like catsup. Admittedly these sauces contain sodium, but one can use them with restraint and end up in a more favorable balance than many people do using salt alone for seasoning. Some dietary sauces contain limited amounts of sodium.

The type of food used is also important. If you eat mostly fruits, vegetables, and cereals and don't add salt, you will have a fairly restricted sodium diet. Most animal products do contain considerable amounts of sodium. Mature beans are an excellent source of protein and contain little sodium. Mature white bean seeds, raw, contain about three-fourths as many available calories as protein in the separable lean of the equivalent weight of round steak, raw. They have equal weights of protein content, but the protein in the meat is more readily digested, accounting for what difference exists. The amount of sodium in 3½ ounces (100 grams) of some common foods is as follows:

	Milligrams
Beans, white mature seeds, raw	19
Beef, round, separable lean, raw	65
Skim milk	52
Enriched white rice, raw	5
Wheat, soft red winter, raw	3
Bananas	1

By concentrating the diet on beans as a major source of protein, limiting meats and all other animal products, using adequate amounts of vegetables and fruits, and avoiding salt seasoning to excess, one can appreciably decrease the dietary intake of sodium. In some individuals if this regimen lowers the blood pressure significantly, it can be an important factor in preventing atherosclerosis. Remember, the pulmonary artery seldom develops any great amount of atherosclerosis, and one reason is its low blood pressure.

sixteen

Exercise

There is a lot of truth in the saying "If you don't use it, you lose it." Exercise or physical activity is a means of preventing disuse. Disuse is a major factor in causing many of the changes in the body we call aging. Physical activity is essential to maintain the strength and function of the musculoskeletal system, including bone and muscle mass. Bones that are not used tend to decalcify. If a leg is put in a cast, the leg bone loses calcium, and, of course, the size of the muscle also decreases.

As muscle mass shrinks, the amount of vital hormones declines. The amount of steroid hormones from the adrenal gland and sex glands diminish with age, but in proportion to the decrease in muscle mass. It is not definitely known whether increasing the muscle mass will increase the amount of hormones and what the overall effect will be upon the body. It is known, however, that the muscle mass can be increased in middle-aged, inactive people by appropriate exercises. With an exercise program, there are many medical indicators of improved health and well-being. It is possible that the level of physical activity is a significant factor in maintaining optimal functions of the endocrine glands to provide life-giving hormones for continued youth and vigor.

Patterns of muscle movements are integrated with the nervous system. The finely coordinated movements of the concert pianist, for example, respond to a memory pattern in the brain or to a visual stimulus which is processed through the brain. Or again, if a leg is removed, the nerve cells related to its function undergo changes. There are numerous other examples to illustrate the interrelations between the musculoskeletal system and the nervous system. It is well known that a stroke or damage to the central nervous system can cause a leg or any portion of the musculoskeletal system to cease functioning properly. Conversely, the functions of the musculoskeletal system affect the memory organization and fundamental patterns of response, ultimately resulting in a chemical reorganization within the nerve cells.

Although there are many gaps in our knowledge of the interrelated functions, it has been established that the musculoskeletal system and its function are linked to the functions of both the nervous system and hormone production. The nervous system and endocrine system likewise influence each other. Thus, the musculoskeletal, nervous, and endocrine systems are synchronized, and physical activity influences all three.

ELIMINATION OF ADRENALINE BUILDUP

Physical activity really affects the entire body. The muscular contractions require fuel, which is supplied by the nutrient elements in the diet, after they have been appropriately processed. Exercise uses a number of other products of the body. Among these are the stores of adrenaline and related materials secreted by the adrenal glands. Basically, adrenaline is the emergency hormone which mobilizes the body for fight or flight. It makes the heart beat faster, mobilizes the sugar reserves, and causes trembling and sweating. It is the chemical product of the sympathetic nervous system and is important in the transmission of nerve impulses to the sympathetic division of the autonomic nervous system.

Adrenaline is a powerful substance and has many useful medical purposes. It can relieve an acute asthmatic attack or be used as a stimulant during an emergency in the functioning of the heart. Whenever a person is under emotional or psychic stress—for example, in a threatened automobile accident—the excess adrenaline and related products are stored in the brain and heart. Exercise causes these stored products to be metabolized. This is an important outcome because if they remain in the heart it will beat faster and the likelihood of irregularities of the heart will be enhanced. They also act on the heart much as a buildup of carbon does in the automobile engine, decreasing its efficiency; that is, the heart muscle becomes an oxygen burner, using more oxygen than it ordinarily requires.

The buildup of adrenaline products in the brain likewise affects its function and even a person's emotional response and mood. This may be one reason why people often feel better after mild exercise. Many individuals know that if they come home from a sedentary office job feeling "dead tired" and engage in some physical activity they will feel better than if they sit down and rest in front of the TV. The physical activity helps clear away the buildup of adrenaline products accumulated through the day's stressful events.

WORK FOR THE HEART MUSCLE

Exercise assists in maintaining optimal function and health of the heart and circulation. It must be used properly, however; never forget that exercise can kill as well as cure. Physical activity requires that more oxygen be delivered to the working muscles. Transporting this greater amount of oxygen is the job of the heart and circulation. It's easy to understand, then, that physical activity makes the heart pump more blood or work harder. The capacity of the heart to pump blood is increased by working it, just as the strength and size of any other muscle in the body are improved by using it. A distance runner needs to develop not only the muscles in his legs but the strength and capacity of the heart muscle to pump enough blood for him to run. Individuals who undertake very little physical activity do not allow the optimal capacity of their heart and circulation to be achieved.

THE VITAL ARTERY NETWORK

Proper physical exercise increases the circulation to the heart muscle by developing the network of small arteries between the two main arteries to the heart. This network is important in providing adequate blood flow to the individual muscle fibers. In the healthy physically fit individual the network is extensive, and during vigorous physical activity it enables large amounts of blood to be circulated to the working heart muscle fibers. In the absence of a well-developed network, the amount of blood siphoned to the heart muscle, and hence the work capacity of the heart is limited. A well-developed network also helps to protect the heart from the effects of blockage in any one branch of the artery system by a buildup of fatty deposits. In fact, if an artery is blocked in one spot and the individual survives, the network to detour blood around the blocked artery is further developed to provide a new blood supply to this area of the heart muscle.

The increased circulation to the heart muscle brought about by exercise not only helps protect one from a heart attack but also improves his chances of surviving a heart attack if it occurs. The greater vascularity of the heart muscle is comparable to that noted in the skeletal muscles. If these are exercised and developed, the circulation to them is increased.

INCREASE IN VOLUME CAPACITY OF THE HEART

Adequate amounts of proper exercise will also increase the volume capacity of the heart. Remember that the heart is a muscular organ and acts as a reservoir for blood between beats. If the heart has to pump more blood, it actually starts enlarging its chambers so that more blood can be stored for each beat. This is a normal healthy response. It is similar to the increase in volume of the lungs that can be induced by breathing exercises. If a heart has a very small capacity, its ability to increase the amount of blood it can pump is limited, and consequently the amount of oxygen that can be delivered and the amount of physical activity that one can do are limited too. Clearly, the volume capacity of the heart is an important factor in a person's ability to perform strenuous or lengthy exercise. In individuals who are free of significant blockage in the arteries to the heart muscle it is probably the single most important factor controlling the amount of physical work that can be done.

The heart does sometimes enlarge with disease, but this is a compensatory mechanism to try to overcome some mechanical defect in the heart. For example, if a valve to the outlet of the heart is partially obstructed, the heart has to work harder to eject blood past the obstruction. In essence the heart is worked and it enlarges accordingly. The normal increase in size and capacity of the heart with physical exercise in healthy people is a healthy finding and shows optimal heart function. An indicator of this is the heart rate. The individual with a relatively rapid resting heart rates is likely to have a small heart with limited capacity. The healthy individual with a normally slow heart rate probably has a heart with larger capacity and a greater range of function.

CIRCULATORY EFFICIENCY

Physical fitness increases circulatory efficiency. That is, the heart and circulation of a person in good condition do less work for a given physical task than those of a person in poor condition doing the same task. Both may use about the same amount of oxygen if the task really requires the same amount of energy, but to deliver that oxygen in the unfit individual the heart has to pump a great deal more blood; thus there must be an increased blood flow to the heart muscle. The reasons are not entirely clear but are undoubtedly related to the small arteries that channel blood to the different parts of the body. In the well-conditioned athlete a major portion of the blood pumped by the heart is sent directly to the working muscles and a smaller portion of it is sent to muscles that are not being used. In this way the maximum amount of oxygen can be withdrawn from the blood pumped by the heart. Many complex mechanisms exist in the body that provide for transporting the increased amount of blood pumped by the heart directly to where it is needed as opposed to sending it equally to all parts of the body.

EXERCISE AND ATHEROSCLEROSIS

Of course exercise influences the heart and circulation indirectly through its metabolic effects. To the extent that exercise decreases obesity and lowers the amount of fat particles in the blood, it helps to prevent the buildup of atherosclerosis which causes blockage of the arteries. It therefore improves the circulation all over the body—in the legs, the kidneys, the testicles, or wherever. Since atherosclerosis can even affect the balance and hearing mechanisms, to the degree that exercise prevents atherosclerosis, it can help maintain optimal function of the ears. Whenever one loses body weight, he also finds it easier to engage in a lot of normal physical activity without overloading his heart. The excess fat that a person carries around is truly an extra weight. Obviously the man who walks a mile carrying 50 pounds of excess fat must work harder, and his heart must pump more blood and work harder too. If the heart has a limited capacity because of disease or other factors, getting rid of the extra 50 pounds of fat means the body has to work less during that mile walk and the heart has to work less. Even an individual with limited capacity of the heart can walk more after he has lost excess fat than he could before and still not overload his heart. To the extent that exercise induces fat loss, it will improve exercise capacity whether or not the work capacity of the heart is increased.

BLOOD PRESSURE

Exercise tends to affect the small arteries throughout the body which are important in regulating blood pressure. Either through the exercise activity itself or through associated fat loss, changes occur in a number of individuals that result in a lowering of their blood pressure at resting conditions. During exercise the blood pressure normally goes up. In individuals in poor physical condition it usually goes up more rapidly than in those in optimal physical condition. Thus, exercise is often a useful adjunct in treating people with elevated blood pressure.

BREATHING CAPACITY

Just as exercise requires the heart to pump more blood, it also requires the lungs to provide more oxygen. Increased breathing exercises the lungs and helps maintain lung capacity. Not only are the lung sacs themselves filled and emptied rapidly during moderate exercise, but the muscles in the chest wall that are responsible for expanding and contracting the chest cavity are also put to more vigorous use. There is a considerable body of evidence to suggest that regular, adequate amounts of exercise help keep up the functional capacity of the lungs.

BLOOD FORMATION

The level of physical activity influences the body's capacity to form red blood cells. Each day a small number of red blood cells are destroyed as they succumb to the wear and tear of being tumbled through miles of blood vessels. The greater the physical activity, the more rapidly the blood circulates, and consequently the more red blood cells are destroyed each day. These are replaced regularly by the bone marrow and blood-forming organs of the body. With regular levels of physical activity the blood-forming organs produce the same amount of red blood cells that the body destroys. Thus the number of red blood cells is kept in fairly constant balance.

During periods of long inactivity, red blood cell destruction decreases and the blood-forming organs cease to produce as many red blood cells. They become relatively inactive and sluggish compared to their state in a very active individual. I observed this effect in studying many healthy young men placed at bed rest to evaluate the probable influence of weightlessness during space flight. When the men got out of bed and resumed normal physical activity, the old red blood cells which had accumulated were suddenly destroyed. The bone marrow had become accustomed to producing a small number of red blood cells and was unable immediately to replace the destroyed cells. As a result most of these young men tended to develop a sudden anemia caused by resuming normal physical activity. In the course of three to four weeks of normal physical activity the bone marrow would regain its level of productivity and a new balance would be established. At this point the anemia would disappear.

In other studies—of dogs—the bone marrow was found to be yellow, filled with fat, and inactive in caged dogs not allowed to exercise. Dogs exercised regularly developed a rich, red marrow characteristic of active blood cell production. Exercise is apparently important in maintaining optimal bone marrow function.

TYPES OF EXERCISE

Different types of exercises serve different purposes. Understanding all of these is necessary in setting up an exercise program to meet specific goals. Exercises can be divided into two general types, isometric and isotonic. Isometric exercises are those which are done without causing any actual movement of the muscle; they are muscle-tensing exercises. To illustrate: Tense the muscles in your upper arm. The biceps will be contracted on one side and the triceps will be contracted on the other. These two muscles contract against each other. While the arm is held in a constant position with essentially no movement, the muscles shorten slightly with the tensing but the forearm is not moved. The muscles are put under load by use of the antagonistic muscle groups that balance each other's force. Tensing muscles in this way can cause them to increase in size just as weight lifting does. Whenever a muscle is placed under tension, it will gradually increase its size and endurance. Isometric exercises are effective for this purpose.

The body is so constructed that one group of muscles acts against an opposite group. By means of the principle of tensing groups of opposite muscles one can put most of the muscle groups in the body under load and so gradually increase their size and endurance. The amount of energy used by these exercises is relatively small compared to running or exercises that involve lots of body movement. Nevertheless, they do require some energy. Since contracting the muscles in this way does cause the blood pressure to rise, they are not totally innocuous in individuals who have heart disease and must limit their activity. The sudden rise in blood pressure makes the heart work harder and is undesirable, for example, in patients with very high blood pressure. Hand gripping and even vigorous hand shaking will also cause a rise in blood pressure, which is one reason a politician needs to have a good heart and circulatory system.

Isotonic exercises involve actual movement of the muscle or lengthening and shortening of the muscle. To take the upper-arm example again: If you straighten the arm so that the triceps at the back of the upper arm is contracted, the biceps is lengthened. If you bend the elbow now, the biceps contracts as the triceps lengthens. Exercises involving movement of this sort are isotonic exercises. Naturally they include almost all forms of body movement, most forms of calisthenics, and activities involved in any physical sport. Although there is no clear distinction, you can divide the isotonic exercises into two general types, weight-lifting exercises and endurance exercises.

In weight-lifting exercises the effort is usually very short in duration and involves more of the strength of the muscle than it does its endurance through a period of time. A weight lifter's muscles become thick because the cross-sectional area determines the muscular strength needed to lift the weight. Endurance exercises are those like running or activity during which the actual weight or tension exerted on the muscle at any one time is not maximal but the action is repetitive and continuous. Long-distance running, long-distance swimming, skiing, bicycle riding, and most competitive sports are excellent examples. Endurance exercises require the delivery of large amounts of oxygen, and the heart therefore has to pump a great deal more blood. Although weight-lifting exercises tend to raise the blood pressure sharply, they do not require the constant delivery of significantly increased amounts of oxygen as do endurance exercises. Both exercises are useful in maintaining optimal health, if properly undertaken.

CALORIE EXPENDITURE EXERCISES

All exercise programs should be designed for specific goals. One goal is control of body fat. While exercise is useful here, many people do not appreciate its limitations in achieving this goal. A rather large amount of exercise has to be done to reduce fat primarily by this means. A 150-pound person will need to walk nearly 60 miles to use the calories in a pound of body fat. A pound of body fat contains 3500 calories, and a 150-pound man will use 60 calories more while walking a mile at a speed of 3 miles per hour than he would have used at rest. Of course, lumberers, ditchdiggers, or football players will use an enormous amount of calories, and in these instances the physical activity is significant in utilizing all of the calories ingested.

The 150-pound individual uses approximately 70 calories each hour during sleep. Size and weight, of course, and many other things influence the metabolism, including the activity of the thyroid gland or any illness. During fever the metabolism is markedly increased, and many calories are used. It is for this reason that individuals with fever tend to lose weight.

Sitting quietly, the average (150-pound) person will use approximately 100 calories an hour; standing, he will use 110 calories per hour. Walking at 3 miles an hour on a level grade under optimal conditions he will use 250 calories in an hour. Seventy of these calories would be used in the sleeping state, leaving 180 calories to be used for exercise or 60 calories per mile. A person weighing 200 pounds would use 100 calories in walking a mile at this speed, about 78 of these for the exercise. A 100-pound individual would need 63 calories to walk a mile at this speed, 45 of which would be utilized for the exercise.

Using the 150-pound person as a standard individual walking at a rate of 3 miles per hour, one arrives at the figure of approximately 60 calories per mile which I have cited frequently as an exercise equivalent, since walking is a common form of activity. To judge how much energy is really required by other physical activities, they can be equated to the exercise equivalent (EE), it being always kept in mind that one unit or one exercise equivalent equals one mile or 60 calories.

The reason people are able to eat as much as they do is that the body uses a lot of energy in rebuilding and replacing the cells. This is the constant rejuvenation process, and it requires energy even if one is not actually doing any physical work. An average individual can be assumed to use about 1500 calories during a 24-hour period even if he engages in no physical activity whatsoever but rests quietly or sleeps the whole time. Therefore an average person should be able to eat 1500 calories a day without adding fat deposits. Most of the calories eaten above this amount, however, must be expended by exercise in order to avoid fat deposits. High-calorie foods require a great deal of exercise to prevent fat deposits.

Exercise is useful and enables one to eat a more satisfying diet. If an average person walks an hour a day at 3 miles per hour, in a year's time he will have utilized 65,700 calories or the amount of calories found in 19 pounds of body fat. A 200-pound individual would use the calories in even more pounds of body fat, while a 100-pound person would use less.

The important point here is walking *every day*, which emphasizes a key word: *consistency*. Exercising moderate amounts every day in a period of time will result in a decided reduction of excess fat deposits. Sporadic exercise or short-term crash exercise programs are not very effective. Few individuals are going to walk 60 miles a day, and if they did they would probably lose only a pound of fat although they might lose a lot of water initially. But walking an hour a day 365 days a year can bring about a significant reduction in body fat.

To use exercise properly one must be careful not to add calories to the diet at the same time. A small addition of food items eaten consistently throughout the year can negate a modest exercise program. A list of food values in terms of exercise equivalents illustrates this point:

	EE (Miles)
Sugar, 4 level teaspoons =	1.0
Butter, 1 tablespoon =	1.7
Whole milk, 1 cup =	2.7
Bologna or frankfurters, 3½ oz. =	5.1
Bacon, raw, 3½ oz. =	11.1

The combined effects of a sensible diet and physical exercise program go a long way toward achieving satisfactory fat reduction.

There is a great difference in how many calories are used by different forms of physical activity. Office work and housework use too few calories to be helpful in fitness or in prevention of obesity; they are thus classified as relatively sedentary occupations. The following list indicates the number of calories used for various activities:*

Activity	Calories per hour	EE (Miles)
Sleeping	70	0.00
Lying quietly	80	0.06
Sitting	100	0.50
Standing	110	0.66
Office work	145	1.25
Housekeeping	150	1.33

* Adapted from L. E. Morehouse and A. T. Miller, *Physiology of Exercise* (St. Louis: C. V. Mosby Co., 1963).

Walking, 2 miles per hour	170	1.60
Walking, 3 miles per hour	250	3.00
Bicycling, 5.5 miles per hour	190	2.00
Dancing, moderate	250	3.00
Dancing, vigorous	340	4.50
Swimming		
Breaststroke, 1 mile per hour	410	5.66
Crawl, 1 mile per hour	420	5.83
Backstroke, 1 mile per hour	500	7.16
Sidestroke, 1 mile per hour	550	8.00
Football	1000	15.50
Horizontal running, 7 miles per hour	870	13.33

Despite calorie restriction with an exercise program, some people cannot lose weight. Even so, they may be losing fat, which is the real goal. The aim is not to decrease the body weight and certainly not to decrease muscle mass, but rather to eliminate body fat deposits. In the process of converting fat to muscle there may be no appreciable change in the reading on the bathroom scales. Theoretically, if you converted one pound of fat to muscle, you would actually gain weight. Here is how it works. One pound of body fat contains five times as many calories as one pound of lean muscle. If by exercise you built up your muscle mass and converted one pound of body fat to muscle, you would actually gain 4 pounds. In the course of a diet-exercise program individuals often increase their muscle mass at the same time they are eliminating body fat stores. Basically, they are changing their body composition. The waistline may shrink, the clothes may fit a lot better, and the overall body proportions may change, but the bathroom scales may read the same.

Similarly, you can be completely inactive and convert muscle mass to fat while eating far more than you should, yet not gain any weight according to the scales. An examination to determine how much fat there is underneath the skin is therefore a better guide to whether or not you need to be on a reducing, diet-exercise program. Daily weighing is useful and often stimulates people to continue their program, but it is no substitute for seeing how much fat is deposited under the skin. Thus a simple weight table leaves a great deal to be desired. An individual on a proper diet with a vigorous exercise program will gradually develop a body composition in which only a limited portion of the body weight is fat. Good examples are the pentathletes or endurance athletes mentioned in Chapter Fifteen on diets. These men did not appear to be skinny or underweight, yet they did not have any evidence of significant fat deposits under the skin, around the buttocks, waist, or other area, as are commonly observed in less active individuals.

EXERCISES FOR THE CARDIOVASCULAR SYSTEM

To work the heart muscle and develop its capacity, one should use exercises that require delivering a lot of oxygen to the body or at least an increased amount of oxygen over a span of at least 15 minutes. For this reason endurance exercises are the most useful in developing the cardiovascular system. Ordinary walking falls into the endurance category. If one walks at a reasonably vigorous rate (there is no need to overdo it) over an appreciable time—for example, an hour—he will use more calories than if he jogs slowly for 10 or 15 minutes. The heart will be gradually increasing its work, and it will undergo some degree of conditioning.

Walking exercises are possible for almost everyone unless he has a serious medical problem. I always recommend regular walking before a vigorous exercise program is begun—for both young and old. Individuals who have been very inactive will need to improve bodily functions before they can safely and painlessly advance to more strenuous exercise. Those who are used to walking can test themselves. If they can walk an hour vigorously without tiring unduly or having difficulty and do so repeatedly over several days, they can usually go on to more energetic exercise. Individuals who have been quite inactive should begin by walking only about 15 minutes at a time. After following this regimen for several days, they can gradually increase the length of the walking period until they have demonstrated that they can walk continuously for one hour without unusual fatigue, pain, or other difficulty. This level of activity in itself would be a significant improvement for many people. Having maintained walking exercises for two to three weeks, they can then progress to jogging, running in place, running, or other more vigorous exercises.

Jogging is fine for developing the capacity of the heart and circulation if it is done properly. As with all forms of exercise, the rule is not to overdo it and to undertake the exercise consistently. The individual who has demonstrated his walking capacity will have little difficulty implementing a jogging program. Walking will already have developed the muscles in the ankles and legs, strengthened the tendons, and tuned up the bone marrow for blood formation.

There is a right and a wrong way to jog. When you jog, do it slowly.

Really, jogging is a slow trot. You should trot flat-footed; that is, let the heel hit the floor first so that the tendon and ankle are not unduly jarred. People who run on their toes keep the calf muscles tensed, and the jogging jars the ankle tendons and can lead to ankle tendon injury. Jog or trot at a pace that is comfortable—well below the level of becoming breathless. Individuals who already have a walking program can start jogging a hundred steps in the course of their walk, counting each time the left foot hits the turf, and then gradually increase the jogging steps at a rate of 20 steps a day so that each five days there will be an added 100 steps in jogging. In the course of time they will finally be jogging the entire period of time rather than walking.

I recommend that all individuals who anticipate starting a jogging program have a medical checkup and receive their doctor's okay for jogging exercises. Then, I like to emphasize one precaution: *Always trot at a slow rate. Do not try to set records.* A number of people have dropped dead as a result of jogging. In almost every instance that has been documented, death has occurred because the person repeatedly tried to beat his previous time. Men seem to be the worst offenders in this regard. If they are able to jog a mile in ten minutes, they are striving to jog it in nine. If they can jog it in nine, they are pushing for eight. It really makes very little difference whether jogging a mile takes nine or ten minutes or only eight minutes as far as health benefits are concerned, and it can be dangerous for the person to push himself too far. As individuals get older, particularly men, they are very likely to have some fatty deposits in the arteries causing some clogging, even if a good diet-exercise program has been followed carefully. For this reason undue exertion is unwise. Smell the flowers along the way, and don't compete against anyone else or against yourself. Competitive athletics are for trained athletes and unless you are in this category, they are not for you. Young vigorous people require years of training to become outstanding athletes. Since most people will not be competing in the Olympics, their goal should be to improve their health and to maintain fitness at a level which will enable them to enjoy normal physical activity.

Running in place can accomplish the same things as jogging. This simple exercise is done by standing in one spot and counting each time the left foot hits the floor. Raise the feet well off the floor so that the knees are well bent. As in jogging, it is important that you do not run on your toes but allow the foot to sink normally to the floor or even initially step on the heel. Run at a rate that is comfortable, usually between 50 and 100 steps a minute. Speed is not the object. Developing endurance is the object. This type of exercise can cause severe shin splints and sore legs in the individual who takes on a crash running-in-place program. It is well to start with only 100 steps and if there is no soreness or stiffness to add 20 steps each day. In this way the number of steps will gradually be increased to a meaningful amount of exercise. Running in place 1000 steps a day is comparable to jogging and can be done in the house in all kinds of weather, away from the neighborhood dogs and poison ivy, and in an air-conditioned, air-filtered room.

Individuals who have reached the point of being able to jog or run in place for long periods may choose to progress to straight running. This is a good form of endurance exercise for those who are qualified and is useful in building up the capacity of the heart and circulation. Sprint running or speed running is not necessary, and as indicated in the preceding tabulation, running at a speed of 7 miles per hour will consume an appreciable amount of calories—though not so much as to allow one to have an unlimited dietary intake. Consistency remains the key to success.

A good indoor exerciser is the stationary bicycle. You can put it in front of the TV set and exercise while watching the news or your favorite program. A useful model is one that permits you to adjust the load or tension on the wheel. Thus you can increase the work load as you train. The heavier the load, the more like weight lifting the exercise will be. If you want to develop large thigh muscles, gradually add to the load. For endurance, use a lighter load and exercise longer. As with all other forms of exercise a gradual buildup is desirable. You should not overdo, and you should be consistent in the effort. The use of a stationary bicycle has the advantage of an indoor exercise and it can often be of value to people who have trouble maintaining their balance. Modified pedaling devices can even be used while one is lying on his back.

Dancing, swimming, tennis, and all other forms of athletics are good endurance exercises. All of them can be dangerous if done to excess by someone who is not trained or conditioned so that he avoids stressing his heart and circulation. The danger of competitive sports in older people is that they will get carried away and extend themselves beyond their usual capability. Exercise, whether it is jogging or playing tennis, is most effective when it is done consistently and the person doesn't allow himself to reach the point of peak exertion. *It is the unusual effort or straining one-self to the utmost that induces most heart attacks or sudden deaths from exercise.*

Regardless of the kind of exercise program embarked on to improve the cardiovascular system, I would like to emphasize strongly that one should begin by walking and gradually build up to an optimal level of exercise consistent with one's health.

A guide to how much a person should do is the heart rate. Adequate levels of exercise for cardiovascular conditioning can be achieved with heart rates that do not exceed 120 beats per minute. If the rate is over 140 beats per minute, you are overdoing things unless you are following a program prescribed by your doctor. If you notice any difficulty with the heart rate, stop the exercise. Stop exercising, too, if you notice any chest pain. Again, if you become unduly fatigued or breathless, it is time to stop. And last but not least, don't fight the clock. You will have a lot more time for living if you don't keep watching time while you are exercising.

BODY STRENGTH AND POSTURE

Endurance exercises are not enough to maintain optimal health. They are very useful for the cardiovascular system and to meet goals in caloric balance, but they are not sufficient to keep up muscle strength in large portions of the body or to help in the constant war with gravity. The postural changes with increasing age are markedly influenced by muscle strength and physical activity. In general, with increasing age the joints tend to be bent—for example, at the elbows, knees, and hips—with the muscles responsible for bending being shortened or contracted. The opposing muscles designed to keep the joints straight lose their strength. This is part of the reason the older person loses stature and walks along with knees slightly bent, hips bent, elbows bent, and neck spine curved with the chin jutted forward.

The loss of muscle strength in the long back muscles allows the spinal column to bend forward particularly in the chest area, contributing to the buffalo hump or dowager's hump so common in middle-aged American women and not uncommon in slightly older American men. If you observe your older acquaintances, you will see that frequently their spines between the shoulders are curved forward, their shoulders are allowed to slump, becoming rounded, and their heads project forward with the chin stuck out. The loss of muscle strength between the shoulder blades is partly responsible for the round-shoulder effect. A great deal can be done to prevent this by means of proper exercises.

In general, an exercise program designed to retain youthful posture and full range of youthful musculoskeletal function is directed toward preserving the proper length of the bending muscles and adequate strength of the lengthening muscles. Simple contracting or tensing of the muscles helps build their strength. Moving the joints through their full range of action helps maintain the length of muscles and tendons. The shortening of tendons with age influences the posture. Part of the reason the knees and hips are bent is because the tendons used for bending become shortened, losing a degree of their youthful elasticity.

Our daily living patterns neglect to provide much use for the arms and shoulders in the way that primitive man originally used them. There are no grapevines to swing on in modern civilization. The body is constantly subjected to forces of gravity bending and beating it down to earth level. Even picking up a heavy load tends to compress the spine. Exercises that stretch the muscles controlling the spine are almost nonexistent. Only a few people such as trapeze artists and acrobats are involved in activities that lengthen the muscles of the spine and put stress on the spine in the opposite direction from that normally caused by gravity.

Any number of exercises can be devised to develop the strength and retain the full range of motion of muscles throughout the body. The ones suggested in the following discussion are merely exemplary. *It is important to realize that tensing, contracting, or stretching of the muscles can be disabling if it is overdone. I want to give a word of caution that these exercises should be approached carefully. They are not as simple as they seem. Do not overstretch, do not overcontract, but proceed gently.* Don't do too many to begin with. It is enough to do each exercise once until you learn them and have some appreciation for what they can do; then you can increase the number of each exercise.

Be satisfied for time to produce improvements. You cannot expect a bent spine to straighten with a few days of exercise. Many bent spines will never be corrected. Most of these exercises are better for prevention than they are for cure. Once defects have occurred, more vigorous efforts are needed under professional supervision. Some individuals with joint and muscle problems will find it impossible to do these exercises. Anyone with a damaged joint should not try to force it but should consult his doctor concerning the advisability of any specific exercise he wishes to undertake which uses that joint.

Usually doctors recommend that patients with defects in the lower spine not do any exercises that arch the back in a backward fashion or that involve twisting from side to side. So, if you have a defect in your spine, eliminate these exercises until you have gotten your doctor's advice.

For the vast majority of healthy individuals this set of exercises will go a long way toward maintaining body posture and strength in the mode characteristic of youthfulness. It is well to do the various body-strengthening exercises barefooted so as to develop the strength of the feet. As a matter of fact, individuals who run in place indoors or do indoor running exercises will find running barefooted excellent for building the strength and power of the feet muscles. The loss of muscle mass in the feet in later years decreases the cushioning effect on the bones and joints and is responsible for certain foot complaints in older people.

A good time to do the muscle strengthening and lengthening exercises is immediately after having done one of the endurance exercises. The body will be warmed up, and the muscles will be in optimal condition for stretching and contracting.

1. Toes
Sit in a comfortable chair and cross your legs. With the foot of the top leg
a. Curl your toes as tight as possible.
b. Bend your toes upward as far as possible.
c. Spread your toes as far apart as possible.
Repeat the desired number of times, then change feet and repeat for the other foot.

2. Ankle
Sit with legs crossed.
With the foot of the top leg
a. Rotate the foot at the ankle joint letting the toes inscribe a circle, first clockwise, then counterclockwise.
b. Bend foot upward as far as possible
c. Bend foot downward as far as possible.
Cross legs the other way and repeat exercises for the other ankle.

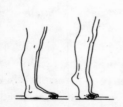

3. Calf
a. Stand flat-footed with feet together, then rise up on your toes, contracting the calf muscles.

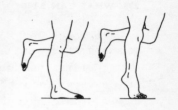

b. Stand on one leg (you may need to balance yourself with a hand against the wall or on a chair), then rise up on the toes, contracting the calf muscles. After the desired number of exercises change to the other foot and repeat.

4. Ankle Stretching

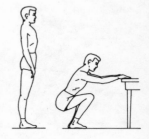

a. Stand flat-footed. Bend at the knees as if beginning a knee bend **but** leave the heels flat on the floor. Bend as far as comfortable. You may want to brace yourself with the back of a chair or the edge of a table for support.

b. Kneel on your right knee with your left foot flat on the floor and the left heel near the right knee. Put your hands on the floor in front of you. Let the weight of your chest rest on your left knee. Now rock back and forth trying to keep your left heel on the floor. Keep your leg muscles relaxed. The purpose is to stretch the muscles and tendons, so keep your leg muscles relaxed. Change to kneeling on the left knee and repeat the procedure for the right ankle.

c. Squat with both feet as nearly flat on the floor as you can. Keep your knees together. You may need to balance yourself with your hands. Lean forward enough to prevent strain on the knee joints. Not everyone will be able to put the heels on the floor with this position, and some will need to be partially on their toes, particularly women used to wearing high-heeled shoes. Don't worry about it. Just sit this way awhile with each exercise session, and gradually the tendons and muscles will stretch enough to let your foot ease to the floor. After you can sit flat-footed, you will soon no longer need to balance yourself with your hands.

5. Deep Knee Bends

Squat, keeping your knees together. Keeping feet in place, rise to full height, then return to the squatting

position. You can put your hands on your hips or your head, or stretch them out for balance.

6. Thigh Stretch

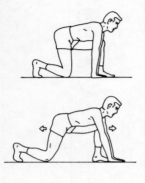

a. Kneel on your right knee with the left foot positioned in front far enough so that the left knee bends at a right angle. Place your hands on the floor with the left hand inside the big toe of the left foot. Now move your right knee back and your hands forward to stretch the spread between the thighs. Then rock back and forth on your knee. Change to the other knee and repeat the exercise. The object is to obtain maximum stretch front to back of the hip joints.

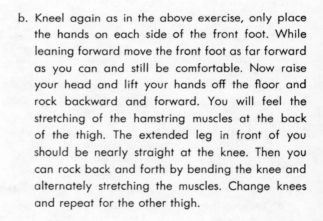

b. Kneel again as in the above exercise, only place the hands on each side of the front foot. While leaning forward move the front foot as far forward as you can and still be comfortable. Now raise your head and lift your hands off the floor and rock backward and forward. You will feel the stretching of the hamstring muscles at the back of the thigh. The extended leg in front of you should be nearly straight at the knee. Then you can rock back and forth by bending the knee and alternately stretching the muscles. Change knees and repeat for the other thigh.

c. Lie on your back with your feet in the air while supporting your hips with your hands to raise your feet as high as possible. Now, keeping your legs straight, let your legs fall apart sideways as far as possible, forming a Y. Bring the feet back together and repeat.

d. Stand behind a chair or a table of the right height so that you can use your hands to help support you. Keep the heels together **but** turn the toes and and knees out as far as you can comfortably. With the heels flat on the floor, and using the hands for support, start a knee bend and squat as far as you can, then rise up to your original position. Keep your buttocks in. You may not be able to bend very far at the beginning, but with time you will be able to squat quite a distance keeping the knees out in the form of an open knee bend.

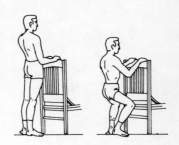

7. Thigh Lift
Stand beside a wall and place your right hand against it. Keeping your legs straight, raise your left leg out as far as possible. Return it to original position, then repeat. Turn to the opposite side and repeat for the other leg.

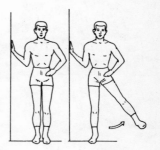

8. Thigh Rotation
Stand beside a wall with your left hand against the wall for support. Swing the right foot forward, out, and back, drawing a circle with the toes. Repeat, rotating the foot in the opposite direction, backward, out, and forward. Change your position against the wall and exercise the other leg the same way.

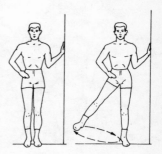

9. Spine
a. Stand straight with your feet together. Hold your hands above your head and stretch as tall as possible. Let your hands fall to your sides, relax, then repeat the stretch.

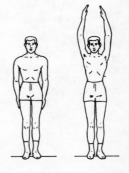

b. Standing straight with your hands resting on the front of your thighs, lean forward as far as possible, letting the hands slide down the thighs and finally allowing them to hang freely or actually touch the toes. You can bend your knees when you begin this exercise if you need to, and in the course

of time your muscles will stretch enough so that you can touch your toes without bending your knees. Rest in this position with the hands and head hanging down to stretch your back muscles. Straighten up and repeat.

c. Stand up straight and hold your hands straight above your head. Now bring the hands down and forward in an arc to touch the toes. Bend the knees if you need to. Rise up, keeping the arms straight, to the original position.

d. Stand upright with the arms outstretched from the sides to shoulder height and with the feet spread apart. Now, holding the arms straight swing the arms forward and backward so that the spine twists at the waist from right to left. (If you have a defect of your lower spine, check with your doctor before doing this exercise.)

e. Stand upright with the feet far apart and the hands held straight out from the side. Now bend forward and twist the shoulders to touch the right toe with the left hand, then rise up and turn to touch the left toe with the right hand. Return to original position and repeat.

10. Grinds

Stand straight with the feet slightly apart. Place your hands on your head with your fingers interlocked. Now rotate the hips by jutting the pelvis forward, to the side, backward, to the side, forward. Use your trunk muscles to do this and sweep as wide a circle as

possible. Stop and rotate the hips in the opposite
direction.

11. Bumps

Stand with the feet slightly apart and the knees
slightly bent. Place your hands on your head with
your fingers interlocked. Swing the pelvis forward as
far as possible and tighten your seat muscles. Relax
and swing the hips backward. Repeat the forward
motion and continue this forward-backward movement, tightening the seat muscles with each forward
thrust.

12. Sit-ups

a. Lie on your back with your feet straight and your
   arms lying straight above your head. Now sit up
   bringing your hands forward to touch the toes or
   as nearly so as you can comfortably. Return to
   the original position and repeat.

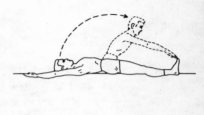

b. While on your back, bend your knees and keep
   your feet flat on the floor with the heels drawn
   up toward your buttocks. Let your knees fall apart
   sideways and then do sit-ups as before. This exercise is more difficult since you will be using mostly
   your abdominal muscles. The preceding exercise
   also uses the muscles that normally bend the hips
   without putting such a large load on the abdominal
   muscles. If it is impossible to do this exercise, you
   will have to continue with other abdominal muscle
   exercises such as the previous one, the head lift,
   and voluntary abdominal contractions until you
   can do this exercise.

c. Use a chair or sofa. Lie on your back and put your
   feet on the seat. The knees and the hips should be
   bent at a perpendicular angle. Keeping this position, do your sit-ups. This exercise, like the preceding one, will use the abdominal muscles
   without benefit of the hip-bending muscles and is
   harder than sit-up exercise 12a. You may need to
   develop your abdominal muscles to do this one.

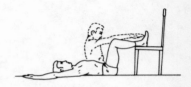

Both it and the preceding one exercise chiefly the upper abdominal muscles and have little effect on the lower abdominal muscles.

13.   Back Extension

Lie on your stomach. Hook your feet under the edge of a heavy sofa or other furniture and stretch your hands out as far as possible in front of you. Holding the arms out stiff, raise your head and upper body, arching the back. Return to original position and repeat. (If you have a defect of your lower back, check with your doctor before doing this exercise.)

14.   Leg Lifts

These exercises help to strengthen the lower abdominal muscles.

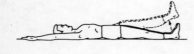

a. Lie on your back with your feet together. Now lift the feet off the floor keeping them together. Hold this position with your feet in the air for a few seconds and then return to the original position. Repeat.

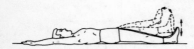

b. Using the same position lift the feet off the floor. Then spread the feet apart, bring them together, and then lower them on the floor. You put the maximum load on your muscles by keeping the feet only a few inches off the floor while you are spreading them apart.

15.   Leg Tensing

While lying on the floor with legs stretched out, contract all the muscles in the feet, legs, thighs, and hips as tight as possible, making them rigid. Hold them contracted for the count of five, then relax and repeat as desired.

16.   Abdominal Contractions

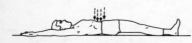

a. While still on your back suck in your abdominal muscles as tight as possible and hold the contraction for the count of five. Relax and repeat as desired. Make an effort to contract the lower abdominal muscles during this exercise.

b. While on your back bend your knees up. Pull your abdominal muscles in as far as possible, then push them out—in this manner alternately contracting and relaxing your abdominal muscles.

17. Head Lift

While lying on the floor lift your head up and touch your chin to your breast bone, then return to the original position. Repeat as desired. This exercise is good for the "pit of the stomach" as well as neck muscles.

18. Push-ups

Lie down on your stomach with your legs outstretched, feet together, and hands at the sides of your chest with your elbows bent. Now keeping the back straight push with your arms until your elbows are straight. Return to the original position. Repeat at will. You can do the same exercise bending at the knees. This is easier for beginners or those with a long way to go.

19. Respiration

Sit comfortably, perfectly upright with your hands on top of your head and your fingers interlocked. Take in as much air as you can and slowly exhale all the air you can. Rest a few seconds and repeat. Take your time between breaths to prevent overbreathing and a feeling of faintness. Try to do five deep breaths this way. **Do not hold your breath!**

20. Abdominal Contractions Standing

Stand upright. Suck in your stomach muscles as tight as you can and hold them in for as long as is comfortable, then relax for about 15 seconds and repeat. This exercise will help to control abdominal muscle tone and to prevent a lower pot or a bay window.

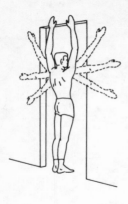

21. Chest Muscle Stretching

Stand in an ordinary doorway and stretch your hands up to the top of the casement. Now lean forward stretching your muscles across the front of the chest. Move the hands outward along the sides of the door jamb, leaning forward with a rocking movement with each new position of the hands. In the final position the hands should be at the level of the lower rib cage. By using all of these different positions, from above the head to the sides, you will stretch all parts of the muscles across the chest. If you can't reach the top of the door jamb, start at whatever level you can reach. Don't overdo your forward lean. Go just as far as is comfortable. In time you can do much more, but it may require patience.

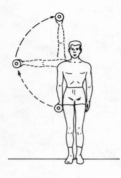

22. Arms and Shoulders

For these exercises a light weight (5 or 10 pounds) will help, or you can hold a heavy book in your hand.

a. Hold the weight in one hand, the hand hanging at the side. Raise the arm straight out from the side and up above the head, keeping the elbow straight. You will be using exclusively the muscle on top of the shoulder. Let the hand go back down to the original position. Build up your strength to do the exercise at least five times. Repeat for the other arm. Individuals who have very weak shoulder muscles can start with no weight and gradually increase the weight—for example, by using progressively heavier books.

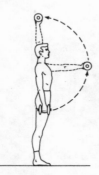

b. Start with the weighted hand hanging at the side. Raise the arm straight out in front of you and up as high as you can, then let it return to the original position. Build your strength to the level that you can do this five times at least. Repeat the exercise for the other arm.

c. Rotate the weighted hand around and around in as large a circle as possible, first clockwise and then counterclockwise. Repeat for the other arm.

d. Use a set of hand springs. Holding the springs from each end with your two hands in front of you, stretch the springs by pulling the arms backward, bringing the springs down to the chest.

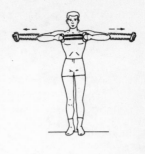

e. With no weights or springs simply rotate the arms (elbows straight) around and around in a big circle. Rotate them in such a way as to swing them upward and forward, then downward and backward.

f. Hold the arms straight out from the sides, elbows straight, hands at level of shoulders. Now simultaneously pull both arms backward by contracting the muscles between the shoulders.

23. Total Body Tension

Simply stretch out on the floor on your back. Now contract all the muscles you can in your body simultaneously, making arms, legs, and trunk muscles stiff. Hold this position to the count of five and relax. Repeat several times.

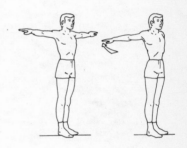

24. Face

These exercises are difficult to describe but the purpose is to tense or contract all different muscle groups in the face that you can, thus increasing their size and strength and helping to prevent facial sagging. They cannot prevent facial wrinkling entirely but they do help some and they give the face more shape with a more youthful appearance. They also give the face more expression.

a. Simply raise and lower the eyebrows as far as possible. Hold the eyebrows up as high as possible for a few seconds.

b. Close both eyes as forcefully as possible and keep them tightly closed for a few seconds. Relax and repeat as desired.

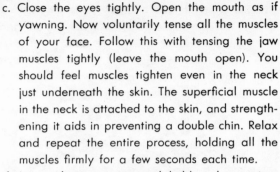

c. Close the eyes tightly. Open the mouth as if yawning. Now voluntarily tense all the muscles of your face. Follow this with tensing the jaw muscles tightly (leave the mouth open). You should feel muscles tighten even in the neck just underneath the skin. The superficial muscle in the neck is attached to the skin, and strengthening it aids in preventing a double chin. Relax and repeat the entire process, holding all the muscles firmly for a few seconds each time.

d. Leave the jaw open and held under tension. Now open and partially close, open and partially close, repeatedly, always keeping the jaw muscles tight. This action should exercise both the jaw and superficial throat muscles.

25. Neck

Do these exercises slowly. Speed is no object, and fast movement can make you dizzy.

Stand or sit upright.

a. Tuck your chin in as far as you can, touching the breastbone. Straighten your head to normal position and repeat.

b. Turn your head and try to touch your right shoulder with your chin. Now walk your chin around to the opposite shoulder and back again. Repeat as desired.

c. Rotate your head, making a circle as wide as you can with the tip of your chin. Repeat, rotating in the opposite direction.

All of the above exercises strengthen the muscles that prevent the neck from curving excessively and throwing the chin out as is often seen in old age.

d. Bend over, putting your hands on the seat of a chair, bed, or sofa, with your head hanging down. Repeat the head rotation exercise with the head down. This is one of the few ways to allow the neck muscles to be stretched using the head as a weight.

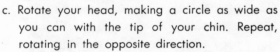

e. Stand upright and tilt the head to the right side as far as possible and then to the left as far as possible. Repeat as desired.

Note: Head rotating may cause you to feel dizzy at first. Don't overdo it and, gradually, training will diminish the dizzy feeling.

26. Hand

These exercises help to avoid having a bony hand often seen in advancing years.

a. Make as tight a fist as possible. Relax; stretch thumb and fingers out as far as possible. Repeat at will. Change hands and repeat.

b. Hold hand out with fingers and thumb outstretched. Tense all the muscles as tight as possible in the outstretched position. Repeat for the opposite hand.

c. Start with thumb and fingers straight and together, then spread apart and close, repeating as desired. Exercise the other hand.

27. Chin-ups and Hanging

In his early development man did lots of climbing and swinging. Tree climbing was often necessary. These activities gave the entire spine a chance to hang from the shoulders, lengthening or stretching the trunk muscles in a way that is difficult to do in any other fashion. Rope climbing, trapeze work, and similar activities have similar effects. You can use any suitable bar or support to chin yourself. Small bars available in most sporting goods stores can be put in a doorway for this purpose. Ideally one should have a chinning bar or other device that is high enough to hang from at arm's length without dragging the feet on the floor.

a. Grasp the chinning bar in both hands and hang loosely, allowing all the muscles in your body

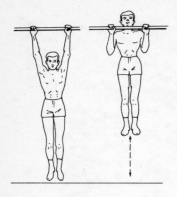

to stretch. At first a short period of hanging may make your arms and shoulders sore. Contract your arm muscles slightly if you need to in order to diminish the stress on your elbows.

b. Grasp the bar in both hands and pull your body up until your chin touches the bar, then let yourself down to the original position. Repeat at will.

seventeen

Habits

Living habits have a great deal to do with health and length of life. Some habits may have more effects upon the cells and how they function than is now recognized. Our habit patterns have changed drastically over the past several centuries. Not only have we stopped exercising so much and begun eating more, but we have started smoking large numbers of cigarettes, consuming large amounts of alcohol, drinking increased amounts of coffee and other stimulating drinks, and more recently enlarged our consumption of drugs.

CIGARETTES

Cigarette smoking is a twentieth-century problem. In the United States in 1900 only 4 billion cigarettes were manufactured; now the annual amount exceeds 580 billion. Prior to the twentieth century the chief use of tobacco was for pipes, cigars, chewing tobacco, and snuff. The ubiquitous cigarette got its start with the cigarette machine which was developed in 1870. Between 1900 and 1910 the annual production was only 4.2 billion a year. In the 1920's it was 80 billion a year. From 1925 to 1929 the average consumption of cigarettes per person annually was already 1285. From 1935 to 1939 it was 1779. After World War II it rose sharply to 3459 and reached a peak of 4287 in 1966.

In the early 1950's numerous reports began to appear about the adverse influence of cigarette smoking on health, and in 1964 came the report by the U.S. Surgeon General's Advisory Committee. A U.S. Department of Health, Education, and Welfare publication states,

> The Surgeon General's committee came to several conclusions, and these have since been accepted by the major medical and scientific organizations of the world. These conclusions were that cigarette smoking is a cause of

lung cancer, that it is associated with heart disease, that it is the most important cause of chronic bronchitis, and that it substantially increases the risk of premature death. In short, as the Committee reported, cigarette smoking is "a health hazard of sufficient importance to warrant appropriate remedial action."

Since then a growing body of information has linked cigarette smoking to a vast array of illnesses and premature death. If you want to improve your chances of living longer, you should not smoke, particularly if you are a man—men are apparently more affected by cigarettes than women. Men who want to know how smoking affects their longevity will be interested in the data from the American Cancer Society's study. Young men may live as much as eight years longer if they do not smoke than men the same age who smoke two packs of cigarettes a day or more. The life expectancy for each age group according to the number of cigarettes smoked is as follows:

		Number of Cigarettes a Day			
Age	Nonsmokers	1–9	10–19	20–39	40+
25	48.6	44.0	43.1	42.4	40.3
30	43.9	39.3	38.4	37.8	35.8
35	39.2	34.7	33.8	33.2	31.3
40	34.5	30.2	29.3	28.7	26.9
45	30.0	25.9	25.0	24.4	23.0
50	25.6	21.8	21.0	20.5	19.3
55	21.4	17.9	17.4	17.0	16.0
60	17.6	14.5	14.1	13.7	13.2
65	14.1	11.3	11.2	11.0	10.7

Death rate and illness have a direct correlation with cigarette smoking in both men and women. In general, the more cigarettes you smoke and the earlier you begin smoking, the greater the incidence of death and disease. Fortunately these correlations can be partially reversed, and the longer the period of time that elapses after quitting, the less likely you are to be affected. Even 10 years after stopping cigarette smoking there is a slightly greater incidence of death in former smokers than in nonsmokers. Cigarette smoking correlates with early death. A third of all deaths of men between 35 and 60 years of age would not have occurred so soon in nonsmokers. As a general expression, for every 10 deaths among nonsmoking men there are 17 deaths in an equal number of men who smoke.

The sum total of illnesses in smokers is much higher than in nonsmokers. Smokers are away from their jobs because of sickness one-third more of the time than nonsmokers.

What do cigarettes contain that is related to these health hazards? Tobacco contains nicotine, which is known to be a cellular poison. It can be used as an insecticide. Ninety percent of the nicotine in smoke that is inhaled into the lungs is absorbed into the body. To illustrate the difference in smoking habits on the effects of absorption of nicotine: Only 25 to 50 percent of the nicotine in smoke is absorbed by the body if it is only drawn into the mouth and then expelled. Cigarettes also contain a variety of tars and assorted chemicals, and last but not least, smoking produces carbon monoxide. Chronic smokers often have 5 to 10 percent of the hemoglobin in their blood stream bound chemically with carbon monoxide. Cigarette smoke contains about 1 percent carbon monoxide, pipe smoke 2 percent, and cigars 6 percent. Carbon monoxide acts as a poison by combining with the hemoglobin in the blood, thereby preventing the hemoglobin from carrying oxygen and causing asphyxiation.

Lung Cancer and Other Problems

Lung cancer used to be a relatively uncommon problem in the United States. In 1930 there were only 3000 deaths from it while in 1965 deaths had risen to 50,000. Lung cancer is directly correlated to smoking in men. It is the second most prevalent cancer in men, comprising 18 percent of their cancers, and is exceeded only by cancer of the skin (which is usually curable if detected early). Lung cancer is twice as common in men as cancer of the prostate (10 percent of cancers in men). The increase in lung cancer in men parallels the increase in cigarette consumption. Over 90 percent of all men with lung cancer are smokers. Women seem to be less affected by lung cancer, and it is thought that female hormones may offer some protection to the lungs against cancer.

There have been numerous efforts to establish an early diagnosis of lung cancer because it is deadly and usually impossible to cure. Early x-ray detection is helpful, and new methods to discover cell changes that precede the formation of a mature cancer are hopeful. Clearly, however, the one best approach to the problem is prevention, and most cancers of the lung can be prevented by not smoking.

In addition to lung cancer, cigarettes take a heavy toll by causing bronchitis and emphysema. The overdistended emphysematous lung, no longer able to act as a ventilating organ, literally slowly chokes its victim to death. As the body is progressively starved for oxygen, chronic fatigue and disability ensue. No part of the respiratory system seems to escape the toxins from tobacco smoking. Sinusitis is much more common in the smoker than in the nonsmoker.

Smoking is the chief lung pollutant. The air inhaled by the smoker is polluted with nicotine, tars, and carbon monoxide. It is little wonder, then, that the smoker is poorly equipped to tolerate the air pollution of modern cities. Much of the problem with air pollution is the increased amount of carbon monoxide, which differs in no way from the carbon monoxide in cigarette smoke. For the smoker, the first step toward correcting his polluted environment is to stop smoking. If he does not stop smoking, cleaning up the environment around him will not eliminate his exposure to pollution.

Cigarette smoking has also been correlated with other cancers: cancer of the bladder, possibly cancer of the pancreas, and, in heavy drinkers, cancer of the esophagus.

Nervous System

Nicotine (and hence smoking) is both a toxin and a stimulant to the nervous system. It can actually paralyze certain parts of the nervous system when administered in sufficiently large quantities. It also causes the adrenal gland to release adrenaline, the powerful chemical that prepares one for flight or fight. Since adrenaline arouses excitement, the overall effect, along with the nicotine, is to cause tremor and in some instances convulsions. Acute nausea, vomiting, and even death can occur with acute exposure to nicotine. It acts on the brain to make the body retain water for as long as two to three hours, inhibiting the normal urinary elimination process.

Chronic cigarette smokers gradually develop a tolerance to nicotine. In this way they escape the acute symptoms that the nonsmoker experiences when he first begins smoking. Even so, the chronic effects of cigarette smoking are comparable to chronic poisoning, which is reflected in the function of the nervous system and the parts of the body influenced by the nervous system.

Circulation

Chronic cigarette smoking and a physical fitness program have essentially the opposite consequences. The adrenaline which smoking causes to be released is stored in the heart and brain, diminishing the efficiency of the heart muscle fibers. Through this mechanism, and possibly its action on the nervous system, chronic cigarette smoking is associated with an increased resting heart rate, whereas physical conditioning slows down the resting heart rate. The faster heart rate of the smoker in turn diminishes the heart's capacity and limits the ability of the heart to pump blood with each heartbeat. Moreover, during exercise the small heart of limited capacity is not able to increase the amount of blood it can pump with each beat to anywhere near the proportions seen in the well-conditioned heart. The small rapidly beating heart is apparently more prone to irregularities, and some of these in their severe form are a common cause of death.

Nicotine has been shown to have a direct effect on the heart muscle, increasing its irritability, even without the added effects of the small fast-beating heart and its tendency to develop a significant irregularity. An appropriate exercise program helps to eliminate some of these adverse effects of smoking. At the same time it is clear that smoking limits the ability to achieve maximum benefits from the exercise program.

Dr. David Spain and Dr. Victoria A. Bradess of Valhalla, New York, did postmortem examinations on men with heart attacks and those who died suddenly. They found that for every death of a nonsmoking male under age 50 there were 16 deaths in men who smoked more than a pack a day. It is well established that the more one smokes and the longer one smokes, the greater the correlation with sudden death or a heart attack. This is the case in both men and women. Moreover, smokers are less likely to recover from an acute heart attack or survive for any length of time after initial recovery from the heart attack. The chances for long-time recovery are greatly improved in individuals who stop smoking after their attack as compared to those who do not stop.

Increased heart rate from whatever cause seems to be associated with a significantly increased rate of heart attacks and sudden death. In general, men with resting heart rates above 80 beats per minute have a greater likelihood of a heart attack or sudden death than comparable men with resting heart rates below 70 beats per minute. This observation may be related to the point that the fast-beating small heart with limited capacity will probably develop serious irregularities which can cause sudden death, whereas the slow heart rate with maximum capacity and long healthy heart muscle fibers seems less prone to irregularity. In fact, individuals who have minor irregularities of the heart (occasional skipped beats) often eliminate them with a sensible exercise program.

Digestive System

Cigarette smoking influences the digestive tract. As a rule it increases the activity of the intestines, causing more rapid and forceful contractions. Particularly in the beginning smoker, it may even cause diarrhea. Obviously for individuals who have an irritable or active colon or any of the forms of colitis, cigarette smoking is an aggravating factor. Peptic ulcer is more widely found in smokers than in nonsmokers. A recent explanation is that cigarette smoking interferes with the complex mechanism responsible for producing alkaline digestive juices in the small intestine just outside the stomach (duodenum). These alkaline juices are supposed to neutralize the acid juices from the stomach. In their absence the acid juices can start ulceration in the duodenum, leading to the common duodenal ulcer. Regardless of the actual mechanism, it seems well established that peptic ulcer is increased in cigarette smokers, and individuals who have this problem or related symptoms of ulcer are well advised to refrain from smoking.

Skin

Although the mechanism is not clear, heavy cigarette smoking is associated with premature aging of the skin. This manifests itself principally in deep wrinkling of the face. The crow's-feet at the corners of the eyes are particularly marked and deep. Some investigations suggest that the faces of heavy cigarette smokers appear to be as much as 20 years older than they actually are.

Effects on Others

Many cigarette smokers resort to the statement that it is only they who are suffering from their habit. This is really not true. They impose the bad effects of their smoking on other people. To begin with, children are twice as likely to smoke if their parents do. Cigarette smokers influence others to smoke. Parents who do not want their children to smoke cigagrettes and subject themselves to the health hazards discussed should seriously consider the impact of their habit upon their children.

Cigarette smoking also affects the birthrate of babies. Dr. Marie Louise Lubs of Denver studied evidences of prematurity of babies in smokers and nonsmokers. Even though the babies were delivered at full term, a higher number of those born to smoking mothers had decreased birth weight and other signs of prematurity. Other studies suggest that the children of smoking mothers are more likely to undergo convulsions or epileptic-type seizures later in life. It appears that cigarette smoking during pregnancy does affect the development of the fetus, which is exposed to the toxins from cigarettes. The full scope of the damage of this poisoning effect has not been completely analyzed.

We all suffer from the secondhand smoke of the smoker. The nonsmoker feels acutely uncomfortable in a room filled with smoke and for good reason. He does not have the tolerance to tobacco that has been built up by the chronic smoker. In addition to the tars and irritating substances which affect the nose and eyes, the smoke in the room may contain an appreciable amount of carbon monoxide. Tests have shown that in a room of smokers the carbon monoxide level may be as high as 20 to 80 parts per million. (The accepted upper level of carbon monoxide in industry is only 50 parts per million!) In other words, anyone closeted in a room of heavy smokers is subjected to carbon monoxide poisoning of at least a mild degree. The nonsmoker will not have acquired a tolerance to this. The chronic smoker can take it because 5 to 10 percent of his hemoglobin is already bound up with carbon monoxide, and he literally suffers from chronic mild carbon monoxide poisoning for which he has made some adaptations. Even mild carbon monoxide poisoning can lead to headache and general malaise.

In addition to the carbon monoxide effect, studies of the sputum obtained from nonsmokers who live in close association with smokers have shown lesser degrees of the same changes seen in smokers. Certain types of cells that are brown stained because of cigarette smoking are common in smokers. Some of these cells are also seen in nonsmokers if they live with smokers. Such cells disappear when the nonsmoker is removed from this environment or when the smoker stops smoking. Changes in sinus secretions are also observed in the nonsmoking individual who is constantly exposed to the smoker. The evidence seems clear that the nonsmoking individual is affected somewhat less by the toxic effects of cigarette smoking but in the same manner as the chronic smoker. Then, of course, there are a host of individuals with medical problems such as allergies, hay fever, and asthma who are quite intolerant or even hypersensitive to cigarette smoke. They find it most disagreeable and sometimes even dangerous to be exposed to cigarette smoke.

Obviously, clean air is essential for good health and hence long life. Clean air is free of pollutants, which include tobacco smoke with its carbon monoxide just as much as automobile exhaust fumes with their carbon monoxide. The full scope of cigarette smoking's influence on health is not fully defined because there are so many other aspects of our living patterns that are also injurious to health. Its effect may be even more serious than is generally appreciated. In any case the evidence is sufficient to justify the report of the Surgeon General's Committee in 1964 which stated unequivocally that cigarette smoking was "a health hazard of sufficient importance to warrant appropriate remedial action." So, if you want to stay young and avoid wrinkling of the face, sudden death, heart attack, emphysema, and a multitude of other disorders, one of the best things you can do for yourself, if you are a smoker, is to stop. The sooner you stop, the more rapidly you will begin to return to a better state of health and the better will be your chances of reversing the adverse effects of cigarette smoking.

ALCOHOL

Drinking alcoholic beverages is not one of the recently acquired habits of man. Apparently alcoholic beverages have been around since the dawn of history, but they are none the less dangerous to health. The early fermented beverages were relatively lcw in alcoholic content. When the Arabs introduced distilling to Europe during the Middle Ages, however, alcohol was acclaimed as the long-sought "elixir of life" and the remedy of almost all diseases (not unlike cortisone and numerous other so-called miracle drugs). In fact, the very word *whiskey* comes from Gaelic *uisge beatha,* which means "water of life."

Far from being an elixir of life, alcohol through its effect on the liver and other organs is probably responsible for more deaths than anything else except heart disease and cancer. The National Council on Alcoholism (NCA) states that 30,000 deaths a year are due to alcohol. The principal mode of death is cirrhosis (scarring and damage of the liver), which is the third most common cause of death in young and middle-aged adults. However, cirrhosis of the liver can arise from a number of disorders other than alcohol. In addition, alcohol is involved in more than half of the nation's over 60,000 traffic fatalities each year.

These grim statistics don't even begin to tell the whole story about alcohol and its role in causing human misery. In the United States about 79 percent of all men and 63 percent of women have drunk alcohol or do drink alcohol occasionally. Figures vary, but 80 to 85 million Americans are thought to qualify as "drinkers," and 4 to 5 million of these are alcoholics. The NCA claims that there are 6.5 million alcoholics, and some estimates run as high as 16 million. The American Psychiatric Association believes that over 9 million Americans are so dependent upon alcohol that the habit is ruining their career or home. Willard O. Foster, coordinator of alcoholism programs in Maryland, estimates that there are 10 times as many alcoholics as drug addicts.

There is considerable disagreement about what constitutes an alcoholic. The use of alcohol is so much a part of the social fabric of our culture that it is difficult to establish definitions that are any more than arbitrary classifications. Being incapacitated by alcohol is not necessarily an indication of alcoholism. By most standards Winston Churchill consumed enough alcohol in various forms to put many self-respecting alcoholics to shame and yet he led Great Britain to victory in World War II and was a towering figure on the stage of history. But for every Churchill there are countless others mired in alcoholic failure.

The example of Churchill's long life is often cited as evidence that drinking doesn't affect one's health; however, Churchill's health left much to be desired, since he had at least one heart attack and several strokes and died disabled by senility. His last days actually were what most of us would like to avoid.

Despite the social and cultural aspects of alcohol and various arbitrary definitions of alcoholism, we can be fairly specific about the biological effects of alcohol on the body.

Alcohol is a food, each gram of which contains 7 calories. It can thus add appreciably to a person's caloric intake and contribute to obesity. Only fat contains more calories per gram than alcohol. Pure alcohol has more calories than pure sugar or pure protein. In addition to supplying calories (without benefit of vitamins, minerals, or other essential nutrients), alcohol stimulates the appetite, partly through causing the brain to release inhibitions and partly through stimulating the secretion of digestive juices. Alcohol is a significant deterrent to meaningful dietary programs designed to prevent fat. In addition, some alcoholics, particularly those in poor economic circumstances, often drink rather than eat. These individuals end up with significant dietary deficiencies which accelerate the development of liver disease and other bodily damage.

Alcohol also has a direct action on the cells. It is freely soluble in water and attacks the living cell by causing it to lose its water and coagulate its protein. Since the protein elements in the cell are essential to its function, clearly alcohol cannot be doing anything to promote the health and longevity of individual cells. By drying out the cells and coagulating their vital proteins, it can lead to cellular death. Apparently there are other mechanisms through which alcohol acts as a cellular toxin. The advent of the electron microscope made it possible to look directly at the damage it does to cells. It injures the muscle fibers of the heart as well as other cells in the body.

The effects of alcohol do not end here. Dr. Melvin H. Knisely, a world authority on the phenomenon of "sludging," believes that this is a major factor in how alcohol damages the body. Normally the millions of red blood cells in the body circulate freely in the blood without clumping or sticking together. In some way alcohol affects the red blood cells so that they tend to stick together or "sludge." Dr. Knisely and his colleagues observed that sludging was common after the ingestion of even small amounts of alcohol. They began their studies by looking at the small blood vessels in the back of the eye that can be readily observed with an ophthalmoscope (the special lighted instrument the doctor uses in examining your eyes). They could literally see the red blood cells pile up on each other and clog those small blood vessels. The more an individual drank, the more sludging and plugging would occur. When he drank to the point of stupor, the red blood cells actually clogged up enough of the vessels to cause tiny hemorrhages in the back of the eye.

Further investigation revealed that the sludging phenomenon occurred throughout the body. Basically, when the small blood vessels are plugged with the clumped red blood cells, circulation through them stops. If a large number of these blood vessels are plugged, the organ involved does not get sufficient oxygen. Because of oxygen starvation, cellular deterioration begins and small hemorrhages occur.

Just as these events are observed in the back of the eye, they also occur in the brain. Dr. Knisely believes that alcohol induces multiple small hemorrhages in the brain and by the sludging action causes numerous small areas to be oxygen starved. It is true that on an examination after death individuals who have drunk alcohol for many years show small patches of destroyed brain cells throughout the brain. Whereas the liver, if damaged by the plugging of vessels, can regenerate itself up to a point, the brain cells cannot. The overwhelming evidence is that the continued drinking of alcohol irreparably harms the brain cells. The amount of harm is directly related to the amount and frequency of the drinking.

Alcohol is known to impair the heart. Individuals who drink an appreciable amount may have sufficient heart damage to develop congestive heart failure with old-fashioned "dropsy" or an accumulation of fluid in the abdomen, legs, and lungs. Their heart failure is entirely analogous to the advanced heart damage from other causes. The main difference is that if they are kept away from alcohol entirely, the heart will recover and congestive failure will disappear. Unfortunately, many people who have the alcoholic habit to such a degree as to produce this response return to the bottle and return to the hospital in heart failure.

Even individuals with heart diseases from other causes do not tolerate alcohol well. Alcohol was once thought to be good for anyone who had heart disease, particularly in regard to preventing chest pain. It was supposed to increase the blood flow to the ailing heart muscle. This claim has not been proved; on the contrary, in people with heart disease, small amounts of alcohol can further impair the function of the heart and cause even more difficulty.

The liver has a surprising capacity to regenerate itself. Nevertheless, long-continued consumption of alcohol can lead to replacement of liver tissue with scar tissue and eventually a shrunken, inadequately operating liver and possibly liver failure. It has been argued through the years that liver damage occurs only in individuals with deficient diets. Certainly a dietary deficiency, particularly insufficient variety of proteins and vitamin B_1 (thiamine), increases the likelihood of liver injury from alcohol ingestion. But even individuals on apparently satisfactory diets who consume excessive amounts of alcohol are susceptible to liver disease.

Alcohol is a powerful stimulant to the stomach to pour out acid pepsin juice. It is this response to alcohol that accelerates the development of ulcers. No one with a peptic ulcer should use alcohol in any form. Alcohol is especially toxic to all of the soft mucous membranes of the body, including those of the mouth and gums and the lining of the digestive tract. It can literally burn these tissues. Inflammation of the lining of the stomach or "gastritis" in heavy drinkers is due to this action. Alcoholic gastritis may not yield any evidence with an ordinary stomach x-ray. Individuals who drink a great deal of alcohol are often examined for the possibility of ulcers, and when none are found their problem is ignored. Instead, attention ought to be directed to the probability of underlying gastritis which causes the aching pain and sometimes burning in the pit of the stomach.

The organ that is perhaps the most sensitive to alcohol is the brain. It is true that the change in the function in the brain is similar to that seen at altitude or on exposure to oxygen-poor air, which is consistent with Dr. Knisely's observation. In a sense alcohol is an anesthetic to the brain if ingested in sufficient quantity. It is not an excitant any more than decreased oxygen is. What really happens is that alcohol releases the inhibitions in some of the functions of the brain, allowing people to become garrulous and overactive and engage in activities that their usual social conscience would prohibit. This response is apparently due to a derangement in the way signals are sent through the complex switchboard within the brain itself. The switchboard is responsible for integrating speech, movement, judgment, and the functions of the different parts of the brain. It is not surprising, therefore, that alcohol causes individuals to lose their coordination and skill. Continuous use brings alcoholic blackouts and other medical problems including rum fits and DT's. Eventually, senile changes of the brain ensue.

Many people are content with the thought that only those who drink large amounts of alcohol are going to have difficulties. This is not true. The sludging phenomenon described by Dr. Knisely was noted in individuals who had drunk as little as one beer. Of course sludging was more extensive and more serious, the more alcohol one had ingested. Nevertheless, small changes in circulation are apparent with minimal drinking. It is possible but not definite that drinking as little as one beer merely causes a temporary oxygen starvation without permanently damaging cell function. Whether or not this is the case depends on how severe the plugging of the vessels is—in other words, how severe the oxygen starvation is and how long it lasts. Nerve cells can withstand oxygen starvation for only short periods of time. Thus, the individual who is only a light drinker but drinks regularly may indeed be providing the basis for progressive, continuous destruction of cells in the brain which cannot be regenerated or restored.

Dr. Gerhard Freund at Gainesville, Florida, has experimental evidence that moderate drinking leads to decreased learning capacity. He fed mice a chocolate-type food with and without alcohol. He eliminated the possibility that the mice would have any dietary deficiency. The alcoholic mice got an amount of alcohol equivalent to what the "executive drinker" inbibes—the man who has one or two cocktails at lunch and several in the evening, a common practice of the American executive. When the phase of alcoholic ingestion had been terminated and learning tasks were presented to the "executive drinker" mice and the abstaining mice, the former could not learn whereas the latter could. The implications are obvious: *The continued use of relatively moderate amounts of alcohol impairs learning capacity.*

All of these observations point to an important fact for individuals interested in living their normal life span in good health and free of senility. The more you drink, the more frequently you drink, and the more years you drink, the more brain damage you will have with a consequent loss of judgment and mental ability—in short, senility.

DRUGS

Only a limited amount of information is available on the influence of drugs on aging. The drug habit is relatively new in the Western culture. Its full effects on aging will probably not be known for several decades. Nevertheless, some tentative information is available.

Amphetamine Group

The amphetamines are the "uppers": bennies (Benzedrine), speed (Methedrine), Dexedrine, and Dexamyl. The amphetamines and caffeine belong to the same group of stimulants called analeptics. Caffeine is the stimulating ingredient in coffee, tea, and colas. The amphetamine group stimulates the nervous system, increasing alertness. They are useful medicinally in treating certain problems of old age. They are also useful in treating depressive states and in hyperactive children or those with related disorders. In other words, used properly, they are not all bad. Used indiscriminately for social purposes, however, they can cause problems. Since all lead to increased heart rate, chronic use has the opposite effect of physical conditioning. The higher heart rate results in a small heart with a limited capacity to pump blood. "Uppers" can also raise the blood pressure and in large doses have been known to cause heart attacks. Any of the amphetamine group increases the likelihood of irregularities of the heart, and chronic use can lead to palpitations and rapid heart action.

Individuals using amphetamines in large quantities or over long periods of time may develop delusions (sometimes violent) and other evidence of psychic disturbance. Chronic use or use of large doses can cause brain damage which may be irreversible. In small amounts these drugs, like caffeine in the coffee drinker, probably will not bring about any obvious change unless one begins to look at the secondary effects related to increased heart rate and altered heart rhythm. It is well to keep in mind that individuals with a resting heart rate of over 80 beats per minute have a much higher incidence of heart attacks and sudden death than individuals with resting heart rates below 70 beats per minute.

On the positive side, the amphetamines are useful in controlling appetite and inducing weight loss. However, many authorities feel that this effect is merely transitory and wears off within a few days and that the chronic use of Dexamyl and other products as appetite suppressants can lead to the adverse findings of prolonged amphetamine use.

Marijuana

Very little is known about the long-term influence of marijuana. Some of its effects have been compared to those of alcohol, which over the long term are not very beneficial. Dr. Harris Rosenkrantz and Dr. Yugal K. Luthra of the National Institutes of Health have recently demonstrated that very large doses of marijuana can produce permanent brain damage in rats. Seizures, convulsions, and death were observed. There was loss of brain protein and RNA. Certainly any substance that interferes with the RNA in the brain is capable of significantly altering the brain's function and integrity and perhaps even altering the programmed life expectancy. These studies, however, did involve large quantities of marijuana, far in excess of the amount that would ordinarily be used in marijuana smoking. Nevertheless, they raise a danger signal concerning the possible long-term implications of excessive marijuana use.

Barbiturates

Barbiturates are the "downers." This group of drugs includes phenobarbital and Seconal, and their long-term effects are still to be discovered. However, when combined with alcohol, relatively small amounts are dangerous and can cause death.

LSD

LSD has not been used long enough for its effects on longevity to be determined. It is known to cause damage to the chromosomes and hence offspring in individuals who have used it. It has medicinal utility in treatment of psychiatric disorders, but it is a dangerous drug and the very fact that it can alter chromosomes suggests an effect at the cellular level which in turn could influence the timetable or longevity. Both time and additional studies will be needed to learn the impact of the taking of LSD on longevity. One may hope that its use in society will be so limited as to render these studies unnecessary.

Coffee, Tea, Colas, and Cocoa

Most people who drink coffee, tea, colas, and cocoa are startled when you tell them they are chronic drug users. A drug is a drug whether it is taken as a pill or a shot or dissolved in liquid and sipped as a drink. The use of a liquid vehicle to administer a medication is as old as medicine and continues—for example, in the familiar cough syrup. The cultural drinking of coffee, tea, colas, and cocoa is a drug habit, and the principal drug is caffeine, although varied amounts of other drugs are also contained in these beverages. When you urge someone to have a cup of coffee with you, you in fact, become a drug pusher. The same applies to the other drinks. Caffeine and the amphetamine or speed group of drugs—"uppers"—belong to the same group of drugs called analeptics.

Caffeine is a powerful nervous system stimulant. As such it acts just the opposite of the way sedatives and tranquilizers do. It makes little sense to wash tranquilizers down with a cup of coffee or a cola drink. Caffeine stimulates the thought process and even increases activity. In small amounts it increases the speed and accuracy of typists. In larger doses (1000 milligrams) it may even cause delirium, ear ringing, tremulousness, and flashing lights. Caffeine stimulates the stomach to pour out acid pepsin juice. It is this action that aggravates or contributes to peptic ulcer formation. Even in animals (animals normally don't have ulcers) large doses or repeated daily small doses cause changes and ulceration in the digestive tract. That burning in the pit of the stomach with or without an ulcer is often due to too much coffee, tea, or cola, and the proper treatment is not tranquilizers but stopping the coffee, tea, or cola habit.

The effect of these drinks on the heart is partly secondary through their action as a nervous system stimulant and partly direct through their action on the heart muscle and blood vessels. In any case the work of the heart is increased because bodily activity is accelerated, requiring more oxygen and hence more blood circulation. The caffeine tends to increase the heart rate significantly in some people; I have seen many young healthy individuals with resting heart rates 15 to 20 beats higher than normal associated with coffee drinking. Cessation of the habit has led to a return to lower heart rates. In this regard, caffeine has the opposite effect to physical conditioning. Continued regular usage of caffeine and related drugs leads to a rapidly beating small heart with limited functional capacity. Such a heart is particularly prone to irregularities, including extra or skipped heartbeats. In some individuals regular use of any of the beverages containing caffeine or related drugs will cause important irregularities of the heart including attacks of rapid heart action. A small rapidly beating heart is associated with an appreciable rise in heart attacks and sudden death. The chronic use of any of these drugs can contribute to this problem. It is important to emphasize again that individuals with resting heart rates of over 80 beats per minute are much more likely to have a heart attack or die suddenly than those with resting heart rates below 70 beats per minute.

These beverages will also significantly increase the level of blood pressure in some people. Since the lower the blood pressure (within physiological limits) the less likelihood there is of atherosclerosis, this is an important consideration even in people with so-called normal pressure levels.

Coffee has not been a longtime habit in Western civilization. It originated with the Arabs and was introduced to Europe in the seventeenth century. The consumption of coffee in the United States has grown since the beginning of the twentieth century parallel to the increase in heart disease. The average consumption of coffee per person before World War I was only 9 pounds a year. By World War II it had risen to 16 pounds per year—about what it is today. Only the Scandinavians use more coffee than the people of the United States. The Swedes use 30 pounds of coffee per person a year. The United States now consumes over 70 percent of the world's coffee supply.

One cup of coffee, depending on how it is brewed, contains from 100 to 150 milligrams of caffeine. Since the toxic level may be as low as 1000 milligrams, it is clear that anyone who is drinking from six to ten cups of coffee a day is getting approximately a toxic dose of caffeine. There is a great deal of difference in individual sensitivity, and tolerance is developed. Some people will have adverse reactions (a sleepless night) to as little as one cup of coffee while others can drink quantities of it and sleep like a log. In very sensitive individuals, a single cup of coffee is sufficient to precipitate irregularities of the heart. Obviously individuals who have irregularities of the heart or a fast resting heart rate or any evidences of digestive disturbances, including peptic ulcers or just plain burning in the pit of the stomach, should not take coffee in any form.

Some of the other ingredients of coffee contribute to these problems, particularly the flavor oils in the coffee, which may be irritating to the digestive tract. Thus, using a decaffeinated product is satisfactory for many individuals to avoid the effects of caffeine, but others are also adversely affected by the other ingredients of the coffee bean.

If the individual who has been drinking a lot of coffee stops suddenly, he will have withdrawal symptoms: a moderate to severe headache and drowsiness with loss of energy. These symptoms can be readily relieved by taking one cup of coffee. To avoid the problem the heavy coffee drinker should gradually decrease his intake of coffee, perhaps to only two cups a day as a starting point, then only one cup a day, and finally none.

Tea is a much older drink in our society. It was a common drink in China in the eighth century and was brought to Europe with the spice trade. Like coffee, it contains appreciable amounts of caffeine. How much depends on the way it is brewed, but a single cup of tea may contain from 35 to 150 milligrams of caffeine. Because of the other related drugs that it contains, it is sometimes a more powerful stimulant to the heart than coffee, particularly if brewed fairly strong.

The *cola* drinks are a twentieth-century addition to our culture. They provide the liquid vehicle for caffeine. A 12-ounce bottle of cola drink usually contains about 50 milligrams of caffeine. As such it is one-half to one-third as effective as a cup of coffee.

It is not generally recognized that *cocoa* is also a stimulating drink. One cup of cocoa usually contains about 50 milligrams of caffeine plus related drugs. Thus, it is more stimulating than a 12-ounce bottle of cola. Cocoa originated with the Aztecs of Mexico City. The Spaniards discovered that the Aztecs were making a drink from the cocoa beans and adding vanilla to it. Vanilla also came from Mexico City. In the 1700's the English added milk to it, and hence we have cocoa. While the milk may help to neutralize some of the acid produced by the caffeine stimulation of the stomach, in sensitive individuals with digestive disturbances, it may not, and therefore it is not recommended for them.

The effect of these beverages on the aging process is not known. However, because of what they do to the cardiovascular system, particularly causing persistent higher heart rates, they may be an important factor in increasing the incidence of cardiac irregularity, heart attacks, and sudden death. Individual susceptibility to this reaction is probable. The fact that the drug effect of these beverages is the opposite of physical conditioning strongly suggests that they are not beneficial in preventing aging or any of the diseases commonly associated with the aging process.

eighteen

Psychosocial Functions

Although much has been written about the mental changes and social problems of aging, little has been said about preventing them. To the extent that any measure maintaining good health prevents changes in the brain, it is a preventive measure. Exercises for the mind, however, and a preventive remedy for social problems are more a pious hope than a reality. This is not to say that you shouldn't try to delay or prevent psychosocial problems, and the proper time to begin is early in life. The goal is to retain the rational function of the mind as long as possible.

Many individuals make death plans. There are few persons of means who have not arranged for death insurance to be paid to their survivors. Countless others have made provision for their heirs through "estate planning." Despite all of this concern about what is to be done after death, what is to be done before death seems to get scant attention. Few individuals give serious consideration to their own personal lives in later years or to the steps that need to be taken to ensure a satisfactory social psychosocial functions. The preoccupation with the events to follow death seems somewhat premature unless those that precede it have been planned for.

The function of the mind is dependent upon the functional state of the entire body. Loss of hearing and eyesight minimizes the normal sensory input to the brain. Disease of the arteries that limits circulation to the brain affects its cells. The prolonged use of alcohol harms the brain. Indeed, brain damage from any toxin, illness, or injury will affect its function and decrease the likelihood of optimal function in advancing years.

The loss of brain function can take many forms, including loss of memory for recent events. We are all familiar with the older person who tells the same story over and over. This is the classic example of retention of long-term memory but impairment of short-term memory. The individual can remember events from the far past well enough to recount them, sometimes in detail, but his short-term memory is not good enough to recall having just told the story, so he repeats it. Retention of memory facilities, both long-term and short-term, should be a goal of a preventive program.

Most individuals are anxious to avoid the psychological and psychiatric problems which occur in aging. The actual mechanics of the brain may change, giving rise to frank delusions. Personality changes and depression of varying degrees are common. Part of the problem stems from the life changes faced by older people. They lose their usual social position because of mental or physical failings and sometimes because of personality changes. Attitudes of society, for example, as regards the mandatory retirement age, are important social factors. Older people often lose their ability to make meaningful contributions either in terms of gainful employment or in other activities of organized society. They no longer feel needed as their children have grown up and assumed their own responsibilities. The children may even have disappeared from their immediate daily emotional contact. In addition, there is the obvious loss of physical prowess and often sexual adequacy. The older person going through this combination of events is thrown into a stage of dependency not greatly different from that he experienced in infancy. Assuming a dependency position in society actually precipitates an identity crisis. These complex situations, both psychological and sociological, bring on depressions.

What can one do about these problems of old age? There seem to have been very few organized programs to evaluate whether it is possible to keep these unpleasant events from occurring. No major program has tried to establish what can be done to avoid loss of memory by memory training or to judge the effectiveness of different social measures. The proposals made in this chapter, therefore, are based on generalizations developed from a concept of learning, sociology, and what happens in later years. They present a working format of the ideas which can be implemented to help cope with the problems of later years. It is important to understand that these efforts should begin early in life because action started once one is already in the grip of senility often comes too late. It is at least partially true that in the older years we become more of what we were in younger years, so developing the proper psychosocial environment, attitudes, interests, and mental capabilities in early life helps us maintain these same qualities later.

PREVENTING ISOLATION

The isolation of age is related to sociological factors including family, occupation, and decreasing abilities. It is most distressing to older people, yet much can be done to avoid it if the problem is tackled early enough. The first and most obvious place to begin is with the family. Maintaining good family relations, not only with parents and brothers and sisters, but with the younger members supplies a social continuity which is important in later years. Older social systems provided for the continuity of generations which helped each generation to cope with its own peculiarities. This is not always the case in modern society. Develop these relationships if they are available to you. If they are not, make meaningful substitutes for them: find friends. Community life in many societies has afforded ample friends for most people. The tribal customs of the American Indians furnished continuous contact among individuals in a wide range outside the immediate family circle. The same was true of the old manor house, in which numbers of families lived together and directed their various skills toward the complete functioning of the whole.

The modern isolated family unit has lost these external strengths, a loss that has been accentuated as individuals have become disinterested in community affairs. The most satisfactory replacements for these needs are meaningful friends. Each individual will find friends according to his own interests if he makes the effort. In order to avoid social isolation it is a good idea to develop new friendships regularly, with people who are younger as well as those who are older than oneself. Set up a positive program of trying to make one new good friend a year. It goes without saying that to establish friendship one must be a friend. This process helps to develop the characteristics that in the long run prevent isolation.

Closely related to finding friends is belonging to organizations. These literally are social vehicles which can be very successful in combating isolation. Many older people find both the church and politics meaningful ways of participating in organized society. In the child-rearing years the organizational structure around the children is fine, but once the children are gone, participation in it often becomes limited or lapses completely. When you seek to become active in organizations, do so in some that will give lifetime meaningful contact. Join at least one organization which is made up predominantly of people your own age. The reason is simple. In groups that are comprised of all different ages the older people are frequently shunted aside from leadership and participation roles as time progresses. On the other hand, if all the members of the society or organization are in your general age group, you can expect to be an active participant through the years. The drawback, of course, is that age takes its toll, and such organizations are likely to cease to exist in time. Consequently it is equally wise to join an organization which includes mixed age groups. This will also provide you contacts with individuals older than yourself, your own age, and younger than yourself. Making younger friends will add a "psychological youth treatment" to your aging psyche.

Don't neglect the idea of accepting a leadership role in some organizational structure: helping educate underpriviledged children, perhaps, or simply supervising playground activities or acting as the adult sponsor for some young people's group. If you provide the proper mix and don't get penned in with organizations that have limited life spans such as those tied strictly to a man's business function or to having children, you can find psychological insurance against social isolation.

One of the striking features about the long-lived Abkhasians in Russia is their social structure. In four-generation families the oldest members, even those who are centenarians, have a sense of belonging. They always feel that the younger generations need what they can contribute. The lesson here is that one of the things that help keep people mentally young is a feeling of being needed or a sense of responsibility. By exposing yourself properly you can encourage this. If you happen to be talented in a special area, you might wish to teach, but do take on some activities that require responsibility. Do something that you know your failure to do will disappoint or adversely affect someone. The intention is to prevent suffering or unhappiness, and knowing what will happen if you don't do it will give you a sense of responsibility.

Even writing letters to people who are lonely and need personal contact is helpful. Many shut-ins welcome communication with other people. One meaningful goal, if one has the energy for it, would be to establish telephone friendships with shut-ins. Simply calling older people who don't often receive visitors makes them happier and helps to remove their sense of isolation.

Of course, the more talents you have, the more things you can do that will give you a sense of responsibility. To be wanted you must have something to give. If you look at a man like Konrad Adenauer, who served as chancellor of West Germany until he was past 90, you will know that he must have had a feeling of responsibility and satisfaction in being needed. Despite his 90 years his country still depended upon his leadership. Not everyone can be an Adenauer, but in their own way individuals who make the effort can find tasks which require responsibility. This course of action sometimes takes courage. It calls for taking on liabilities, and usually they are personal liabilities if anything personal is going to be achieved.

IMPORTANCE OF GOALS

Plan long-range goals. Many people drift aimlessly through life and in their later years have no particular "reason for living." Having a goal is important. The goal you select should be long-term enough to require some meaningful effort on your part. The businessman who plans carefully for the financial aspects of his retirement had better plan equally carefully for some goals after retirement as well. Each person will have to define what his own goals might be. One good approach is to plan a second career. The working individual should begin developing a second career long before the time of retirement so that he will be able to acquire some skill and aptitude in it. Photography is one example, or, if you are exceptionally talented, you might go in for painting or other forms of the arts.

Women too need a second career. Most women's career is their home and children. A high percentage of older women are widows. Their children are gone, and they are left in isolation. Their work as a homemaker is essentially over, and unless they have done something to develop a second career they may feel goalless. A woman who is clever with a needle and thread may be able to make and sell her handiwork. Women can become successful photographers or writers or go into business in their later years. The best approach is to capitalize on one's best talents.

While making long-range goals, couples should think seriously about what to do after the husband comes home for retirement, particularly in the American society where the home is not the man's castle, but the wife's. This is where she has practiced her occupation. She has lived here on a 24-hour basis and has arranged it primarily for her function. When the husband comes home at age 65 and sits in her house and listens to her television set and disrupts her routine, she is usually not too pleased. Similarly, the man is somewhat unhappy because he feels uncomfortable. He misses the trappings of his office (his home away from home) or his job. He may not have any distinct portion of the house that he really feels is his own. In general the situation produces more togetherness than either one is able to cope with. Unfortunately, it is economically impossible for everyone to have sufficiently spacious living quarters to maintain a degree of privacy and periods when he can be alone or work on his own thing. It is wise to plan your living patterns ahead of time, however, to do what can be done about this possible area of conflict.

Hobbies serve a real purpose. They are ways of learning to do more things, and again it is important to remember that if you wish to be wanted you must have something to offer. The problem with the hobby idea is that too often it falls into the category of basket weaving, which is not much of a challenge for a man who has been president of General Motors. Nonessential basket weaving just doesn't do much for one's psyche. But one can develop meaningful hobbies, some of which in turn set the stage for a second career. Raising animals or pets is a good example. One individual might wish to raise horses; another, dogs; another, cats; still another, all three. The dog fancier may eventually have a kennel. There are dog shows with social contact. Breeding and selling animals may even provide financial return, and in any case there is an emotional contact between people and animals. Pets are excellent emotional support for people in all age groups; think of a child's first dog or the dog that brings the old man his slippers. They help relieve the sense of isolation, and I strongly recommend them.

Gardening can become a meaningful hobby. If you have been a company president and accustomed to lots of activity you may end up extending it into a commercial project and selling organic foods or having your own greenhouse. At the very least you can raise part of your own food, and the whole process of growing things becomes interesting and involves one's mind.

All of these suggestions are intended to provide means to help solve the sociological problems of aging. Many others could be added to the list. The idea here is to indicate some of the directions that people should begin to take early in life to provide "social insurance" against the isolation of aging.

MEMORY EXERCISE

What to do about the memory deficits and learning problems of old age must at this point be strictly theoretical. Efforts to date to stave off these problems have been primarily directed toward maintaining physical health—by preventing atherosclerosis or other diseases. One theoretical approach is to take advantage of Hebb's theory of learning. According to Hebb, when you learn something, connections are formed between different "neurons" in the brain, and as these connections are reinforced an organized pattern develops, which he called a "cell assembly." If you learned a series of interrelated things, this was a "phase sequence" or the normal thought process.

The important element of Hebb's idea is that learning involves structural changes in the cells. Numerous studies since the original theory appeared have supported the idea that chemical changes occur in the cells with the learning process. What we learn through our eyes, ears, nose, or touch provides signals to the brain which in turn affect the chemical organization perhaps even of the DNA and RNA in certain cells of our nervous system. Knowledge and cellular chemistry are closely related.

The importance of this concept in preventing deterioration of the functions of the brain is that it offers a means of exercising the brain which may be just as vital to these chemical mechanisms as physical exercise is to the chemistry of skeletal muscle. What effects could be achieved by using memory training and modern teaching techniques with older people? While much effort is directed toward developing programs to quickly advance the brains of young people, nothing has really been done so far to reinforce the learning and memory capacities of their elders. Lacking this knowledge, about the only thing you can do is "exercise the system": set up your own program of memory training and learning.

For memory training one approach might be to memorize something new at regular intervals even if it is a very short verse a day or something else which you want to learn. If Shakespeare interests you, pick out some long passages and learn a few lines a day until you have memorized the chosen segments. Or you might wish to memorize something else. But the process of memorizing helps reinforce the brain's chemical mechanism to memorize.

It is important to realize that Hebb's theory of learning also means that individuals who have developed "phase sequences" have the building blocks to learn more. This is the basic concept to explain why learning may be difficult at first but as times goes on becomes much more rapid. The various "phase sequences" are the foundation for new learning experiences, not only in youth but as the years pass. The problem is that once formal education is stopped many individuals stop having sufficient stimulus to develop cell assemblies and phase sequences; consequently learning processes become progressively more difficult.

That the complex nervous system can be kept intact, including its memory, is well exemplified by concert pianists who have reached advanced age and are still masters of their field. To play the intricate scores they must retain the complete memory pattern of the music in the brain as well as all the mechanisms that enable them to respond to the memory pattern. One reason individuals well past their 80's can continue to perform at this high level is that their memory patterns have been constantly reinforced by the continuing action of playing the piano. Similarly, you can no doubt gradually increase your scope of knowledge and your memory capability by making it a point to learn and remember something new each day.

To retain one's memory it is a good safeguard to start early in life to develop memory mechanisms. The young person with a "poor memory" can improve his memory pattern by using memory techniques. Numerous books are available to the general public on this subject, and many of them will provide different concepts which are useful in helping one to improve his memory. A simple one is the word association pattern, illustrated as follows: Assign a number to each of five objects and memorize this list as your basic word list. It might be:

1. Apple
2. Shoe
3. Tree
4. Door
5. Hive

Once you have memorized your own list of five objects with their numbers, you can literally play games when you need to remember things. If someone were to give you a list of five items in order, you would be able to recall any one of them when he asked for the number. Suppose you were given the following:

1. Apple
2. Flower
3. Dollar
4. Hammer
5. Vase

You could form a mental picture association between your word list and the five objects you have been asked to remember: a gun shooting the apple off a boy's head, a flower growing out of the shoe, dollars growing on trees, a hammer pounding on a door, or a vase set on top of a beehive. Such association mechanisms as memory aids are useful, and developing a number of them to a high degree early in life will help you in your memory patterns if you use them as the years advance.

An important aspect in memory and learning training is to expand as many of your capabilities as you can. Get the most out of your life's experiences. When you read or listen, do so with the intent to recall what you have just been exposed to. If you read something, at the end of the page ask yourself what are the main ideas you have read. Try to pick the points out of something you have just read so that you can relate them. You might even wish to jot down the principal facts you learned from a particular article or story after you have finished it. You can do likewise when you listen to a program or a lecture.

When someone is talking on a subject ask yourself what main points he is really making. Try to separate these out of the flow of words and conversation. At the end of a social evening sit down and try to recall the salient ideas that came up during a discussion. By training yourself to pick out the key points from the things you have read or heard or seen, you will quickly develop a facility for learning and retaining facts. *Unless you are able to identify the main points—for example, in an article that you have read—it is unlikely that you are going to remember them, so the first step is recognizing the real message. The second step is remembering it.*

SELF-IMPROVEMENT

Closely related to all this is setting educational goals for yourself. Some may be arbitrary. If you have never been very good in geography, make a decision to sit down and learn the main geographical areas of the world. You would not have to memorize the names of the capitals or anything as rote and unproductive as that, although these could be used for memory training if you chose, but you would be developing an organized concept of the geography of the world, its regional temperatures and climates—in short, starting to understand the world in which you live. You can do the same with history, literature, music, or almost any field that arouses your curiosity. Having this kind of information you will be more interesting to other people. One of the reasons older people fall into isolation is that, not having enough to offer, they are not interesting to anyone else. Usually they simply haven't bothered to continue to learn anything. This problem can be avoided with a self-improvement program.

EMOTIONAL TRAINING

Aside from the social and intellectual training mechanisms which are important in psychosocial aspects of aging, one must consider emotional conditioning. As one gets older there is a great tendency toward "inwardness." This is closely related to the hypochondriacal nature of many older people and what is often described by young individuals as their "self-centered attitude." To get the most out of life you must have some emotional return, and you get it by being interested in other people. You must, therefore, learn to care—or, expressed more completely, learn to love. Like intellectual capacity, emotions need to be exercised. In many societies individuals develop flat emotional responses because they are trained to do so. The steel-eyed hero of the West who felt no emotions beyond wondering where the nearest water hole was for his horse developed this personality characteristic by emotional conditioning. Gradually hardening oneself not to respond emotionally and not to demonstrate emotions limits one's capacity to have an emotional experience. There is a physical analogy: If you bind the feet too tightly, they can't develop. Likewise if you bind the emotions too tightly, they will not develop.

It is difficult to tell people how to learn to care or how to learn to love, but it is important to realize that you must work at it. You must make a genuine effort to listen to other people's problems, to allow yourself to become involved in other people's needs, to encourage that spark of feeling that flickers inside you and hope that it grows to the point of being a genuine emotion. This is one of the things that grandparents often give to grandchildren. The realization that their grandparents love them will lure grandchildren to their side even when they are old, wrinkled, and physically not very attractive, at least in the eyes of the grandchildren. The old picture of the grandparents sitting by the fireplace rocking and telling the youngsters stories of the past exemplifies the principle of having something to give. The grandparents had love to give and also the knowledge of past experience, both of which were needed and wanted by the grandchildren. This is the essence of belonging. The person who makes a constructive effort in the emotional area early in life and learns how to give emotionally and not just materially will reap the benefits of this capacity in later years.

EXERCISE OF THE PSYCHOLOGICAL SYSTEM

The key to preventing the psychosocial problems of later years, then, is to develop your social capacity, goals, and interests; to develop your memory and learning capacities; and to develop your emotional capacities —in short, to constantly exercise the psychosocial system.

nineteen

Cures: Facts and Fantasies

Man's quest for immortality has spawned innumerable treatments for old age and ways to regain lost vigor. Most of these have been straightforward quackery practiced on the gullible and hopeful, but buried within the mountain of unscientific efforts are some useful ideas. One thing seems certain: The wonder pill or injection that prevents or reverses aging has not yet been found.

Apparent improvements after so-called youth therapy often owe their success to "the art of medicine" or "faith healing." The mind does wonderful things for the body, and faith in a form of treatment often does effect an improvement, however short-lived it might be. This is precisely the reason scientists evaluating drugs and treatments in clinical research insist on control subjects (not receiving therapy) and even go so far as to design experiments in which neither the doctor nor the patients know who is getting the real medicine and who is getting a sugar pill. Meaningful results must eliminate the bias of both the patient and the doctor. A patient markedly impressed with the doctor will often improve from the favorable psychological factors involved in the relationship.

Another factor in some forms of therapy is change in the patient's lifestyle. Better dietary habits, proper exercise, elimination of tobacco and other bad habits, stimulation of a new interest in life—all improve many people's health and overall response. Of course, nature being what it is, some patients recover in spite of their doctors rather than because of them.

LEGITIMATE MEDICINES

A number of medicines are legitimate, proper therapy in maintaining youth and vigor. Basically, all medicines and treatments which tend to restore health increase longevity, or at least that is their goal. Taking female hormones is a good example since they will delay the characteristic changes of the menopause and many of the changes which normally follow the menopause. To the extent that female hormones prevent drying up of the female sexual organs, loss of femininity, and even degeneration of the bone from osteoporosis, they may be thought of as youth medicine. This is not to say that the female hormones necessarily prolong the life span, but they do accomplish in part some of the major goals of youth therapy in extending the physiological state of the middle years, those years in the female when she is capable of reproduction. Of course, giving female hormones does not preserve her ability to have children, but many of the other aspects of femininity are retained.

Similarly, in those men who undergo bodily changes and it can be demonstrated that there is a significant decrease in male hormones, administering testosterone often contributes to the retention of bodily vigor and many of the desirable aspects of the middle years. Furthermore, in the overall hormone field, insulin used in the treatment of diabetes is clearly a lifesaving hormone in some instances and may prolong life and health. Thyroid hormone appears to be quite important, and as decreased amounts are formed in later years there is some evidence that giving replacement thyroid hormone is helpful. The administration of hormones in individuals who have normal hormone levels and normal endocrine functions has no useful effect on the body and can be harmful.

Medicines to prevent specific diseases closely associated with aging may also be thought of as youth pills. The various medicines which have been developed to help prevent atherosclerosis are in this category. To date, none of them have proved to be spectacular in that area. Most scientists think that the first step in preventing atherosclerosis is proper dietary and exercise measures, which have been discussed. Nevertheless, even when these measures are carried out conscientiously, there are a small number of individuals who are not significantly benefited. They continue to have high levels of fat particles in their blood stream and so are predisposed to atherosclerotic blockage of the arteries.

Many different medicines have been proposed to lower the fat levels in the blood. Some purport to bind the cholesterol and fatty products in the intestinal tract and keep them from being absorbed; others, to speed up the process of metabolic destruction of cholesterol and fatty products; still others, to block the formation of cholesterol and fatty particles that would be carried in the blood stream. Most of these medicines have been unsatisfactory. The effects of some have been minimal or questionable. Not all have been entirely safe. One, Mer-29, was used extensively for a few years until it was discovered that it could cause cataracts and baldness and gave other evidences of serious toxic effects on the human body. After these observations were made, the drug was withdrawn from the market. To significantly alter the basic mechanisms of the body by chemical means that are not really directed toward replacement or correction of actual abnormalities always offers the possibility of an adverse response. This is what sometimes makes the treatment worse than the disease.

In recent times two medicines worthy of mention have been used. One, dextrothyroxine (Choloxin), is a chemical variation of the thyroid hormone. It speeds up the destruction of cholesterol and fatty particles and hence lowers the blood levels. Some few individuals have significant improvements from this medication. In many other instances the changes effected are minimal. The other and perhaps more popular medicine is clofibrate (Atromid-S). It is not known exactly how clofibrate works. Its toxic effects in usual doses are negligible, but it will cause nausea, diarrhea, and abdominal discomfort in some people. It has not been used long enough for its total effect on the body to be fully evaluated. In addition to lowering cholesterol and fat particles in the blood, it prolongs the normal blood-clotting mechanism. This feature may be of importance in its possible role in preventing blood clots or thromboses associated with heart attacks. Some initial enthusiastic reports have claimed that clofibrate decreases the rate of heart attacks by as much as 50 percent. The studies were done in young men, and no association was made with a decrease in cholesterol as compared to an untreated control group. Initial results await verification and studies of other age groups before any sweeping conclusions can be drawn about the general uses of clofibrate in preventing heart attacks. Nevertheless, it is a promising medication.

Much of the enthusiasm for developing a pill which will prevent atherosclerosis is directly related to people's inability to stay on a diet and maintain a proper exercise program. They would rather take a pill than concern themselves about diet and exercise. This may well be a very shortsighted philosophy since *it is doubtful that a pill alone is going to eliminate the necessity for healthful living patterns.* Proper diet and exercise no doubt do much more for the body than just help forestall atherosclerosis. Restriction of calories has been shown to be associated with a significant increase in life span, particularly if initiated in youth. Taking a pill to lower the cholesterol and fat particles while at the same time stuffing oneself is not likely to extend the life span nearly as much as will adherence to dietary restrictions. The ideal medicines will probably be those that correct residual defects in the body chemistry of one who has already corrected the undesirable aspects in his life style, namely, overeating, lack of exercise, smoking cigarettes, drinking alcohol, and other unhealthy habits.

THE SEX GLAND TRANSPLANTERS

Aside from these legitimate enterprises in medicine to improve health and preserve life, there have been a host of less legitimate efforts directed toward "rejuvenation." Whereas women equated aging with loss of "beauty" and frequented the cosmetic rejuvenator, men equated aging with "loss of manhood." Sexual incapacity and aging seem to have been synonymous in the minds of many men and indeed many physicians. To most of the victims of these early charlatans the one clear-cut sign of rejuvenation was an erect penis. Since in numerous instances impotence is psychological, the confidence such victims got from the operation often produced the desired effect. In other instances the effects were temporary, and in still other treatments resulted in severe damage to health.

One of the most prominent rejuvenation charlatans was Dr. John Brinkley of Kansas, who became world famous with his goat gland transplants. The post–World War I period was the heyday of the transplant rejuvenators. Actually, respected scientists had demonstrated years before that testicle transplants would rejuvenate sexual activity. Transplanting testicles to the gizzard of an old rooster regenerated his hen-chasing instincts. But it remained for John Brinkley and his ilk to capitalize on testicular transplants. Because testicles do contain testosterone, no doubt some few individuals did get transitory hormonal effects, thought the effects may have been fairly weak.

Brinkley chose the goat because of its well-known sexual capacities. The victim's scrotum was incised and the cordlike epididymis freed from the body of the testicle. Then a goat gland was stuffed into the space and sewed in place. After the operation the man's scrotum was literally packed with goat glands. Following a careful on-site review of Brinkley's activities, the Kansas Medical Society revoked his license to practice medicine.

Brinkley was a powerful political figure in Kansas. I well recall in my early childhood there the story of his running for governor. He was, in fact, said to have been elected except for technicalities in how the votes were counted. Thus he was denied the governor's chair and finally thwarted in his efforts to flout the medical profession's curtailment of his activities and protection of the public.

Brinkley ran his own radio station and let it be known that for an additional sum of money he could even obtain a human testicle from a healthy man under 35 years of age. In all, John Brinkley is said to have transplanted 16,000 impotents before he was forced to flee south of the border to continue his fraudulent enterprise.

Brinkley had his European counterpart in Serge Voronoff, of Russian origin, whose base of operation was in France. Voronoff was not a total fraud. At the onset of World War I he published a paper on the successful transplane of a thyroid gland in a 14-year-old Corsican cretin. Voronoff also believed that the way to prevent aging in men was to augment their testicles. He felt that the decline in testicular function was associated with the other general evidences of bodily decline. He had a good basis for his opinion since he had been physician to the eunuchs of the harem of Khedive Abbas II in Egypt. He noted that the eunuchs seldom lived past 60 and when they died they looked like centenarians. However, more recent studies support the idea that male castrates live longer than intact males (see Chapter Ten, "The Sexual System").

Voronoff, like Brinkley, was a flamboyant character. At the beginning of this career he advertised for human donors. Reportedly only two responded, and they wanted exorbitant prices for one of their precious testicles. The absence of human donors led him to use chimpanzees, and for years he transplanted chimpanzee testicles into the scrotums of the rich and hopeful. Many returned for retread jobs.

There were many other impostors who used operations, injections, and any device they could dream up directed at improving a man's masculinity. There were also some serious attempts by legitimate physicians. Dr. Leo Stanley of San Quentin prison did experimental work in which he took the testicles from young hanging victims and transplanted them into senile lifers, apparently with encouraging results. He also experimented with goat gland serum injections.

CELL THERAPY

The idea that adding new tissue to old would combat aging had some basis. In the early 1930's the famous French physiologist Alexis Carrel demonstrated that he could keep tissues in the laboratory alive and vigorous indefinitely by simply constantly adding new young cells to the old cells for nourishment. Many scientists, including the eminent German pathologist Rudolf Virchow, subscribed to the idea of a "life bearer" cell, and Carrel's experiment illustrated that young cells in some way did have a life-bearing function.

Carrel's work was the direct forerunner for still another youth doctor, the celebrated Paul Niehans, who introduced "cell therapy" for rejuvenation. Niehans had carefully observed the attempts of his colleagues in this field, including his associate, Serge Voronoff. If Niehans had been educated in more recent times, he might well have been one of the giants in medicine. As it is, he was a curious mixture of fraud, genius, and capable physician. He apparently had both the intellectual and the educational background to become a respected successful physician within the legitimate practice of medicine. He had mastered the elements of several different specialties. It is entirely possible that he suffered from the same problem that afflicts even some of the greats in medicine, the "messiah" complex, for he felt that he was God's answer to medicine and it was his role in life to be the high priest of all physicians, emancipating man from suffering, disease, and death. Individuals afflicted with this psychological makeup often are blind to their own errors and the inadequacy of their research design to permit the conclusions which they make. In short, emotional and psychological motivation overrides their innate capabilities.

In any case, Paul Niehans was close to being a legitimate youth doctor. He credits the beginning of his famous cell therapy with a near accident occurring in April, 1931. The story goes that a young Swiss surgeon had accidentally removed the tiny parathyroid glands on each side of the thyroid at the time of surgery. These glands regulate the calcium balance in the body, and when they are removed, tetany and convulsions ensue. According to Niehans's story, the patient, a woman, was almost in extremis when he was called in for consultation. He came to the operating room equipped with freshly removed parathyroid glands from a young steer. These he cut into very small pieces and irrigated with a salt solution. Filling his syringe with the solution, he injected the material into the chest muscles of the woman. Almost immediately her spasms and convulsive contortions ceased and she returned to normal, making a rapid recovery. Thereafter she lived to a ripe old age.

The basic idea of cell therapy is to inject a preparation of young cells into the aging body, in hopes that they will do what the young cells did to the old tissue cultures in Dr. Carrel's experiment. A whole family of young cell therapists have been spawned by Paul Niehans's work. Today the cells that are used are obtained from sheep fetuses, usually about one month before their expected birth. Young cells of the liver, heart, and most organs are obtained in this way. For the endocrine glands, the pituitary, testes, adrenals, parathyroid, and ovaries, mature young animals are used because these glands are too small or undeveloped in the fetus. The fresh cells are cut into very small pieces and suspended in a salt-water solution which has essentially the same chemical content as the fluid in human blood. This preparation is then injected into the buttocks of the patient. Sometimes the preparation is lyophilized, a process of freeze-drying. In other instances a frozen preparation is used.

The idea is that the organ in the body that is not functioning properly, supposedly because of aging, is benefited by the injection of young cells of the same organ. Thus, if a person's heart is not working well, the injection of young heart cells would literally rejuvenate it and return it to a younger and more vigorous state. Of course, that patient has to be diagnosed correctly to determine which organs are in need of rejuvenation.

There are many dangers inherent in this procedure at the hands of the novice, as was evidenced after Paul Niehans had been invited to attend Pope Pius XII. The publicity that followed the Pope's recovery encouraged many other doctors to try the same thing. Some patients were injected with cells that were not sterile and contained bacteria. Others reacted to the foreign protein, having what is called an anaphylactic shock or a severe allergic-type reaction sometimes resulting in death. There were many other complications.

To his credit, Niehans never really claimed that one could live indefinitely with cell therapy. He only proposed that the adding of young cells to the old body would improve its state so that one's life span could be enjoyed in better health. Along with his program went changes in life habits. He encouraged his patients to eliminate tobacco and in general improved their life patterns. His personal relationship to his patients had a strong psychological effect. He was by all accounts a supremely confident man. He was also careful in the selection of his patients.

Although cell therapy as practiced and advocated by Paul Niehans is certainly not the answer to preventing aging or reversing aging, somewhere within the vast amount of unplanned research effort are a few ideas worthy of exploitation. This assertion is well supported by Carrel's young cell transfusion studies. Whether there are some weak chemical elements that influence the body or whether some form of reactivation of basic cellular mechanisms indeed takes place is not clear at this point. Sophisticated, well-planned research at the cellular and biochemical level is required. For the moment it suffices to state that Paul Niehans's *cell therapy is outlawed in the United States because it has not been found to achieve most of the things it has been claimed to do.*

One is led to suspect that a lot of Dr. Niehans's reported successes were directly related to his impact on his patients' way of life and psychological mechanisms. It is unfortunate that a man of his capability did not have the advantage of modern training in research techniques and the advances in biochemistry and molecular biology of more recent vintage. Sophisticated medical research is a relatively young science, and most physicians trained before World War II have had little opportunity to become masters of it. The real explosion in medical research responsible for much of our current knowledge came in the wake of World War II, at the end of Niehans's career and not at its beginning.

MORE TRANSPLANTERS

Cellular therapy or transplanting cells or their products into the body is not the only kind of transplanting that has been used to stem the ravages of age. Even the simple blood transfusion is a form of transplantation. It also points up some of the dangers in transplants since individuals can be transfused only with compatible blood. A person who has type A blood cannot accept type B blood. Transfusion reactions can be fatal. The compatibility of one's tissue with other tissues has been under constant assault with the advent of more sophisticated procedures. Some of the early transplants were skin transplants. Then medical science went on to renal operations in which whole kidneys were successfully transplanted. Here again careful tissue matching is the key to success. Transplanting kidneys in identical twins is much more likely to have a favorable outcome than transplanting kidneys between unrelated individuals.

It is easy to understand that the complex gene system of each cell, made up of highly complex chemical structures, creates an individuality of cells which is not necessarily compatible with that of someone else's cells. The body has a natural mechanism to reject foreign objects which is closely related to the body's immune mechanism.

Some of the early successful transplants involved transplanting human arteries. Arteries blocked by atherosclerosis were simply cut out and replaced with arteries from other individuals. One of the pioneers in this form of rejuvenation is Dr. Michael E. DeBakey of Houston, Texas. Like Paul Niehans, he seems to be totally dedicated to the idea that he must save humanity. He possesses the high energy level of most of the "youth doctors." In the years that I worked in the Houston Medical Center I observed that DeBakey proceeded full speed ahead with unshakable faith in his efforts regardless of questions raised by other scientists. Niehans prided himself on the fact that no one had ever died at his facility. DeBakey, similarly, was determined that no one should die "in the operating room"—although determination alone was not sufficient to prevent some deaths—and, in fact, seemed to have the idea that whenever he operated on anyone the patient should automatically be improved.

Stories in Houston at the Baylor medical complex strongly suggest many difficulties with the original aortic grafts similar to some of the problems in cell therapy. One problem was preventing bacterial contamination of the newly implanted arterial graft. The host of troubles experienced by the "grafters" soon led to the development of artificial devices, and the new plastic materials for replacing blood vessels have been highly successful. DeBakey and his colleagues deserve full credit for stimulating these developments, for countless lives have been prolonged because of them. Moreover, the feasibility of using artificial devices to replace body structures has also been proved.

With successful kidney and artery transplants it was foreseeable that the next big goal was transplanting the human heart. The rejection of artery grafts and of transplanted kidneys had provided ample reason for caution in proceeding to this effort without sufficient preparation. A person could reject a transplanted kidney and still have his life maintained by an artificial kidney machine outside of the body, but no such device existed for the heart. If the one and only heart that the patient had ceased to function, death was inevitable. Pioneering in the attempt to solve the complex problems of heart transplants was Dr. Norman Shumway. As a surgery resident at the University of Minnesota, he shared the fruits of his laboratory research with his colleagues. One of these was Christiaan Barnard, subsequently to become famous with the world's first heart transplant.

Already the news value of heart surgery had become plain. Surgeons and physicians around the world were cognizant of the fact that whoever successfully accomplished the world's first heart transplant would win a niche in medical history. DeBakey had demonstrated the amount of publicity that could follow a spectacular surgical effort. He had already tried to use an artificial device to replace part of the heart's function. The worldwide headlines he received for the first effort to implant an artificial heart in a human being dwarfed any of the publicity ever achieved by earlier transplanters Serge Voronoff and Dr. John Brinkley.

Heart transplants were a long way from Voronoff's first successful transplanted thyroid at the beginning of World War I. The first direct attempt in a human subject, Louis Washkansky, was made by Dr. Christiaan Barnard at Groote Schuur Hospital on December 3, 1967. A second, more successful transplant, again by Dr. Barnard, was done on the famous Dr. Philip Blaiberg on January 2, 1968. At the time, I was a professor of medicine at Baylor College of Medicine in Houston. Excitement ran high in the academic corridors, and it was a common impression that Dr. DeBakey was disappointed in being displaced from the public headlines as the number one pioneer in heart surgery. His chagrin with Dr. Barnard was short-lived for soon thereafter his junior colleague, Dr. Denton A. Cooley, startled the world with a sudden series of heart transplants—three in less than two days.

Dr. Cooley had learned his lessons well from his mentor and received full news coverage on a national and worldwide basis. Public coverage of the transplant spectaculars rivaled that of the nation's effort to land a man on the moon. With Dr. Cooley's sudden preemption of the limelight, the long-existing feud between the old surgeon and the young surgeon had gone public. Rivalries between physicians are not new; in fact, they were commonplace among the "youth doctors," who fought for public notice and wealthy clients. There were daily rumblings around the Medical Center as the animosity between the two surgeons grew. Months elapsed and still Cooley's transplants were the talk of the world. Eventually, Dr. DeBakey weighed in with *his* spectacular, "harvesting" the organs from one patient to provide a heart, kidneys, and lungs for four different recipients. The series of competitive events was capped by Dr. Cooley's first complete replacement of a human heart with an artificial device. In April, 1969, he and Dr. Domingo Liotta replaced both of the heavy ventricular muscle pumping chambers of the heart with an artificial mechanism designed by Dr. Liotta and were able to keep the patient alive on it for more than 60 hours.

The heart transplant saga had a predictable result. The rejection problems observed earlier in animal studies and in other organ transplants plagued the surgeons. Many patients, since they were extremely ill to begin with, died immediately after surgery. The lucky ones survived about six months. The problem of rejecting foreign tissue was not controlled, and the vast majority of these individuals suffered heart rejection. A few, like Dr. Philip Blaiberg, lived for reasonably long periods of time after surgery, but these were exceptions.

Transplant programs sprang up all over the world and became something of a status symbol for medical centers. This reaction was not dissimilar from the upsurge in cellular therapy by many different physicians after the notoriety of Dr. Niehans's treatment of Pope Pius XII. Despite the early failures in heart transplants, there were some successes. Louis B. Russell, Jr., an Indianapolis schoolteacher, was leading an active life five years after his successful transplant on August 24, 1968. Eventually, the rate of success will be higher, when the problems of tissue rejection are solved and more is known about the cellular mechanisms within the body.

Some of the drawbacks inherent in the program were apparent from the clamor at the Houston Medical Center. There were constant questions about whether the heart that Dr. DeBakey had transplanted into a recipient was really any better than the one removed. It is understandable that obtaining donors with healthy hearts is very difficult since a large number of individuals who die would have been vigorously treated prior to their demise. Thus, the hearts that were available were often soaked with drugs and no doubt in some instances did indeed have inherent defects. Competition over the source of donors also became manifest.

Aside from all of these difficulties, neither a perfectly developed artificial heart nor a successful transplant program will really solve the problems of heart disease and its impact on aging. The simple truth is that as many as one-half of the individuals who have a heart attack die before they can be brought to a suitable medical facility. None of those who drop dead suddenly are going to be helped by these measures. Death can strike a young, vigorous-appearing man without warning and I might add without any significant findings on a very comprehensive medical examination. The idea, then, that heart transplants and artificial hearts will solve the problem of heart disease is a gross exaggeration. The real solution to heart disease will be found in preventing it.

The vast majority of people who die of heart disease today have atherosclerotic blockage of the arteries to their heart muscle. The same disease occurs throughout the body. Replacing a heart damaged by this process offers no protection whatsoever from the continuation of the atherosclerosis in the brain and the subsequent senility which is sure to develop. The goal is to prevent or reverse atherosclerotic blockage of the arteries, whether it affects the arteries that supply the testicles or the brain or the kidneys or any other part of the body. The goal will not doubt be achieved as a result of long-continued, well-planned research which is not likely to provide spectacular headlines of the type characteristic of the artificial heart and heart transplant era.

AUTOINTOXICATION

Not all youth doctors have relied on surgical procedures to work their miracles. Perhaps one of the earliest real scientists to tackle the problem of aging was Elie Metchnikoff. In many regards he deserves the title of father of gerontology (science of aging). He was a Russian who had emigrated to Paris where he became head of the Pasteur Institute. Far from being tainted with quackery, so commonly associated with doctors involved in youth medicine, he was a premier scientist who along with the German Paul Ehrlich won the Nobel Prize in 1908 for his work in immunity. Metchnikoff used science and his microscope to begin a real definition of changes thought to occur with aging and various methods claimed to combat it. In the course of these investigations he discovered that white blood cells phagocytized germs and he began to lay the groundwork for modern immunology.

Understandably, with Metchnikoff's interest in germs and immunology he started to look at infections as a possible cause of aging and finally centered on the colon, since it normally harbored a multitude of bacteria. His studies gave rise to the "autointoxication" theory, and in its wake came unethical doctors removing patients' colons or devising procedures to eliminate the infectious source sapping the life force. In the United States doctors turned to treating patients by eradicating "foci of infection." There followed a great wave of tonsillectomies, adenoidectomies, wholesale removal of teeth and any other portion of the body that might harbor unwarranted germs. Metchnikoff himself recommended *Lactobacillus bulgaricus* yogurt as a means of removing autointoxication from the colon. Yogurt enthusiasts multiplied, and the idea took hold that yogurt would cure everything from acne to constipation. While the lactobacillus may indeed change the acid-alkaline base in the colon and affect the type of germs living there, it does not, unfortunately, increase the life span and has no relationship to preventing aging.

Metchnikoff's early theories of immunology are really the forerunners of the autoimmune theory often advanced as one of the important mechanisms of aging. Dr. Roy L. Walford of the University of Southern California has used Imuran, a substance that suppresses the normal immune reaction, to increase the life span of mice 10 weeks longer than that of the control animals. The role of autoimmune mechanisms in producing aging is a highly regarded current concept.

GEROVITAL

In the post–World War II heyday of youth drugs, one of the most famous was Gerovital; similar or related medicines were Impletol and H3. All of them are really procaine, the same medicine that the dentist uses when he is injecting a substance to prevent pain. The high priestess of the Gerovital craze is Ana Aslan of Bucharest. She claims a slight variation in her Gerovital or H3 from the chemical structure of simple procaine (Novacain).

Like most other youth remedies, Gerovital has been claimed to cure everything from baldness to impotence and all the wrinkled skin in between. The story is that Ana Aslan's success with Gerovital began when she relieved the arthritic pain of a young man. Severely disabled with arthritis of the knee, he experienced instantaneous relief when she injected procaine into the artery in his leg. Repeated injections rehabilitated him and allowed him to return to normal life.

Ana Aslan has even asserted that Gerovital will restore natural hair color. Her claims, however, have not been adequately supported by reputable scientists. Gerovital and related youth compounds have been outlawed by the FDA until recently, even for importation. This action speaks for itself about the limited effectiveness, if any, of these medicines in preventing or reversing aging. In 1973 the FDA approved studies of Gerovital to investigate its effects in combatting depression. Its use as an antidepressant may be valuable but this has nothing to do with all the extravagant claims about its use in preventing aging.

In defense of Dr. Aslan's work, it must be stated that a number of her older patients have shown remarkable improvements. The results are not necessarily attributable to Gerovital, however. Apparently Dr. Aslan is a dedicated doctor who places the interest of her patients foremost. Many of her older patients may do better because it is the first time they have received any form of genuine care. All are treated with proper exercise programs and careful diets plus intellectual and manual labor for those who are able to do it. Older people are likely to improve markedly when someone else takes an interest in them and they are introduced into meaningful activities once again. Diet and exercise, of course, are considered by all reputable physicians to be useful measures in maintaining good health.

The failure to prove that Gerovital is an important anti-aging medicine does not detract from the overall important uses of procaine and related medicines when indicated. Procaine injections for the relief of pain have been found beneficial in the hands of qualified physicians, particularly for the relief of musculoskeletal pain. Of course, procaine is effective as a local anesthetic in numerous situations, from dental work to suturing small skin wounds. Related chemicals derived from it have proved to be some of our best medicines in treating irregularities of the heart.

TEMPERATURE CONTROL AND ANTIOXIDANTS

It has been shown in experimental settings that the life span can be prolonged by freezing or cooling. Simply by lowering body temperatures, fish will live longer than at higher temperatures. Further, some medicines under study may yet prove to have valuable applications in aging. Dr. Denham Harman, a biochemist at the University of Nebraska, has put forward the "Free Radical Reaction Aging Theory." He believes that certain chemicals or energy sources are prone to oxidize or act with the basic structure of the complex chemicals within cells and that, in the course of time, these actions cause fundamental cellular changes that lead to aging. Although his theory is somewhat complex, in practical terms it means that items which slow down oxidation help to prolong life. Some of these so-called antioxidants are common preservatives such as are used in bread to prevent staleness. In one of his experiments using butylated hydroxytoluene (BHT), an antioxidant, Harman was able to significantly increase the life span of mice. Over half of the mice fed BHT were still alive at 22.4 months while over half of the group not receiving BHT were dead at 14.9 months. Although antioxidants are not currently available for prevention of aging, Harman's studies perhaps point the way toward other substances that one day may be useful in this area. While the process of aging is probably much more complex, the mechanism of antioxidants, decreased temperature, and near starvation in extending life may all be a matter of just simply slowing down the life processes.

VITAMIN POPPING

Not unrelated to the antioxidants is the concept of megavitamins. Actually vitamins A, C, and E are antioxidants. The idea is to overwhelm the body with large amounts of vitamins, far in excess of what is normally required to meet bodily needs as would be found in an ordinary balanced diet. The superconcentration of vitamins is supposed to enable the cells to repair basic cellular mechanisms and thereby regain their youth. Studies are still very much in the research area, and there is no hard evidence at this writing to substantiate that huge doses of vitamins are useful in preventing aging or are otherwise beneficial to individuals receiving an adequate normal diet.

NOT SO MAGIC MEDICINE

Hope springs eternal that the magic medicine will one day be found. A celebrated rejuvenator is Dr. Johan Bjorksten, who until lately was better known for his theories than for his research achievements. Like other rejuvenators and transplanters he has amassed a sizable fortune. It is hoped that some of Dr. Bjorksten's concepts will point the way toward a medicine or medicines which will help prevent aging. Bjorksten is the father of the cross-linked theory of aging. In recent times his research efforts have been supported under contract by the Upjohn Company. Indicative of the enthusiasm of doctors and writers for the youth panacea was an article in the *Ladies' Home Journal* a couple of years ago in which Patrick McGrady, also author of the popular book *The Youth Doctors*, implied that as a result of Dr. Bjorksten's work the youth pill was just around the corner.

According to McGrady, Bjorksten had used a unique method of studying elements that attack collagen or fibrous material and devour it. These bacteriophages were found in the soil and related to the mechanism of digesting dead animals. Obviously they must contain some enzymatic substances capable of reversing the changes at the points where protein chains were stuck together or cross-linked since they were able to break down protein completely. If an extract were made from the bacteriophages, the long-awaited youth pill would be in the wings awaiting adequate funding to provide immortality for all. McGrady advanced the idea that Upjohn had decided not to continue to underwrite Bjorksten's work beyond the initial five-year contract because an additional 10 years and millions more dollars would be required to develop the elixir of youth and prove to the Food and Drug Administration that it was effective and satisfactory.

It is probable that McGrady's enthusiasm for youth medicine led him to overemphasize the likelihood of an immediately available youth pill. To dispel some of the resultant clamor the public relations office of Upjohn released its own statement concerning his article in the *Ladies' Home Journal*:

> While it is indeed true that such research was conducted by a very able and respected scientist, the impression that there is now a product waiting around the corner which will add years of longevity and completely rejuvenate the aged population is an unwarranted impression.

. . . The scientific studies by Dr. Bjorksten added considerably to the understanding of cell metabolism, genetic transfer, and DNA-RNA chemistry. However, as in most basic research, the information must be considered as only a small piece in the total realm of total scientific understanding.

Hopefully, through such research as advanced by Dr. Bjorksten and the Upjohn Company, inroads will be made into the puzzle of aging. Most likely, however, these inroads will be made step by step, slowly, and with cooperation by researchers the world over. In a scientific endeavor of this magnitude, the possibility of an immediate youth pill as insinuated in the article is quite remote.

The McGrady article typifies the problem constantly facing the public about "youth pills." There is more unrestrained enthusiasm than there are available facts. The truth is that at this writing no simple easy shortcut to perpetual youth—by medicine or surgery—exists. Important medicines and methods are at hand for maintaining health, and the evidence is abundant that improvement of living patterns will significantly improve health and life span. While these more arduous efforts to achieve a more limited goal may not be so glamorous as a magic pill, they are, nevertheless, the most useful procedures we can offer at this time. When the basic function of the DNA-RNA mechanisms and the factors that determine their capacity to perpetuate themselves are understood, then a real opportunity for immortality will exist.

PART IV

The Future

twenty

Get Ready for Immortality

Many people alive today will have the opportunity for a greatly prolonged life span. Even immortality now seems possible. The basic secrets of life are already known. In 1953 when the young scientists James Watson and Francis Crick solved the chemical structure of DNA, they excitedly told their colleagues they had discovered the secret of life, and indeed they had. Despite the understanding of DNA-RNA, mRNA, and repressors and inducers that shut them off or turn them on there still remains much to learn about how to activate the system and ensure perpetual regeneration.

The complex DNA-RNA system enables the cells to build a fantastic number of combinations of chemical compounds and hence variations in living cells which determine what kind of creatures will be the end result. It is very much analogous to a cryptographic problem. Although there are only 26 letters in the alphabet, the possible combinations of these fill several dictionaries in different languages. The DNA-RNA protein synthesis scheme has many more building blocks which can form simple or complex chemical compounds. To build a living system such as man from the basic chemical components would indeed be a horrendous task, but not impossible. Whatever else life is, it is an integration of complex and simple chemical compounds into the whole. It is not necessary to begin with the basic chemical elements, however, since the compounds of life are all around us. Our cells already contain the individual complex DNA-RNA molecules. These can be used to build life, and immortality is possible if the life processes can be altered. We already know that some living cells have the characteristics of perpetual regeneration and hence immortality. What is already known is the important basis for unlocking the remaining parts of the puzzle.

Now that it is possible to manufacture DNA, to make genetic copies of living creatures, and to induce genetic changes, man may be very close to having all the information he needs to achieve immortality. A major effort such as that expended to land a man on the moon could well reward the long search for life everlasting and it could be accomplished in this century. With this achievement it would be possible for people to remain in the mature youthful state they enjoyed in their early 20's and for the DNA-RNA machinery of older people to resume regeneration and repair, replacing diseased, damaged, and exhausted protoplasm with new tissues; in short, to grow young again.

Inevitably some voices have been raised questioning the moral advisability of achieving immortality, or making genetic copies of humans, or "tinkering with life." Throughout history *our* theological considerations and *their* superstitions have proved to be a poor basis for scientific considerations. Whenever theological concepts have been given precedence over emerging scientific knowledge, the situation has not been helpful to man. The history of Galileo's struggle with the leaders of the Catholic Church is an excellent example. The theologians considered it heresy for anyone to disagree with the theological belief that the earth was the center of the universe. If history is any indication of the future, the theological considerations will not prevent the continuous assault of the minds of men on the secrets of life, and eventually achieving the ability to provide immortality. In this sense the moral issue is not relevant. *What can happen will happen*, and immortality can and will happen. Only a few short years ago it was thought impossible to split the atom, but the atom was split. More recently it was thought impossible to orbit men around the earth, and now man has landed on the moon and started mapping its characteristics. So, too, will man eventually unlock the final secrets of perpetuating life.

This achievement would have a major impact upon religion. Religions which offered a reward of life everlasting to the faithful would have to face the fact that life everlasting was possible here on earth or any other region of the universe which man had mastered. The implications would have a far-reaching social and cultural influence on all mankind.

Moral concepts may well determine where and who will achieve immortality first. Societies in which religious ethics forbid tampering with life do not offer environments conducive to this achievement. The emphasis on scientific advance and the deemphasis on religious concepts in the Soviet Union make it most likely, economics permitting, that the Soviet scientists will be the first to reach the capability of immortality and the first to apply it to their society. While the American scientists have been content with more modest goals of preventing heart disease, curing cancer, and dealing with the immediate problems, many Russian scientists have fixed their sights on a longer-range goal, a quantum jump in longevity or nothing short of immortality. The nation which accomplishes and exploits this ability may well be the nation that becomes supreme on earth and dominates the future direction of mankind. A major step in evolution will have been taken. In considering this development we must not lose sight of the possibility that life may and probably does exist elsewhere in the universe, perhaps on a planet like earth which is part of another solar system. Any location where life and evolution have existed may be populated by living creatures who have already solved the basic elements of immortality.

Many people say, "But I don't want to live forever." This attitude is naive since it is usually equated with ideas of being old, senile, and beset with problems. If one has enjoyed any aspect of his life, the possibility of immortality offers the opportunity to experience the pleasurable parts of life and not just its hardships. The body can remain youthful, and the brain can continue in that inquisitive, knowledge-acquiring state that typifies youth.

One of the great advantages of immortality would be the opportunity to further develop the mind. When time is not a factor, one can constantly acquire new knowledge and learn new skills. It would no longer be necessary to be either a doctor or a lawyer or a statesman; one could be all of these and play many roles. Most people learn limited numbers of skills and acquire limited amounts of knowledge because of the restrictions of time and motivation. The brilliant minds that would be possible with immortality would be able to develop the motivation, and time would be no object. Superintelligent people might be able to master the universe from finite to infinite. The question of what man would do with his time isn't important either when one considers the multitude of things to be done, discovered, and explored. No doubt the more brilliant immortal minds would find ways to help motivate and occupy constructively the minds of others.

The opportunity for great minds to live, experience, and create offers fantastic possibilities. What contributions to society could Leonardo da Vinci, with his inventive genius, not have made, in a world that had electricity, engines, new sources of power, if he had lived in a state of youthful being for 500 years?

With his newfound control of life processes, man would literally control evolution. It would be possible to temporarily alter the life process— for example, to develop a respiratory system suitable for exploring the oceans of the earth. Nature already has one example of metamorphosis of life from water to air: in the common tadpole that becomes a frog. The ability to control metamorphosis and evolution could be of major importance in the conquest of other planets, like Jupiter, or the rest of the universe. Such changes can be utilitarian and reversible. Man could have the time, the knowledge, and the means to manage social problems. For instance, the question of skin color could be simply solved: A person could change from black to white and back again with all gradations in between, which possibility might put this arbitrary distinction into its proper perspective.

Unlocking the secret of immortality would answer many medical problems. Preventing, controlling, or eliminating cancer would be possible. The runaway genetic system of cancer cells could simply be converted back to their normal cell characteristics. Even if the genetic apparatus of a cell were taken over by a virus DNA or RNA, the problem could be corrected by controlling the virus DNA or using measures to repress it, perhaps with repressors or related substances. Should it be determined that cancer cells result from loss of DNA, it could be replaced.

Wear and tear arthritis would be eliminated. The worn cells could be replaced with new structures. If a number of cells had been destroyed, inducing the growth elements active in the early years of life could lead readily to their replacement. Remember, the whole body originally develops from the union of one male and one female cell.

Many cases of vascular disease could be cured. Damaged cells in the arteries could be replaced by new cells along the original patterns seen in younger years. The problem of senility and its effects on the mind would disappear. If the same chemical mechanism operative in youth were made available, the sick nerve cells could be rebuilt from new chemical parts.

The ability to replace exhausted, diseased, and injured tissues would not mean that one could abuse the body with unhealthy living habits. Just as a new car can be destroyed in a wreck, so can the delicate chemical machinery of the human body be destroyed, immortality or no immortality. It is likely that acquired aging will still be with those who refuse to follow life-styles that ensure optimal body health, though some of the ravages of unhealthy life styles may be limited by virtue of having young tissues to begin with. The man of 35 who drops dead of a heart attack because of unwise living habits cannot be saved by learning the secrets of immortality. Nor can these secrets protect a person from pneumonia, tuberculosis, and lethal levels of toxic pollutants.

There will be moral and social problems to solve with the advent of immortality. What about a population explosion if people simply don't die? The conquest and colonization of other planets, like Jupiter (many times the size of earth), can solve part of this problem, as can colonization of the seas. One obvious solution is not to add to the existing population. Population control enters into the questions surrounding abortions and birth control. Perhaps it will be possible to genetically engineer people not to be fertile unless their reproducing genes are turned on.

Even some scientists have expressed moral indignation at the thought of cloning, making a genetic copy of an individual, sometimes referred to as xeroxing people. What is so wrong with making a xerox copy of an individual as compared to two people making 10 hybrid copies of themselves using their genetic reproductive equipment? Should a woman who wants to have a child and is married to a sterile man be allowed to have a genetic copy fetus of herself made and implanted in her uterus and deliver her own child? Why should artificial insemination from the sperm of a stranger be preferable to her own genetic copy? Is it more moral for her to adopt a child, which is a genetic mixture of two other people who did not want a child to begin with? Why is the adopted child better than her own under these circumstances? Or could she have a genetic copy of herself and a genetic copy of her husband and thus the couple would have two children which came from their own DNA chemical pool? Should a man who is married to a sterile woman be allowed to have a genetic copy of himself? And would such a child be just as morally acceptable as an adopted child of someone else's sex life? If it is all right for a man married to a sterile woman to have a genetic copy offspring, why couldn't a single man or woman who didn't wish to marry have a genetic copy offspring? The moral issues are not so clearly right and wrong, and it really doesn't matter since, as I suggested, *What can happen will happen.* Nevertheless, society would have to come to grips with these and other questions.

One possible solution would be at some point to say there cannot be any more multiplication of people. This would leave people with a choice of having a mixed gene offspring and forfeiting their own right to immortality, having a cloned offspring and forfeiting their right to immortality, or having neither, and choosing to stay around indefinitely. As a safeguard against sudden complete destruction, people could put some of their tissue in a tissue bank, which would provide a simple cell nucleus and could then be used to produce a genetic copy of themselves if anything happened. It is true that the genetic copy would not be the same person, but even this eventuality might be obviated. All the body is electrochemical material. All knowledge, experiences, and even emotions are chemical. Just as we can transfer music or sound or any electrical impulse to a magnetic tape, we could transfer impulses to the cells to record life experiences and emotions. In this view the body is an empty magnetic tape, and life experiences are stored chemically in the cells. From birth our cells are constantly receiving new recordings. It may eventually be possible to transfer the recorded sum total of life experiences to the genetic copy, thereby providing a duplicate of the original in more than an empty genetic copy sense. There may also be erase mechanisms, making it possible to remove certain recorded experiences. These concepts even raise the possibility of transferring knowledge through a recorded technique—for example, knowledge of a foreign language or the recordings of higher mathematics. Learning transfer may not be too far removed from the processes of immortality.

Some will reject these ideas as far out and not possible or desirable. But they are possible and they will eventually be realized. Man really doesn't have a choice of whether or not he will have immortality. The choice is what to do with it. Unlocking the final secrets of immortality would bring untold blessings to man and make him master of his future and perhaps the future of all things in the universe. How long it will be before these advances in evolution take place depends on the effort that is made, but they can occur in the lifetime of many people who live today. You then have a chance for immortality. It will be necessary to do what you can to preserve your health to live a long healthy life if you are to participate in this greatest of man's experiences. Follow healthy living patterns and maintain a healthy environment, along the lines discussed in this book. Basically, these principles tell you how to get ready for immortality.

Index

74 75 76 77 9 8 7 6 5 4 3 2 1